EXPORTING DANGER

EXPORTING DANGER

A History of the Canadian
Nuclear Energy Export Programme

RON FINCH

BLACK
ROSE
BOOKS

Montréal·Buffalo

This book is dedicated to all the people working for peace. Whether they are struggling for it in their homes, churches, workplaces, community centres, or on the streets, they provide the hope that there will be future generations on this planet. Do not give up.

Black Rose Books No. 0 105

ISBN Hardcover 0-920057-74-8
ISBN Paperback 0-920057-72-1

Canadian Cataloguing in Publication Data

Finch, Ron, 1958-
        Exporting danger: a history of the Canadian nuclear energy export programme

Bibliography: p.
ISBN 0-920057-74-8 (bound). — ISBN 0-920057-72-1 (pbk.).

1. Nuclear industry — Canada. 2. Nuclear nonproliferation.
I. Title.

HD9698.C22F55 1986   338.4'7621483'0971   C86-090226-9

Cover design: J.W. Stewart

Black Rose Books

3981 boul. St. Laurent
Montréal, Qué. H2W 1Y5
Canada

University of Toronto Press
33 East Tupper St.
Buffalo, N.Y. 14230, USA

Printed and bound in Québec, Canada

TABLE OF CONTENTS

TABLES AND FIGURES

TABLES

FIGURES

Acknowledgements

I am indebted to the staff of the Elizabeth Dafoe and Business Administration Libraries, University of Manitoba, Winnipeg, and the Whiteshell Nuclear Research Laboratory Library, Pinawa. Without their assistance, my work would have been much more difficult.

Finding the material, however, was only half of the effort. It had to be turned into something worth reading. I thank Professor Tom Vadney for helping me realize the value of being succinct and the importance of editing. With his help, my garbled prose was untangled.

Most important, I would like to thank Nancy Thorne Finch for the spiritual, emotional, financial, and intellectual support she provided from the beginning of this endeavour. It is unlikely this book would have been completed without her encouragement.

While I also acknowledge the help and support of colleagues, friends, and family, I alone am responsible for any errors or omissions.

INTRODUCTION

Canada has never produced an atomic bomb of its own, but it has played a major role in the proliferation of nuclear technology throughout the world. Canadians have attempted to sell reactors and uranium to at least twenty-five countries since 1945. Many of these nations were to be found in parts of the world noted for political instability, and some apparently have had an interest in the production of nuclear arms. India has utilized Canadian technology to build an atomic weapon. Other nations may have developed the capacity to do likewise. Yet except for the Indian case, the magnitude of the Canadian effort to export nuclear technology and fuel is not widely appreciated. Neither are the reasons why Canada began to sell abroad. It is the plan of this work to examine both matters. Exactly what was the scope of Canada's export activity, particularly in the Third World as the largest potential market? And, given the obvious risks of proliferation, why did the Canadian nuclear industry expand beyond what was required for national security and for domestic energy needs?

The data to answer these questions are to be found in the press, the considerable body of information generated by Canadian nuclear agencies, the debates of the Canadian House of Commons, the findings of parliamentary investigations, and a variety of other printed primary and secondary sources. What emerges is a portrait of a capital-intensive industry critically dependent on government financial and ideological support. Export markets were pursued to help underwrite an expensive though limited domestic nuclear program. But this strategy was not completely successful. The pursuit of export sales often resulted in disastrous financial losses and disregard for effective non-proliferation safeguards. By the early 1980s, the export program still had failed to provide sufficient room for expansion, so that the nuclear industry remained dependent upon the federal government to resolve its problems. Rather than review the industry's inability to achieve viability on its own, the path chosen was to continue subsidizing exports. A review might have threatened the nuclear program's vested interests. Federal assistance, however, perpetuated the historic state and private links that were created when the Canadian nuclear program was first established.[1]

Yet despite the clarity with which the history of the Canadian nuclear program emerges from the plethora of primary sources, there are a limited number of secondary sources that examine the subject in a way which links the social, economic, political, technological, and international factors. What sources are available? The major general work is Wilfred Eggleston's *Canada's Nuclear Story* (1965). But two factors limit its usefulness. First, it was published before the program reached maturity. In the mid-1960s, it was easier to sustain enthusiasm about the industry's future when actual problems could be dismissed as "growing pains." And second, Eggleston's book is an official history, which undoubtedly influenced his favourable portrait of the industry.

Even Eggleston's enthusiasm for nuclear power, however, was to be surpassed. In the late 1970s, when the Canadian nuclear program was in extreme difficulty, a number of pro-industry (even apologetic) sources appeared. These included: Peter Mueller, *On Things Nuclear: The Canadian Debate* (1977); Charles Law and Ron Glen, *Critical Choice: Canada and Nuclear Power, the Issues behind the Headlines* (1978); Allan Wyatt, *The Nuclear Challenge: Understanding the Debate* (1978); and David Peat, *The Nuclear Book: What Happened at Harrisburg? And Can It Happen Here?* (1979). Other works, while supportive of the Canadian nuclear program, provide more information. For example, see: Robert Morrison and Edward Wonder, *Canada's Nuclear Export Policy* (1978); Robert Morrison and Gordon Sims, *Nuclear Power in Developing Countries: A Search for Indicators* (1980); and G. Bruce Doern, *Government Investigation in the Canadian Nuclear Industry* (1978). The tendency to produce pro-industry material, however, was not unique to Canada. It also occurred in the United States. Among others, see: Peter de Leon, *A Cross-National Comparison of Nuclear Research Development Strategies* (1976); and Charles Ebinger, *International Politics of Nuclear Energy* (1978).

There were other authors, however, who began revealing the Canadian industry's problems and critiquing its supposed benefits. These included: Bill Harding, *Nukenomics: The Political Economy of the Nuclear Industry* (1979); Jan Marmorek, *Everything You Wanted to Know about Nuclear Power (But Were Afraid to Ask)* (1978); Doris McMullan, Ian Hornby, Jim Collins, and John McAulay: *The Nuke Book: The Impact of Nuclear Development* (1976); and Simon Rosenblum, *The Non-Nuclear Way: Creative Energy Alternatives for Canada* (1978). Yet problems remained. These sources were generally brief examinations of a very complex industry. For many years, Fred Knelman's *Nuclear Energy: The Unforgiving Technology* (1976) stood alone as the most detailed critique of the Canadian nuclear "establishment" (Knelman, in fact, coined the term). Yet despite the strengths of Knelman's work, it would be incorrect to assume that all aspects had been analysed.

It was not until the early 1980s that another group of authors began examining in detail the Canadian nuclear program (or its various segments) within the social, economic, technological, and international context in which it operated. These include: Paul McKay, *Electric Empire: The Inside Story of Ontario Hydro* (1983); Carol Giangrande, *The Nuclear North: The People, the Regions, and the Arms Race* (1983); Ernie Regehr and Simon Rosenblum (eds.), *Canada and the Nuclear Arms Race* (1983); Walter Robbins, *Getting the Shaft: The Radioactive Waste Controversy in Manitoba* (1984); and Rosalie Bertell, *No*

Immediate Danger: Prognosis for a Radioactive Earth (1985). This study is an attempt to extend a similar approach to the question of nuclear exports. But the void is far from being filled. Many aspects of the Canadian nuclear program still require detailed examination. Uranium mining, worker health and safety, the international corporate connections to Canadian uranium, and public control of the Canadian nuclear program are but a few examples of areas requiring more work. While access to federal records would undoubtedly provide many answers, there is plenty of public material available. It is hoped that this book will encourage others to examine these areas which, in turn, may spark a public debate.

CHAPTER I
CANADA AS
A NUCLEAR POWER

BEGINNINGS

The origins of the Canadian nuclear industry are clear enough. They were associated with the Second World War and the Anglo-American plans to construct an atomic bomb for use against Germany and Japan. The onset of the atomic era can be divided into two periods. The first focussed on scientific research and experimentation. It dates primarily from the discovery of radiation and radium in the 1890s. The second period began with the politicization of nuclear research by various governments, when atomic energy was removed from the laboratory and assumed a role in foreign policy. Key dates included the achievement of criticality (a self-sustaining chain reaction)* at the Chicago pile on December 2, 1942; the secret test explosion at Alamogordo, New Mexico, on July 16, 1945; and the dropping of the atomic bomb on Hiroshima on August 6, 1945.

In Canada, research was conducted on a relatively small scale at the National Research Council (NRC) laboratory on Sussex Street in Ottawa and at the University of Montreal. This first phase continued until 1942, longer than in other countries. In Europe, for example, the shift from the first to the second stage occurred during 1938-39. With the discovery of uranium fission, many scientists began to recognize that vast amounts of energy would be released when uranium was bombarded with neutrons. After the onset of World War II in September, 1938, secrecy became crucial as Britain, France, and Germany continued their individual experiments.

The evolution of tripartite cooperation between the United States, the United Kingdom, and Canada began as early as 1940. At this point, research being done primarily in the British universities. But by the summer of 1941, with the escalation of the war and the advances made in atomic theory, it was decided that all research should be coordinated. Prime Minister W.L.

---

* A list of technical terms and abbreviations has been included. See glossary.

Mackenzie King later stated that the goal was "to find, just as rapidly as possible, the means of producing atomic bombs." To this end, American and British teams, directed by Enrico Fermi and Hans Halban, respectively, were coordinated in an ad hoc manner starting in October 1941.[1]

The inclusion of Canada was a result of two factors. The first was the completion of the British Maud Committee Report on the atomic bomb in July 1941. This supported the views of Otto Frisch and Rudolph Peierls, two influential émigré physicists working in England, that an atomic bomb was possible. The Defense Service Panel of the Scientific Advisory Committee, however, argued that

> large-scale separation plants [for extracting the plutonium] should not be built in Britain, because any interruptions from the enemy action such as bombings would be serious; the plants should be constructed across the Atlantic; perhaps in the United States but preferably in Canada. In the latter case many of the necessary components could be obtained in the United States.

Certain sectors of the British government, particularly the Chiefs of Staff Committee, initially ruled against the transfer to North America. But they soon recognized that for security reasons and capital and resource availability, the probability of a successful bomb design and construction program would be greater outside England. Thus the British heavy water team started to arrive in Canada in September 1942. It was the British decision which signalled the politicization of Canadian atomic research. The Canadian Cabinet authorized $500,000 to facilitate the reorganization and eventual expansion of the National Research Council's Montreal laboratory to accommodate over 300 staff members engaged in military atomic research.[2]

The second reason for Canadian involvement in the war-time nuclear program was the possession of substantial uranium supplies in the Northwest Territories. During the 1930s, Eldorado Gold Mines Limited had struggled to exploit the formidable pitchblende deposits at a site (later named Port Radium) near Great Bear Lake. The intent was to refine the mineral into radium and break into the Belgian-controlled market. But the plan failed, the Great Bear mine was closed, and Eldorado languished near bankruptcy. Instead of radium sales, it was the uranium waste by-product and American government interest which quickly turned around Eldorado's fortunes and drew Canada further into the wartime nuclear project.

In the spring of 1941, Lyman J. Briggs, acting as the chairperson of US President Roosevelt's Advisory Committee on Uranium, ordered six to eight tons (the figures vary) of refined uranium oxide from Eldorado for atomic pile experiments. This was an important beginning. But after the December 1941 attack on Pearl Harbor, American efforts increased dramatically. The US Planning Board's survey of strategic material revealed that Eldorado had over 300 tons of uranium concentrate in Port Hope, Ontario, and several dozen tons of ore sitting on the shores of Great Bear Lake. As well, if the nearby Port Radium mine were reopened, it might produce 300 tons of uranium ore per annum. In January 1942, therefore, the US Planning Board recommended purchasing 200 tons of uranium oxide from Eldorado's stockpile. But by July 1942, when the purchase was made, the amount had been increased to 350 tons, or nearly all of Eldorado's accumulated stockpile.[3]

It was at this point that Canadian government interest increased. Clarence D. Howe, Minister of Munitions and Supply, called his personal friend Gilbert LaBine, an Eldorado director, to Ottawa to discuss the proposed purchase. Howe wanted the Port Radium mine restored to full production as soon as possible. He gave the company clearance for obtaining all required materials, which were in short supply due to the war. By August 1942, the mine was producing ore for the American nuclear bomb program.

The arrival of the British heavy water team and the possession of large uranium reserves and deposits thus involved Canada in the wartime bomb program. Canadian officials — primarily C.D. Howe — worked actively to increase the country's participation. Yet shortly after the politicization of the Canadian atomic program in August-September 1942, the program's expansion was thwarted by a change in the American attitude toward tripartite cooperation.

In Ottawa, Dr. Chalmers J. Mackenzie, President of the National Research Council of Canada and chief Canadian executive of the Anglo-Canadian atomic project, received a letter dated January 2, 1943, from Dr. James B. Conant, chairperson of the US National Defense Research Committee and pivotal figure in the American bomb program. Conant's letter resulted in a unilateral alteration of the US-UK-Canada relationship. Conant argued that the US had to date been most responsible for the application of atomic theory. From this he concluded that a cooperative interchange of technical intelligence should continue only if "the recipient of the information is in a position to take advantage of this information in this war." Since it was evident, at least from the American perspective, that neither Canada nor Britain would produce plutonium-239 or uranium-234, the fissionable materials required for atomic bombs, before the end of the Second World War, Conant's letter informed the British and Canadians that the existing interchange of information would be terminated. The American intent was to stop the reciprocal nature of the information interchange but maintain intact the inflow of British and Canadian research. The letter, in fact, recommended that the Canadian project continue its work on the use of heavy water as a moderator, a material that increases the probability of further fission, "so that Du Pont Company could base their design on this experience."[4]

In *Canada's Nuclear Story*, an official history, Wilfrid Eggleston cites a host of reasons for the radical change in American policy: the increased role of the US Army in the American bomb program, the concomitant demand for secrecy and security, and an Anglo-Soviet agreement for the exchange of new weapons.[5] Yet these reasons were secondary to something more fundamental: Atomic technology, if completed in time, would decisively affect the conflict and have dramatic implications for the postwar period. And two important factors had facilitated the American desire to acquire hegemony in nuclear weapons technology. First, the achievement of criticality at the

Chicago pile on December 2, 1942, had revealed the success of American efforts with a graphite-moderated reactor. Second, neither Canada nor Britain could commit the resources required to develop an independent program.

According to Martin Sherwin, in *A World Destroyed: The Atomic Bomb and the Grand Alliance,* James Conant saw that "the continuation of an equal partnership would be inimical to American postwar commercial interests." Sherwin argues that Conant was important in convincing top American policy advisors of the need to restructure the form of the allied atomic bomb project. The reason becomes clear when one examines the corporations involved in the construction of the heavy water reactors in the United States and later in Canada.[6]

In the US, the Du Pont Corporation was directing the heavy water project at the Argonne Laboratories near Chicago. The only Canadian company able to do the same, however, was Defence Industries Limited (DIL). While DIL was a Crown corporation established early in the war to build and operate large munitions factories, its key personnel had been drawn from Canadian Industries Limited (CIL). CIL, aside from being Canada's largest chemical manufacturer, was a subsidiary of the American Du Pont Corporation and Britain's Imperial Chemical Industries (ICI). Fear that technical secrets might become available to the British ICI via Canada's DIL likely concerned the Du Pont Company and thus served as a reason to defer development of a heavy water project in Canada.[7]

The British were irate over the shift in American policy. Dr. Wallace Akers, a top figure in the UK program, felt betrayed. Despite the numerous British contributions since the late 1930s, suddenly they were being excluded, as "no further interchange of information on any subject nor undertakings to supply material will be considered." The British temporarily considered pursuing an independent course. They soon discovered, however, that the Americans, through a December 1942 deal with Eldorado and previous contracts with Belgium's Union Miniere, had command of all the uranium not under Axis or Soviet control. The Eldorado contract had required formal approval from Ottawa. Howe and Mackenzie knew where Canadian economic interest lay and had no intention of siding with the British against the Americans.[8]

The uranium supply issue eventually was resolved by a form of American benevolence. It was agreed that Canadian and British uranium requirements were not that large. Thus, if the efficiency of the Port Hope refinery and the output at Great Bear Lake were improved, there would be enough uranium for all. Nevertheless, the British still were anxious to secure a free flow of information. At Casablanca, January 14-23, 1943, Prime Minister Churchill complained to the Americans (particularly Harry Hopkins, President Roosevelt's personal aide) that the information exchange still was blocked. It was not until August 19, 1943, at the first Quebec Conference, that Churchill and Roosevelt signed an agreement providing for the resumption of the exchange of atomic energy information. It was decided that the establishment of a Combined Policy Committee (CPC) in Washington with British and

American officials and one Canadian representative (C.D. Howe) would facilitate the exchange process.[9]

If Roosevelt's general position had been that information on the military uses of atomic energy should not be given to anyone—not even an ally—why were the Americans suddenly willing in August 1943 to cooperate with the British demands? Part of the answer lay in the Quebec Agreement. The British agreed to

> recognize that any post-war advantages of an industrial or commercial character shall be dealt with as between the United States and Great Britain on terms to be specified by the President of the United States to the Prime Minister of Great Britain.

This clause guaranteed American control of the information generated by the atomic bomb program, code named the "Manhattan Project." Yet it still did not fully explain the American acceptance of British involvement. To understand this, one must examine the global context in which the shift occurred.

The victory at the Battle of Stalingrad in January 1943 had succeeded in routing the German offensive on the European Eastern Front and, during the following months, boosted Stalin's bargaining power with his allies. It was increasingly evident that the Soviet mobilization had turned the course of the war. Thus it was in the American interest to reinstate Anglo-American atomic cooperation to accelerate the development of a nuclear bomb that could be used in the conflict and gain a substantial lead over the Soviets in the postwar period.

A second reason for the American policy shift is discernible when one considers the other primary subject of debate at the August 1943 Quebec Conference—the date and location of the eventual Second Front in Europe. Churchill had voiced the British insistence on having the Second Front opened in the Balkans. The Americans, however, imposed their decision to land in northern France. This corresponded with the American attempt to weaken British influence in the Eastern Mediterranean. While the United States Atomic Energy Commission's (USAEC) historians tend to dismiss the issue, it is entirely possible that the atomic concessions also served as one trade-off for Churchill's acceptance of the Second Front's opening in Western Europe.[10]

Although the British and Americans had largely settled their differences, the Canadian program still was in limbo. The Montreal laboratory was dependent upon the Americans for supplies of heavy water and uranium metal, and these were not forthcoming. The Canadian laboratory was in desperate need of heavy water for further experiments. It was informed that the American-controlled Consolidated Mining and Smelting Company of Trail, British Columbia, was experiencing technical difficulties in producing heavy water. In fact, the Trail plant's heavy water output was being diverted to the heavy water reactor under construction in the Argonne Laboratory near Chicago. Eggleston cites security concerns as the main reason why the Americans did not favour the Canadian program. While security was crucial, it appears more probable that the situation was not so simple. The American decision not to inform the Canadians that the Trail plant was producing effectively put the Montreal laboratory on hold. This allowed the Americans time to develop their own heavy water reactor program and thus secure American technological independence from the Montreal operation.[11]

Why then, after delaying the development of the Canadian program, did the Combined Policy Committee (CPC), created after the August 1943 Quebec Conference, decide on April 13, 1944, to develop the Montreal heavy water project? Three reasons are discernible. First, the Canadian government had revealed a willingness to increase its financial expenditures to assist the nuclear program. On January 12, 1944, C.D. Howe approved the expansion of the Montreal laboratory. More concretely, on January 28, 1944, the Canadian government had expropriated Eldorado Mining and Refining Limited (its name had been changed from Eldorado Gold Mines Ltd. in July, 1943). With a total payment of $5,271,812.10 for 3,905,046 outstanding shares at $1.35 a share, the federal government claimed control of the second most important uranium mine in the world and the only refining mill in North America. Shortly after, Ottawa established a guaranteed base price for uranium ore and concentrate.[12]

The reasons for the nationalization were clear. Any revenues would accrue to the Canadian federal treasury and, equally important, the guaranteed base price secured American contracts while allaying American concerns that Eldorado could exploit the situation by rapidly escalating the price of uranium. Thus, at a time when the American administration was hesitant about seeing a heavy water program in Montreal, the Canadian government was extremely helpful in expanding its laboratory in anticipation of a contract and had stabilized the supply and price of uranium for the American bomb program.

A second reason for the shift in American policy was that the Du Pont Corporation had had a sufficient lead-time to secure technical independence from any project undertaken in Montreal. Less than two months after the CPC decision, Dr. C.J. Mackenzie visited the Chicago reactor. On June 8, 1944, he noted in his diary that it was

> quite a marvelous show. 'C' [carbon] pile has been in operation now for about a year and is operating by remote control. The 'D' [heavy water] has just been in operation quite recently.[13]

Thus, back in April 1944, any pressure that the Du Pont Company had been exerting to oppose the Montreal program seemed to have decreased.

The third reason for authorizing the Montreal Project is evident when one examines the function of the Canadian reactor project once it was in operation—to allow for further research and to provide plutonium for the US weapons program. The April 1944 decision stemmed from the American recognition that the program needed to be accelerated to aid in the implementation of postwar objectives. It was evident that the Germans were on the defensive on the Eastern Front, and within two months the long-delayed Second Front would be launched in Western Europe. In the view of Fernando Claudin, the Americans were worried that "at the end of 1943 and the beginning of 1944 the USSR was capable of defeating Germany and liberating Europe with no forces but its own and those of the national resistance movements." One must remember that in May 1944, shortly after the decision to go ahead with the Canadian heavy water project, Admiral William D. Leahy, US President Roosevelt's Chief of Staff, argued

> that in the event of a break in the 'grand alliance' and war with the Soviet Union, the United States could at the most defend Great Britain, but not defeat the Soviet Union. In other words, we would find ourselves involved in a war which we could not win.[14]

In sum, there were three reasons for the April 13, 1944, decision to develop a heavy water project in Canada. First, the Canadian government had been extremely helpful by securing uranium price and supply primarily for American use and by preparing to pay for development in Canada. Second, Du Pont was secure in its advances in Chicago. And third, the US wanted to increase its plutonium resources for the postwar period. From the American perspective, it was a happy situation. If the bomb project failed, development in Canada would be at the Canadians' expense; but if it succeeded, uranium and plutonium supplies would be guaranteed. It appears, therefore, that the needs of the American bomb program facilitated the expansion of the Canadian program. But participation also required that Canada comply with various American demands. A prime example was the removal of Dr. Hans Halban, Director of the Montreal laboratory. Halban, a French national, was viewed as a security risk to the Anglo-American atomic alliance. Thus the day after the CPC's decision, C.D. Howe cabled London for the release of Dr. John Cockcroft from his duties in Britain. Within eleven days, Cockcroft had landed in the USA.[15]

The April 13, 1944, CPC action authorized the release of information from the US to Canada previously embargoed by James Conant's letter of January 2, 1943, and resulted in hurried discussions between the Canadian federal government and private industry. The April decision also resolved the earlier difficulty of obtaining uranium metal and heavy water supplies from the US. And, true to its commitment, Ottawa financed the entire project. Work immediately was undertaken to finalize the site selection for the proposed reactors and to secure a contractor. On May 26, 1944, Canadian Industries Limited informed C.D. Howe that DIL was prepared to undertake the design and construction of the reactors; and on July 7, 1944, a contract was concluded. After a number of consultations with the Americans, various site testings, and discussions between the National Research Council and C.D. Howe, Chalk River, Ontario, was selected on August 19, 1944. Nearby Deep River was chosen for the construction of a housing community for the Chalk River staff. The new project was called "The DIL Petawawa Works," to lead the uninformed to believe that it was part of the nearby Petawawa military base. Within two days of Howe's approval of the Chalk River site, US Brigadier-General Leslie R. Groves, the Army's officer in charge of the Manhattan Project, arrived in Canada on August 21, 1944, to review Canadian plans. Discussions involved the plant lay-out, local radiation hazards, priorities for materials and equipment, proposed arrangements for maintaining secrecy, and "matters concerning the US executive."[16]

The CPC's decision resulted in the construction of two reactors and a nuclear research laboratory. The Zero Energy Experimental Pile (ZEEP) was the smaller research reactor, designed in 1944-45 and started up on September 5, 1945. It was a $200,000 pilot plant for the production of plutonium in a heavy water reactor and was the first pile to operate outside the United States. The larger Nuclear Research X-metal, or X-perimental (NRX), reactor was the centre of the Canadian project. Eggleston states that while ZEEP's completion prior to the NRX was preferred, it was not to slow down the latter's construction schedule. It would appear that the NRX's considerably greater plutonium production capacity explained the priorization. The $10-million NRX was not completed until July 22, 1947. While neither ZEEP nor NRX was completed in time to provide plutonium for World War II, the termination of the war, in August 1945, did not significantly alter the Canadian nuclear program.[17]

POSTWAR EXPANSION

It was not until after the war that the Canadian public began to be informed of the nuclear program in Canada. From 1945 on, the public received primarily information that the Government had authorized for dissemination. The Government went to great lengths to advocate the benefits of nuclear technology: improved medical treatments and a potential energy source that would revolutionize the world, as did the combustion engine. Little was said about the NRX's anticipated production of plutonium for American nuclear weapons. Rather than emphasize the sale of plutonium—which was the major source of revenue in the early days—the sale of radioactive isotopes was broadcast as a benefit to humankind. One must be aware of how popular conceptions of atomic energy were molded in the postwar period. Stephen Hilgartner, Richard C. Bell, and Rory O'Connor, in Nukespeak: The Selling of Nuclear Technology in America, argue that after the Second World War and the bombing of Hiroshima and Nagasaki, "nuclear developers used information-management techniques—officially secrecy and public relations—to promote what one called the 'sunny side of the atom.'" The manipulation of language helps explain the public acquiescence to the development of nuclear technology in the postwar period.[18] While it is universally agreed that Hiroshima and Nagasaki radically altered the postwar world, there was also a tendency to view the wartime use of the bomb as justified. It made an invasion of the Japanese home islands unnecessary and saved thousands of Allied lives. To many North Americans, the problem was not atomic energy itself but the apparent unwillingness of the Soviet Union to cooperate with American proposals for international control— as envisioned by the Baruch Plan of 1946. Whatever the rights or wrongs of Soviet behaviour, however, Canadians were exposed to a barrage of propaganda which presented the dawn of the nuclear age in a generally positive light.[19]

In Canada, there appears to have been little question of forsaking nuclear development. The operation of ZEEP was continued, as was the construction of the NRX. The only changes one witnesses in the immediate postwar period were the expansion of the industry and a series of organizational measures. In May 1946, for example, the Atomic Energy Control Act was presented to the Canadian House of Commons by C.D. Howe, Minister of Reconstruction, for the creation of the Atomic Energy Control Board (AECB). This was a historic event in the evolution of a nuclear program in Canada because the new AECB served to guarantee atomic development.

C.D. Howe cited four reasons why Canada was directly concerned with atomic energy: first, uranium was in plentiful supply in Canada; second, Canadian scientists and manufacturers "have taken a very big part" in the development of atomic energy; third, Canada, along with the USA and the UK, possessed "many of the secrets of manufacture"; and fourth, Canada was a member of the United Nations Atomic Energy Commission, formed in December 1945. These reasons translated into: first, existing or potential uranium profit; second, a vested interest by the science community and industry; third, capitalizing on the advantageous position of having acquired the technology; and fourth, a fraternal commitment to our allies to further the development of atomic energy for mutual benefit. To ensure that these four factors were exploited, the Atomic Energy Control Act limited parliamentary control of the Canadian nuclear program.

> The bill permitted the AECB to acquire or cause to be acquired by purchase, lease, requisition or expropriation prescribed substances and any works or property for production... or for research or investigation with respect to atomic energy.

Only the approval of the governor-in-council was needed. This perpetuated the extremely limited character of parliamentary control over atomic energy development. Thenceforth Parliament's control was limited to expenditures. Howe stated that with this control came "the usual opportunity to obtain information about the operations of the project." While this seemed enough, in practice, the ability of members of Parliament to obtain information was severely limited by the amount which C.D. Howe felt willing to divulge. As soon as questions approached a sensitive subject, the reply was that secrecy could not allow the information to be disclosed. Even during the debate or passage of the Atomic Energy Control Act, Howe stated that secrecy would not allow a visit to Chalk River unless the American and British officials agreed. When asked if the proposed bill could be submitted to a committee for further examination, Howe opposed such a step. He argued that the committee would probably request a visit to Chalk River or more information, both of which were not possible at that point.

The bill for the creation of the AECB, aside from limiting parliamentary control, allowed future expansion. The Act provided for the "creation of corporations to carry out certain powers of the board which may be more conveniently performed by separate corporations." This clause was used later in 1952 to establish the Atomic Energy of Canada Limited (AECL).[20]

Thus in the immediate postwar period, the nuclear program was entrenched in the appropriate bureaucratic changes that severely limited public knowledge or possible debate. While still under the veil of almost military secrecy, the program began a long period of expansion. The two most significant events occurring in the first few years after the war were the start-up of the NRX on July 22, 1947, and the announcement of plans to construct a third reactor.

The NRX reactor was a direct outcome of the April 1944 Combined Policy Committee decision. Though intended originally for start-up in July 1945, a variety of delays pushed its completion date to July 22, 1947. Nevertheless, its production of plutonium was reserved for the American weapons program. The reactor was billed as "having the most advanced design and performance of present known reactors." In other words, it produced plutonium at an adequate rate.[21]

But the fanfare over Canadian advances in nuclear technology could only partially compensate for the truth that was harder to accept: the Chalk River project was not a lucrative venture. The prospect of competitive power generation from nuclear energy was still in the future, and the Canadian nuclear program was an increasingly expensive operation. In an attempt to justify the work at Chalk River, it was decided to construct a new reactor specifically devoted to the production of plutonium. Selling this material would increase the project's source of revenue. It also was recognized, however, that should the NRX reactor fail, a back-up would make it easier to keep the Chalk River program alive.[22]

The market for plutonium clients was exceedingly small. The US and the UK were the only possible choices. The British declined a Canadian offer made during the summer of 1949. The UK government was engaged in the construction of three reactors at Windscale, England, for the production of plutonium and did not require the volume that the Canadians wanted to sell.[23] The Americans, however, were willing to purchase the proposed plutonium production. In May 1949, Dr. Chalmers J. Mackenzie, in his new position as President of the Atomic Energy Control Board, discussed the matter with David Lilienthal, head of the United States Atomic Energy Commission (USAEC). By August, the USAEC had agreed to purchase the plutonium from the proposed plant. With the promise of expected revenues sufficient to justify construction of a new reactor[24], Howe authorized the creation of the 1949 Special Committee on the Operations of the AECB. This was a rubber stamp committee which recommended the construction of the proposed reactor and was intended to validate the federal Cabinet's commitment to, and control of, nuclear expansion. On December 8, 1949, the Committee tabled its report, and within two weeks Dr. Mackenzie was informed by Howe that an order-in-council had approved construction of the 60-MWt Nuclear Research Universal (NRU) reactor.[25]

The NRU reactor was the first major development not undertaken as a wartime commitment. Also, while it was built for the production of plutonium for American atomic bombs, it differed in that commercial objectives were increasingly important. As Howe stated in the House of Commons,

> The Chalk River establishment has important commercial possibilities and ... the earnings from this operation will be substantial.... The decision to add a new reactor of commercial capacity had made it evident that the future operation of the property will involve industrial aspects.

As the government research and development agencies and private industrial subcontractors grew and coalesced into what Fred Knelman (in *Nuclear Energy: The Unforgiving Technology*) calls the "nuclear establishment," the prospect of commercial ventures increased in the United States, Britain, and Canada. Knelman's term is extremely useful, as it evokes the bureaucratic and corporate interests which were developing in all nuclear programs. In Canada, the Government's order-in-council, by approving the rationale and cost of the NRU reactor, signalled the beginning of this trend.[26]

The possiblity of commercial ventures arising out of the atomic energy developments was foreseen in the early years. It was not coincidental that the Atomic Energy Control Act allowed for the creation of separate corporations for further development of atomic energy. But by 1951, the prospect of electrical generation from nuclear power was increasing, and the National Research Council, under the direction of the Atomic Energy Control Board, began exploring the matter.[27] With the support of a Canadian utility interested in nuclear power generation and the implementation of the Atomic Energy Control Act's expansion clause, a new Crown corporation was established with a mandate to expand the Canadian nuclear program.

In March 1952, Howe argued it was essential that Atomic Energy of Canada Limited (AECL) be created. It would

> relieve the National Research Council of responsibilities that have become more industrial than research and ... concentrate the management in one agency charged solely with responsibility for expediting development in this expanding field.

If for some members of Parliament it was insufficient simply to justify the creation of AECL as a logical extension of earlier developments, Howe combined this argument with promises of future profits.

It is expected that when the new pile is completed the commercial side of the operation will be self-supporting and that it will in time make a financial contribution to the research activities. However, for a time we will have to ask parliament every year for grants to carry the scientific and development division, in much the same order of magnitude as at present.

But Howe's promotion of AECL also involved distorting reality. Members of Parliament were told that "at the moment there are two broad areas of chief interest [at Chalk River], namely isotope applications and industrial power." This approach effectively emphasized the peaceful and potentially profitable uses of atomic energy at the expense of the foundation of Canada's nuclear program—the production of plutonium for American bombs.

The creation of AECL signalled parliamentary approval for further expansion. The AECB which, according to Howe, "can do almost anything it likes," took the authority it had delegated to the NRC and gave management control of the Chalk River Project to AECL. The new Crown corporation would be responsible for research and development and all Canadian atomic activities. Howe told Parliament that AECL would be administered by nine directors. They would be

appointed by the atomic energy control board with [Howe's] approval. There is no term to their service; they are appointed to serve at will; ... [here would be] four or five men from large electrical power companies, and one or two others from industry generally. [28]

The composition of AECL's Board of Directors suggested two points. First, it was an attempt to involve private industry and provincial public utilities in the Canadian nuclear program. While directorships may have been easily filled, the greater and ongoing problem was trying to involve a variety of companies or utilities in an actual nuclear venture. Second, the choice of Dr. Mackenzie as the first AECL president typified what Fred Knelman calls "the incestuous nature of the Canadian nuclear establishment." Mackenzie was also president of the AECB and had held the same position at the NRC. [29]

The March 1952 creation of AECL implied that everything was developing smoothly. In many ways this was true—until the NRX accident at Chalk River. On December 12, 1952, an explosion within the reactor melted the core. It necessitated cleaning up over one million gallons of contaminated water and dismantling and replacing the radioactive core if the reactor were to function once again. The accident served to test the Government's ability to whitewash problems within the nuclear program. Actually, it was a trial run for a number of later "incidents" that the Canadian government would try to downplay.

The 1952 explosion, however, was singularly important. It was the world's first serious reactor accident. Rather than recognize it as a disaster that could have involved the loss of human life, industry representatives reflected upon it and regretted that the "opportunity to develop [the] first nuclear power

[was] missed by 10 days." In apologizing for the explosion, C.D. Howe stated that the "NRX is an experimental plant designed during the war when there was little if any operating potential." He even argued that AECL was fortunate for

> when the last explosion occurred it was decided that it would be worthwhile to decontaminate the calandria ... to withdraw the calandria for examination and build and install a new calandria which would in effect give us a brand new pile for pile No. 2.... rather than a calamity, the last explosion was perhaps fortunate in that we are able to rebuild the pile.

While possibly effective in downplaying the hazard, such apologies did not explain why an accident could occur in light of the safety devices for shutting down the NRX in an emergency. By offering the members of Parliament a less than objective account of the events, C.D. Howe served to ensure parliamentary approval of expenditures for repairing the NRX and the continued expansion of the Canadian nuclear program.[30]

Given his concern for protecting the nuclear industry, Howe authorized a Special Committee to study the Government's atomic energy projects. It was an important legitimizing tactic, undertaken just two months after the December 1952 explosion at Chalk River. It would thwart fears that the Government was supporting an unviable and dangerous technology that was increasingly expensive and still cloaked in secrecy. Authorizing a Special Committee, however, was not synonymous with a full-scale inquiry. While the Special Committee's area of examination—the Operations of the Government in the Field of Atomic Energy—appeared all-encompassing, this was circumvented by the Committee's inability to call for witnesses and evidence. Selected industry officials were simply presented to the Committee. Of course, Howe offered the Government's excuse for secrecy by saying that

> the work that we are doing at Chalk River is of importance to military developments, and for that reason, and for other reasons, cannot be made a subject of common knowledge. I am sure that the committee will appreciate that fact and will be governed accordingly.

The result was that the 1952-53 Special Committee, as its predecessor in 1949, functioned more as a parliamentary tutorial than as an investigation. As was expected, the Special Committee's final report glowingly approved all developments in the Canadian nuclear program.[31]

THE TRANSITION TO POWER REACTORS

Despite the NRX accident, Canadian nuclear projects continued to develop. The pro-nuclear euphoria had been aided by Dr. Wilfrid Bennett Lewis's 1951 atomic power proposal.[32] Lewis, a British emigre, had directed the Chalk River Project since the summer of 1946 (Dr. John Cockcroft, the previous project director, had been recalled immediately after the War by the UK authorities to head the British program). Lewis argued that research in Canada had developed to the point where it was possible to produce electric power from nuclear energy. This prospect was examined in a nuclear feasibility study launched by AECL in September 1953. The study actually was a concerted effort by the Canadian government to involve provincial utilities in an expensive and risky venture. AECL supplied the technical information and experimental facilities for the study, while the Ontario Hydro Electric Power Commission supplied $100,000 and the personnel (thus training a group of atomic designers).

While the feasibility study was underway, an international event occurred that radically altered the nuclear industries of all countries. In December 1953, US President Eisenhower announced his "Atoms for Peace" policy before the United Nations. The purpose of the program was three-fold. First, by pouring state and private money into a publicity blitz promoting the peaceful atom, the program served to separate, in the minds of the public, reactor construction from weapons production. The former was exalted as a safe, clean energy source "too cheap to meter," while the latter was supported as the technology necessary to deter Soviet advances into Asia, the Middle East, and Western Europe. Splitting the atom into peaceful and military halves was an important prerequisite for the success of the "Atoms for Peace" program's two remaining aims. It opened up information and investment capital for private sources to launch the domestic nuclear power industry. And finally, to facilitate the global expansion of this industry, Eisenhower urged the creation of an international infrastructure that promoted the exportation of nuclear technology to First and Third World American allies. The resultant International Atomic Energy Agency (IAEA), established in 1957, was a UN-affiliated agency with a preponderance of voting power with the Western industrial nations. While responsible for controlling the use of atomic technology, its primary function was to

> encourage and assist world-wide research on and development of peaceful uses of atomic energy and to act as an intermediary for the purpose of securing the performance of services by one member of the agency for another.[33]

The new American program justified and encouraged similar activities within the Canadian nuclear community. Thus in February 1954, it was decided to expand the membership of the original AECL-Ontario Hydro feasibility study. The result was a multi-level investigative group comprised of representatives from AECL, the NRC, Ontario Hydro, and several other power companies. The group's stated purpose was to "provide a medium whereby power producers in all parts of Canada might be kept fully informed of developments in the atomic power field." The expanded committee, like its September 1953 predecessor, was a federal effort aimed at enticing various utilities and industries to involve themselves in nuclear technology. This, in turn, validated the federal government's claim that it did "not intend to get into the business of generating power from atomic energy."[34]

While the investigative group continued its research, C.D. Howe succeeded in having the nominal parliamentary control of AECL further reduced. In 1954, Howe argued that his proposed amendments to the Atomic Energy Control Act of 1946 would "establish administrative machinery and procedures which will better meet the requirements of the present and future program in atomic energy." Actually, the changes increased the independence of AECL's future endeavours in two important ways.

Control of the AECB's research and production operations was transferred to the Chairperson of the Committee of the Privy Council on Scientific and Industrial Research, who could then delegate the work to AECL or private companies. This served further to reduce the AECB's extremely circumscribed function. As Gordon Sims states in "The Evolution of AECL,"

> the relative size of the two organizations militated against effective control. In 1953-54 AECL had a staff of about 1,700 and the AECB a staff of three. AECB's budget for its own regulatory activities was on $40,000 while the research and production appropriation it applied for on behalf of AECL was nearly $20 million.

Sims states that even health and safety regulations were "being administered internally by AECL without AECB supervision." Thus Howe's amendments aggravated an already unbalanced situation.

AECL's power was increased another way. This involved establishing it as the stockholding company responsible for the overall direction of the program, including the approval of operation and capital budgets for Eldorado Mining and Refining Limited and Nuclear Research Limited (the new name given to the Chalk River Project).

The amendments also enhanced the authority of C.D. Howe as the Minister who was the Chairperson of the Committee of the Privy Council in Scientific and Industrial Research. The legislation empowered Howe to decide which companies would receive the work previously done by the AECB. Yet this did not unduly concern the members of Parliament. In fact, M.J. Coldwell, leader of the Cooperative Commonwealth Federation (CCF), thought it "quite justified." But in the event that there were any reservations about his amendments, Howe impressed upon the members that the changes were "following exactly the pattern of organization in the United States." C.D. Howe's control over an increasingly autonomous AECL thus was established at a crucial point in the Crown corporation's evolution. At the international level, with Eisenhower's "Atoms for Peace" program, the initial steps were being taken to establish an international agency advocating the export of nuclear technology. Meanwhile, in Canada, electric power production was becoming technically possible.[35]

By December 1954, the AECL-directed feasibility study had advanced to the stage that the actual design and construction of a 22-MWe reactor was being considered. But by this time, it was also apparent that the February 1954 multi-level investigative group, while possibly having served its information function, had failed seriously to involve any utilities other than the Ontario Hydro Electric Power Commission and the Nova Scotia Light and Power Company Limited. Of the two utilities, only Ontario Hydro could undertake the huge financial and technical risks. Thus it was the sole utility involved in building the proposed Nuclear Power Demonstration (NPD) reactor. AECL hoped that the NPD, which was not expected to produce power at costs competitive with thermal or hydro plants, would provide the operating and cost experience to facilitate the development of larger reactors. The NPD, therefore, was a federal experiment expected to cost between $13-15 million, of which Ontario Hydro agreed to contribute $3-5 million.[36]

AECL experienced similar difficulties in encouraging private industry participation. In December 1954, AECL requested proposals for the design and construction of the planned reactor. Two factors limited the number of potential companies: first, the design, engineering, and manufacturing resources required for such a project were considerable; and second, participation required a financial contribution. It appears that only Canadian General Electric Company Limited (CGE) fulfilled the requirements.[37]

Thus early in the Canadian nuclear program, the federal government recognized the difficulty of attempting to develop nuclear technology in a smaller industrial country. Few utilities and private corporations were capable of undertaking the formidable risks of reactor design and construction. But when C.D. Howe made the announcement on March 24, 1955, that, upon AECL's recommendation, the Government already had authorized the construction of the NPD reactor, little was made of any existing or potential problems.

The NPD was planned as a heavy water cooled and moderated reactor using natural uranium.* While much has been made of the difficulty in choosing a reactor type, it appears there was little room for choice. Two reasons are evident. First, Canada's only major experience had been with natural uranium-fueled heavy water reactors. This was the outcome of several developments: the arrival of the British heavy water team in 1942; large supplies of indigenous uranium; and the April 1944 Combined Policy Committee's authorization of the Montreal project. To have developed a different reactor type would have further increased the cost of the program. The second factor—usually ignored—was the vested interest in the growing community of Deep River/Chalk River. The scientists and bureaucrats involved in a burgeoning nuclear establishment would have opposed any actions which threatened their interests. Emerging from primarily these sectors was the vehemently nationalistic rhetoric trumpeting the wonders of the Canadian-built reactor.[38]

The security of the Canadian nuclear program's proponents, however, was not being threatened. In fact, it was increased after the September 1955

---

* The coolant removes from the fission process the heat that is used to move the turbines which, in turn, generate the electricity. The moderator slows down the fast neutrons and increases the probability of further fission.

signing of a nuclear cooperation agreement with India. The initial outcome of the treaty was the announcement of Canada's willingness to supply India with a research reactor modelled on the NRX—known for its high plutonium production capabilities. The name of the reactor was initially CIR (Canada-India-Reactor). However, Canada was unable to supply the required heavy water, so the Americans provided the material. The name CIRUS was used to acknowledge the U.S.'s heavy water contribution.

The CIRUS reactor, a $9.2-million gift from the Canadian taxpayers, served at least two functions. It was part of the Columbo Plan, which was a program encouraging capitalist development in South and Southeast Asia "as a means of containing communism and offsetting the 'neutrality' of Asia." As John Diefenbaker, the leader of the opposition Conservative Party, later explained, "$50 million a year ... would be cheap insurance for Canada ... to halt communism in Asia." But the reactor also aided the postwar effort of the industrial West to secure Third World markets. CIRUS served to expand the Canadian nuclear industry and offered the hope that future sales might generate some much-needed revenue. [39]

For many people, however, a return on the nuclear investment was not enough. The program's rising costs and continued expansion inspired demands by the federal opposition parties for a full parliamentary inquiry. In an attempt to protect the nuclear program and satisfy the Opposition, C.D. Howe in February 1956 introduced a motion for the formation of a Special Committee to investigate the role of the Government in the field of non-military research in Canada. Howard Green, the Conservative member for Vancouver-Quadra, quickly condemned the motion as insufficient. Green recognized the resolution's three major flaws. First, it asked one committee to study the National Research Council and the atomic energy program. The combining of two fields of investigation for one committee was to occur despite Howe's statements in the year previous. Green quoted Howe's July 15, 1955, comments: "I think it is better to have a committee on atomic energy. I believe it is a big enough field. If other committees in the fields of science are needed, perhaps they could be separate committees." Green realized that with Howe's 1956 motion, the Canadian nuclear program would not receive undivided attention. But other problems also existed. The motion ignored military research. And it did not allow the committee to send for exhibits or witnesses which it felt were relevant. Green was angered by the almost "complete lack of information given to the House." Rather than being fed propaganda and witnesses at the discretion of C.D. Howe, Green advocated the creation of a Parliamentary Standing Committee on atomic energy. Green suggested

we could very well copy at least a portion of the organization... [the Americans] have set up. They have three watchdog committees over atomic energy. One is made up of defence people, a second of scientists appointed from all over the United States, and the third is the congressional committee which is really the congressional watchdog committee on atomic energy.

Green argued that the present Canadian situation robbed Parliament of any effective check on atomic energy expenditures.

Howe, on the other hand, defended the preservation of secrecy, since

> at Chalk River we do a considerable amount of work for the Atomic Energy Commission of the United States having to do with the field of weapons. There is hardly any period when we have not had work of that kind in process at Chalk River. The reason is that the pile there is able to do some work which no other pile can carry out successfully.

In effect, the USAEC was able to conduct military tests in Canada without the examination of American "watchdog committees" and with a Canadian commitment not to allow an investigation into the military aspects of nuclear research in Canada. Was this another example of a smaller country's succumbing to the demands of a larger ally? Perhaps. But the Canadian government's commitment to maintaining secrecy for its own reasons was a more likely explanation. Two facts point to this conclusion. The Canadian nuclear program was completely dependent upon US supplies of heavy water. As well, publicity would have threatened the availability of American technical information. As Howe stated,

> If today this parliament decided that a committee would be appointed with authority to send for papers, I believe the flow of papers to Atomic Energy of Canada Limited would be very sharply curtailed not later than tomorrow.

Thus Howe rejected Howard Green's suggestions as "fatal" to the work in Canada. The Special Committee's mandate, therefore, was limited to the confines of Howe's original motion. [40]

The Special Committee did not affect the development of the Canadian nuclear program. With one firm reactor export and domestic construction continuing, it was committed to further expansion. Proof of this was evident in the April 1957 release of an AECL report advocating a larger reactor. But despite plans for further growth, a problem within the Canadian nuclear program temporarily threatened its future.

A dispute began when Ontario Hydro refused to involve itself further in a relationship whereby Canadian General Electric (CGE) had a monopoly as the commercial supplier of nuclear reactors in Canada. Many companies were willing to engage in subcontracting but, aside from CGE, there were no corporations interested in or capable of undertaking the design and construction of nuclear power reactors. This put AECL in a quandary. Either it would succumb to Ontario Hydro's demands and undertake the sole responsbility for the design and construction of nuclear reactors or Ontario Hydro—the only utility involved—would not participate in future projects.

AECL responded in a statement released in February 1958. The corporation tried to conceal the degree to which it was prepared to expand in order to perpetuate nuclear development and thus secure its own existence. But the rhetoric could only soften the reality. The statement announced the formation of the Nuclear Power Plant Division (NPPD) with the purpose of "designing the nuclear steam supply systems of nuclear stations and for providing management services as required by the customer." Thus AECL had yielded to Ontario Hydro's demands. AECL divested CGE of its monopoly and became a commercial supplier of nuclear reactors in Canada.[41]

Yet little thought appears to have been given to whether the long-term domestic and international markets could support AECL and CGE. Rather than review the development of a nuclear program in Canada, AECL made the changes necessary to satisfy Ontario Hydro. The February 1958 creation of the NPPD revealed three important facts: first, the power of Ontario Hydro was the only serious domestic customer of a nuclear reactor; second, private Canadian industry was unable to establish a competitive nuclear reactor supplier; and third, the Canadian government, acting through AECL, was firmly committed to expanding the Canadian nuclear program to perpetuate the latter's existence.

THE CANADIAN NUCLEAR PROGRAM'S TROUBLED MATURITY

After AECL complied with Ontario Hydro's demands, expansion within the nuclear arena continued. On June 18, 1959, Gordon Churchill, the Conservative government's Minister of Trade and Commerce, announced to the House of Commons the next stage of development in the Canadian nuclear program—a 206-MWe reactor to be located at Douglas Point, Ontario. It was with this natural uranium-fueled, heavy water cooled and moderated reactor that AECL first used the catchy CANDU (Canadian Deuterium Uranium) acronym. According to Churchill, the Douglas Point plant was to be in operation by late 1964 or early 1965, at an estimated $60 million "exclusive of design and development costs." Thus Parliament was denied the total estimated price even though the design and development work had been completed. The studies for the Douglas Point reactor had been compiled from several sources: the initial feasibility study conducted at Chalk River in 1957; the design work on the NPD done by CGE; and the AECL study authorized in 1958 and carried out in Toronto at the Nuclear Power Plant Division offices.

Similar incongruities emerged in the construction of the CANDU at Douglas Point. It was to be a cooperative effort between AECL and Ontario Hydro. AECL was primarily responsible for the design and construction of the plant's nuclear section. Ontario Hydro provided the site, cooperated in the design of the reactor, designed and constructed the conventional sections of the plant, and agreed to operate it as a unit in its power distribution system. While apparently equitable, the actual relationship resulted in AECL's undertaking most of the work, risk, and cost—with Ontario Hydro simply maintaining an option to purchase the reactor. A key agreement divested Ontario Hydro of most of the responsibility:

> Ontario Hydro will buy power produced and will purchase the plant when it has demonstrated that it has suitable characteristics for Hydro's power system. The formula for the purchase price would permit production of power from CANDU that is competitive with the cost of power from modern, coal-fired power plants of a similar size.

With such an agreement, Ontario Hydro had little to lose. And AECL was secure, as it had the support of the Conservative government.[42]

Two facts were revealed by the Diefenbaker administration's approval of AECL's decision to build the Douglas Point reactor. First, there was the speed with which AECL expanded Canadian nuclear development. Back in March 1955, when the St. Laurent government announced before the House of Commons its decision to authorize the NPD reactor, C.D. Howe justified the construction by saying it would provide the operating experience necessary for the development of a large power reactor. But in June 1959, the NPD was still under construction. It was not started up until April 11, 1962, and did not achieve full power until June 28, 1962. Apparently this was too long for AECL to wait. Undaunted, the decision was made to escalate the Canadian reactor program by an order of magnitude—from the 22-MWe NPD reactor to the 206-MWe Douglas Point reactor—and Gordon Churchill, Diefenbaker's Minister of Trade and Commerce, privately authorized the move.

Yet government approval of the Douglas Point reactor was not an only indication of support for the demands of the nuclear industry. It was also an attempt to placate the clamour from Canadian uranium producers. Churchill later stated that he had sanctioned the Douglas Point reactor, without waiting for the completion of the NPD, for one major reason. If it worked,

> then the market for Canadian natural uranium may be assured. This is the target at which we are aiming, and we hope in time that it will support our uranium producing industry at home.

Authorizing the Douglas Point reactor partially succeeded in calming the concern among Canadian uranium producers. At the time of the June 1959 approval, it appeared that the US, the major purchaser of Canadian uranium, would not renew its contract option. The Canadian uranium producers' fears were valid. In August 1959, the United States Atomic Energy Commission informed Ottawa that indigenous American uranium supplies were sufficient to meet their needs.[43]

Churchill's decision to accelerate the Canadian nuclear program was well received. The project further entrenched the nuclear program, provided sub-contracts for private industry, and offered the uranium industry the hope of increased domestic consumption in the future. With the growing concern in early 1959 that the Americans would not renew their uranium contracts, it was unlikely that the Opposition would criticize the Government for succumbing to the nuclear interests. Furthermore, complaints were highly improbable because Lester Pearson, the Member of Parliament for Algoma East (where the Elliot Lake uranium mine is located), was the Leader of the Opposition. Pearson had already expressed to the House of Commons his support for extensive uranium exploitation. In fact, Pearson congratulated Churchill for his decision and proceeded to instill a little fear by stating that

> It certainly is necessary ... that both industry and government at the provincial and federal levels show initiative, drive and planning so we will not be left behind, not only in the international market but perhaps at home.[44]

Pearson's words did not fall on deaf ears. The Diefenbaker administration enthusiastically supported the Canadian nuclear program and worked to reap political gain from increased development. But while the go- ahead for the CANDU at Douglas Point was well received, a second attempt at expanding the program resulted in loud Liberal denunciation. They were not angry with the new project but with the Conservatives' chosen location. The dispute began on October 1, 1959, when Gordon Churchill announced, in Winnipeg, the Government's decision to build a new research centre (eventually named the Whiteshell Nuclear Research Establishment) in Manitoba rather than in the existing communities of Chalk River or Elliot Lake. Later, during the debate in the House of Commons, one member of Parliament quoted from an editorial in the Sudbury *Star* that argued the Conservatives chose Manitoba simply for political reasons:

> Trade Minister Churchill is from Winnipeg South Centre. Prime Minister Diefenbaker is from the west. Premier Roblin of Manitoba is chairman of the Manitoba development authority which has been working in close liaison with Atomic Energy of Canada Limited.

The editor also noted that because Pearson's riding was Algoma East, Elliot Lake was ruled out. Nevertheless, the Government insisted that the choice of a site near Lac du Bonnett, Manitoba, was made for technical reasons. It received an ample water supply from the Winnipeg River, had a firm bedrock, and was close to a university. The Conservatives argued that building the research reactor at Elliot Lake would not substantially have altered the mining community's long-term unemployment situation because of the type of technical employment which the research centre would create.

The Liberal opposition appeared correct in accusing the Conservatives of favouring Manitoba for political reasons, but they failed to notice another reason for the choice of Manitoba. As stated earlier, Ontario Hydro's vehement opposition to the monopoly involvement of a private corporation, Canadian General Electric, in reactor design and construction forced AECL to undertake this task. The NPD, announced in March 1955, was the last reactor in Ontario for which CGE had a major part in the design and construction of the nuclear section of the plant. Yet CGE was awarded the contract for the Whiteshell organically cooled reactor (an oil was used instead of heavy water). It appears, therefore, that the Whiteshell research centre served a number of functions. It satisfied AECL's demands for increased research space while serving the political reasons discussed in the Sudbury *Star* editorial. But also it gave CGE a domestic contract which maintained the corporation's activity in the nuclear program without opposing the demands of Ontario Hydro. Had the centre been built in Ontario, the utility might have demanded that AECL also design and construct organically cooled reactors.[45]

The announcements of the Douglas Point CANDU and the Whiteshell Nuclear Research Establishment revealed the Diefenbaker government's support of the continued development of the Canadian nuclear program. Their support, however, did not compare with that offered by the Pearson Liberals after their 1963 federal election victory. This was evident with the Liberals' December 2, 1963, announcement of the development of a heavy water program in Canada. (Heavy water, or deuterium, exists in nature but requires separation from ordinary, or light, water.) The dependence of the Canadian nuclear program on supplies of American heavy water had long been a point of embarrassment for the federal government. Yet the decision to embark upon a domestic heavy water program was not made simply due to a spark of nationalistic sentiment. Appealing to a sense of Canadian nationalism was useful, but the fundamental reason was economic necessity. The Canadian demand soon would outstrip the American supply. Since large quantities of heavy water would be required in Canada, the anticipated cost of domestic heavy water production would be reduced. This, in turn, would lower the cost of the CANDU reactor.

Earlier AECL investigations into the possibility of building heavy water plants in Canada resulted in the call for private presentations to be completed prior to May 31, 1963. The four companies which submitted proposals were: Deuterium of Canada Limited (Toronto), Dynamic Power Corporation (Calgary), Imperial Oil Limited (Toronto), and Western Deuterium Company Limited (Victoria). On December 2, 1963, C.M. Drury, Minister of Industry, announced that Deuterium of Canada Limited was chosen, as it had

> made an unconditional offer to produce heavy water in Canada for sale at a price which is considerably lower than that of other bidders who fulfilled the conditions established by the government. The proposal by Deuterium contained a commitment that the company would have a substantial degree of Canadian equity participation. Also the company agreed to utilize the maximum possible quantities of Canadian materials and equipment in the construction of the proposed plant.

The contract required that Deuterium of Canada Limited produce "not less than 200 tons of heavy water per year for the first five years of production."

The Government agreed to underwrite the sale at $20.50 per pound and provide a further subsidy of $0.91 per ton of coal used to produce steam and power for the heavy water project. The Government even had a firm commitment that the first 200 tons of heavy water would be available for delivery on or before March 31, 1966, at no more than $22 per pound.

The project was looked upon rather favourably for a number of reasons. For a five-year investment of approximately $41.5 million of taxpayers' money, it guaranteed a supply of heavy water that would abolish the dependence on more expensive American supplies. The plan involved a private company that promised a high Canadian content. Furthermore, it was to be located at Glace Bay, Nova Scotia, thus providing short-term construction jobs, a few long-term maintenance positions, and a guaranteed market for Nova Scotian coal. Nova Scotia was extremely interested. A provincial Crown corporation, Industrial Estates Limited, invested between $25-30 million in the proposed plant. Thus the combined federal and provincial initial investment was estimated at approximately $66.5—71.5 million.

Yet despite repeated infusions of large amounts of money, the Glace Bay Heavy Water Plant became a technical and economic nightmare. It eventually was mothballed as useless. In retrospect, the Pearson government entered the heavy water field without properly considering the potential problems. Atomic Energy of Canada Limited was particularly at fault for inadequately researching the heavy water method used by Jerome Spivak, President of Deuterium of Canada Limited. But why did the Government go along with AECL's hasty choice? Grant Deachman, the Conservative MP for Vancouver-Quadra, offered an explanation. He argued that "if we succeeded in building a plant which produced cheap deuterium, we then had an opportunity to sell deuterium abroad—and not only that, but to sell reactors."[46]

Further evidence that Ottawa and AECL were thinking about future heavy water supplies for reactor exports was brought forward exactly two weeks after the announcement of the Deuterium of Canada contract. On December 16, 1963, Pearson tabled an agreement between India and Canada for the sale of a second and larger reactor. The agreement allowed for the construction of the 203-MWe RAPP (Rajasthan Atomic Power Plant) reactor. This station was of the same size and capacity as the Douglas Point reactor, which was still under construction. The agreement, while not stipulating the use of Canadian heavy water, stated that India should use Canadian uranium and that India would "procure from Canada as much of the material and equipment for the station as is available on reasonable terms and which cannot be procured in India."

The contract for a second Indian reactor seemed to justify all expenditures to date on atomic energy.* Unlike the CIRUS research reactor at Trombay, RAPP was a power reactor export—a Canadian first. The similarity, however, was that it too was heavily subsidized. But of greater importance to the industry, the Indian reactor was not an isolated contract. Within the next

* See Appendix I for a list of federal nuclear energy R & D expenditures.

year, two more projects were announced: the Pickering complex in Ontario and an export agreement with Pakistan.

The new contracts seemed to imply that the Canadian nuclear program had reached maturity. But its growth still was aided by considerable government assistance. The Pickering project was a prime example. On August 20, 1964, the Canadian federal and Ontario provincial governments announced the decision to construct a 1000-MWe nuclear station (comprised of two 500-MWe CANDUs) in Pickering County just outside Toronto. This was to be a cooperative effort among Ontario Hydro, the federal government, and the Ontario provincial government. The total estimated cost was $266 million. Ontario Hydro's financial contribution was relatively fixed at an amount equal to the estimated $120 million cost of the coal-burning station of the same capacity it was building at Lambton, Ontario. It was the federal and Ontario governments that would absorb any cost overruns. Their initial contributions were calculated at a ratio of 1.2 to 1. Thus Ottawa's and Toronto's initial estimated costs were $79.5 million and $66.5 million, respectively. The rationale for government assistance was stated by C.M. Drury, the Minister of Defence Production:

> By reasons of the contingent financial risk in building a very large nuclear power station at this relatively early stage in nuclear development, participation by governments was desirable. No full sized nuclear power station of this type is yet in operation, so there remains a slight measure of uncertainty. This will change when the 200,000 kilowatt nuclear power station at Douglas Point which will soon be completed has shown that it operates successfully.

The Pickering project was a significant development. In a number of ways, it reflected changes within the Canadian nuclear program. First, the station was to be built as a commercial venture. Second, the Pickering contract involved greater participation by Ontario Hydro. This was an important shift that reflected the increased autonomy of Ontario Hydro's nuclear component and the utility's increasing demand for nuclear power at the expense of other energy sources. While AECL designed the nuclear steam supply system, Ontario Hydro had sole responsibility for the remainder of the plant. And third, Pickering was the last domestic CANDU project in which AECL was the project manager. thenceforth, AECL only would assume that role if it were hired. The reason for this shift is obvious; it forced the purchasing utility to bear an increased responsibility for the technological and financial risks.

There was, however, at least one important factor about the August 1964 Pickering announcement that was consistent with the history of the Canadian nuclear program. The two 500-MWe reactors had been authorized before obtaining the operating experience of the previous station which, in this case, was a 200-MWe reactor still under construction at Douglas Point. It would not produce electricity until 1967. But this did not concern Parliament. Representatives of the various parties stated they were "delighted," "glad," and "urging commendation to the Minister of Industry, to Atomic Energy of Canada Limited and to all those responsible for concluding this agreement."[47]

Parliamentary accolades also accompanied the 1965 announcement of Pakistan's decision to purchase a CGE designed and constructed CANDU reactor. The contract settlement for the 125-MWe Karachi Nuclear Power Plant (KANUPP) was facilitated by considerable Canadian government assistance.[48] AECL was also involved. It contributed information and consulting services during the formative period of negotiations. But while the KANUPP reactor contract served to keep CGE in the nuclear field for a few more years, the paucity of export markets was forcing it out of business. Members of Parliament, however, were protected from the reality by optimistic prophecies. Thus C.M. Drury, as Minister of Industry, suggested that

> it is safe to say that interest in the Canadian system is keen; so also is competition from other industrialized nations. But I am sure that an aggressive Canadian industry employing a very sharp pencil, and encouraged by the AECL, should be able to look to markets abroad in the nuclear field in the years immediately ahead.

Yet rhetorical promises of future export markets belied the plans announced in 1964-65. The new policies were intended to create adequate domestic heavy water supplies. AECL officials recognized that until the heavy water constraint was removed, export contracts would be limited. The December 1963 decision to build a heavy water plant at Glace Bay, Nova Scotia, had not resolved the problem. Canada still was dependent upon limited American heavy water exports. To operate the Douglas Point reactor, for example, AECL had to borrow deuterium from the US Atomic Energy Commission. The projected Canadian heavy water requirements were for at least 1,335 tons over the next five years. Yet the projected output of Deuterium of Canada's Glace Bay plant was 200 tons per year for five years and was not contracted to begin deliveries until July 31, 1966. To alleviate the problem, AECL began a program to increase future supply and decrease future demand.[49]

It was decided that building another heavy water plant would resolve the supply crisis. But, once again, the lack of potential contractors complicated the plan. On February 26, 1965, C.M. Drury announced the Government's acceptance of Western Deuterium Company Limited's proposal to produce 300 tons of heavy water per annum (a 50% increase over Deuterium of Canada Ltd.). Yet within two weeks it became known that Western Deuterium could not adequately produce heavy water. Then, in the summer of 1965, the Government announced that the second bidder, Atomic Power Corporation, was not willing to carry over its contract. Finally, in April 1966, the Government announced that CGE had been awarded the contract. After receiving a deadline extension, the company stated, on June 30, 1966, that the plant would be located on the Cape Breton side of the Strait of Canso in Nova Scotia.

By this time, however, the heavy water issue had become more complex. In December 1965, the Pearson government had overreacted when it appeared that there would not be a second heavy water plant under construction. This led to Ottawa's January 1966 authorization of AECL's attempts to double Deuterium of Canada Limited's production at the Glace Bay heavy water plant. The rationale was based on the possibility of export prospects materializing and a belief that an expanded Glace Bay plant would be the only source in production. To criticism that the Government did not know what it was doing, Jean-Luc Pepin, Minister of Mines and Technical Surveys, responded,

> It is quite difficult for Atomic Energy of Canada Limited to state these figures very clearly, because for one thing they depend on contracts which they enter into with other countries of the world. It is quite difficult to know when these contracts will materialize. Second, it depends on production in Canada. It is quite difficult for Atomic Energy of Canada Limited to know whether the contracts entered into by Canadian production companies will be concluded.

The explanation seemed to confirm the criticism.[50]

The Canadian government's attempts to resolve the heavy water dilemma by increasing supply revealed serious planning problems. Yet their tactics for decreasing demand were even more disastrous. On November 4, 1964, C.M. Drury, when arguing that Canada's heavy water supply would be insufficient, stated that "if, during the 1970s, the heavy water moderated power reactors are developed to use boiling light water or light water steam for the coolant, the total requirements of heavy water for each plant will be reduced by about one fifth. He was referring to the AECL investigations aimed at developing a reactor system with a light water coolant to decrease the demand on heavy water, reduce the total cost of the reactor system, and thus increase the Canadian program's competitiveness on the world market. As an added bonus, Drury added that the use of light water would decrease the coolant replacement cost in the event of leakages.

The result of these preliminary investigations was the decision to construct a prototype 250-MWe reactor fuelled by natural uranium, moderated by heavy water but cooled by boiling light water (BLW). This was announced in the House of Commons on May 11, 1965. Exactly why the CANDU-BLW reactor was to be located in Quebec was not explained. Two possible reasons, however, were discernible. First, Ontario Hydro may not have wanted to divest personnel and money from its program on an experimental prototype. Second, and more important, building in Quebec would involve engaging and training Hydro-Quebec officials, thus possibly opening a future market in a second province.

The arrangement among the federal government, AECL, and Hydro-Quebec was virtually identical to the federal government, AECL, and Ontario-Hydro agreement for the Douglas Point station. The plant, eventually called Gentilly I, was to be built by AECL at AECL's expense. Hydro-Quebec

42

would provide the site (which would require AECB approval) and operate the plant as part of its electrical grid system while purchasing the electricity produced. As in the case of Ontario Hydro, Hydro-Quebec was absolved of any liability. Drury informed the Commons that "ownership of the plant will be transferred to Hydro-Quebec when it has been demonstrated that the plant may be operated commercially as a unit in the utility system."

Since the late 1970's, Canadian nuclear officials have not often discussed the Gentilly I reactor. Like the Glace Bay heavy water plant, Gentilly I is the reactor that they would like to forget. A quick review of its performance—or lack thereof—reveals why. In November 1967, Jean-Luc Pepin, Minister of Energy, Mines, and Resources (EMR was created October 1, 1966), stated that AECL expected the plant to cost an estimated $106 million. But by July 1979, AECL announced that the plant would be closed indefinitely. Due to numerous technical problems, the reactor's performance had been dismal. It had

> produced virtually nothing [between 1971 and 1979]. In 1972, its best year to date, it had a capacity factor of 20 per cent but ran at its rated output of 200 MWe for no more than four weeks at a time.

Not only was the plant a financial and technical disaster but it had been an environmental hazard.

> In two days during May 1977 [May 21,22] it managed to spew 10 metric tons of heavy water containing 31,000 curies of tritium (radioactive hydrogen) into the water of the St. Lawrence.

Due to Gentilly I's financial, technical, and environmental record, it is obvious that industry representatives and many academics would try to dismiss the fiasco. James Casterton, for example, a Carleton University researcher, said Gentilly I

> has been plagued with several teething problems which have resulted in numerous shutdowns and AECL has decided to delay efforts to perfect the boiling water variant until some later date.[51]

At the time of the 1965 authorization, one would assume that AECL did not recognize that the Gentilly CANDU-BLW reactor would turn out to be such a disaster. Nevertheless, it was the result of the nuclear industry's attempt to increase the cost competitiveness of the CANDU reactor system and at the same time alleviate the heavy water supply problem. The attempt to boost heavy water supply by rapidly expanding production was undertaken at the same time and with similar results. While it would be a number of years before the Gentilly I fiasco would become evident, there were concerns that the projects to increase the supply would result in a dramatic oversupply. The Canadian nuclear program was capable of such frantic expansion because of two circumstances: the extremely limited public and parliamentary controls; and the world economy throughout the 1960s and early 1970s, which resulted in a voracious demand for energy supplies.

Indicative of the demand for more energy and the ability of Third World countries to embark upon a nuclearization process was the Indian decision to acquire a second power reactor (CIRUS ostensibly was for research purposes). On December 16, 1966, Canada and India signed an agreement which allowed for cooperation in the construction of RAPP-II. This reactor, like RAPP I, was modelled at the Douglas Point Nuclear Generating Station. But the Douglas Point CANDU had only been started up on November 15, 1966, and would not begin providing electricity until January 7, 1967. The absence of an operating history, however, did not seem to generate concern. Instead, Canadian officials were more interested in the rapid expansion of India's nuclear plans which served to validate AECL's export promises, the CANDU design, and the massive federal, provincial, and utility investments.[52]

THE FEDS TO THE RESCUE

The publicity given to the RAPP II contract, however, obscured a looming crisis from public view; there were not enough reactor orders to maintain the Canadian nuclear industry. Domestically, while Hydro-Quebec was cooperating in AECL's Gentilly experiment to decrease heavy water requirements, the utility's major expansion still was with hydro-electricity. Other provinces were considering a nuclear program but not very seriously. Thus the Canadian market was limited to expansion in Ontario. In April, 1967, Ontario Hydro announced its decision to build the Pickering III and IV reactors. This was the second phase of the Pickering project begun in late 1964. The provincial utility and AECL were cooperating on the project, but Ontario Hydro was playing a considerably larger and more independent role.

Canadian General Electric, however, was finding it impossible to maintain its operations in an increasingly unviable field. CGE seemed to be locked out of Ontario Hydro's plans, and the remaining domestic market was not promising. CGE's reactor division had been involved in only the NPD and Whiteshell reactors. Internationally, CGE faced stiff competition from Westinghouse, General Electric (CGE's parent corporation based in Schenectady, New York), and other large corporations. The contract with Pakistan was CGE's only export sale. The company's other major overseas attempts had failed. While CGE allegedly was the successful one of three bidders for the $100-million Finland contract, the deal was not concluded. The excuse offered by one member of Parliament was that the Soviet Union exerted pressure "on the Finland authority to delay the project in order to provide ... [the Soviet Union] with an opportunity to bid on this project." Argentina, CGE's next customer, also chose not to purchase a CANDU. Argentina bought a reactor from the West German Siemans Corporation, apparently, due to more favourable financial arrangements negotiated with the West German government.

In 1968, CGE decided to remove itself from the reactor sales market. This was because of the poor domestic and international sales prospects, international competition, and the loss of its two most recent bids. It is not known if there was pressure from CGE's parent corporation. While CGE was afforded a degree of autonomy, the parent may have instructed the Canadian branch plant to terminate the design and construction of nuclear reactors. From General Electric's perspective, decreasing the number of corporate competitors would increase the probability of the parent company's winning an export contract. While the issue of external corporate pressure on CGE's decision is rather speculative, it is noteworthy that when the decision was made, the Schenectady head office agreed with it. Yet, regardless of possible external factors, the market prospects warranted CGE's 1968 decision.

Under the circumstances, CGE's resolution to withdraw from the design and construction of nuclear reactors was a logical corporate move. Of greater interest, however, was the Canadian federal government's response. On March 22, 1968, Jean-Luc Pepin, Minister of Energy, Mines, and Resources, stated in the House of Commons that a "merger" between CGE and AECL had occurred on the day previous. Pepin described the take-over of the private company's reactor design and construction operation as a one-year contract which he expected would "be renewed for a period of five years." The Minister, however, did not inform the House that the take-over was due to poor market prospects which precluded CGE's continued involvement in the field. Instead, he argued that

> The purpose of the merger is to keep together the nuclear energy design capacity available in Canada partly in view of the possibility of selling Canadian type nuclear reactors in Romania, Finland and elsewhere.

Thus, once again, the House of Commons was denied the knowledge that the industry was not as viable as portrayed. Canadian General Electric Company, the only private firm in Canada that entered the field of designing and constructing nuclear reactors, had just bailed out. Instead of initiating a public review of the situation, the federal government covered up the problems of the international market and, in July 1968, authorized AECL to assume total responsibility for nuclear power marketing. It was a concerted effort to maintain the Canadian nuclear establishment. This was a crucial point in Canada's nuclear program that was denied a public and democratic debate. This was consistent, however, with the nuclear industry's twenty-six-year history.[53]

By 1968, the Canadian nuclear program was at a turning point. While originally developed by the Canadian government and reliant upon American military contracts, by the late 1960s, the industry was becoming a domestic energy supplier. But the CGE action revealed the severity of the market constraints on the industry's future. Thus, in an attempt to resolve the crisis, the Canadian federal government and AECL increased their efforts to maintain the industry with a reactor export program. The limited success of this strategy will be examined in the next chapter.

CHAPTER II

EXPORTING CANADIAN NUCLEAR REACTORS TO THE THIRD WORLD

The export of nuclear reactors and reactor technology has been relentlessly pursued since Eisenhower's "Atoms for Peace" pronouncement at the United Nations in December 1953. The primary reason was that reactor exports aided in the perpetuation of the domestic industry by transferring the original research and development costs to the purchaser. The results were corporate profits in the supplier and client countries. This was a major factor in the Western world's emphasis on nuclear power as the portable energy source essential for Third World industrialization.

But from the Canadian perspective, simple economics did not guarantee international reactor sales for two reasons. First, markets in developed countries were either closed or limited to technology transfers or licensing agreements due to the existence of other highly advanced domestic nuclear programs.* Second, the competition between international reactor retailers made it increasingly difficult to conclude a sale with one of the limited number of Third World countries willing to pursue the nuclear route. This chapter will examine how the Canadian federal government struggled to achieve reactor sales in Taiwan, Argentina, South Korea, and Mexico after Canadian General Electric removed itself from the field. However, to understand the dynamics of a reactor export and, in particular, the receptivity of specific Third World countries toward importing foreign reactors, it is insufficient to examine only the Canadian side. Thus this chapter also will examine briefly the motives of the specific groups within the Third World that have favoured importing power reactors from developed countries.[1]

---

*   For a brief review of Canadian marketing attempts in First World countries, see Appendix II.

TAIWAN

Atomic Energy of Canada Limited's (AECL) first post-1968 contract was signed in Taipei, the Republic of China (Taiwan), with the Taiwan Atomic Energy Commission (TAEC) on September 16, 1969. While important for the Canadian nuclear industry, it was not a major contract for a CANDU reactor. Rather, the AECL-TAEC contract provided for AECL to supply a 40-MWt natural uranium-fueled, heavy water moderated research reactor to be completed by September 16, 1973. The Taiwan Research Reactor (TRR) was a modernized copy of the NRX reactor at Chalk River, Ontario.

AECL officials described the TRR as a turnkey contract in that the corporation supplied, for a fixed price, everything which originated in Canada or at least from outside Taiwan. In the Taiwan example, the research reactor cost $35 million of which 80 percent, or $28 million, was specifically Canadian content. The agreement stipulated that AECL supply all the work necessary for the complete construction, installation, and proper functioning of the research reactor at Hvaitzupa, about 20 miles southwest of Taipei. This included design and construction of the reactor, the first charge of fuel and heavy water, and the training of Taiwanese personnel. Taiwan sent a number of supervisors to Canada for a one-year training program at Chalk River. A Taiwanese design team and senior operating staff arrived in Canada in late 1969, while the main group of operations staff arrived in October 1970. Aside from learning about the operation of a Canadian research reactor, Taiwanese officials acted in an auxiliary capacity at the construction site, supplying power, fresh water, and waste management.

AECL gave the TRR a lot of publicity, for it appeared that a government-directed export program would be viable. But the project involved only a limited number of Canadian companies. Canatom Ltd. of Montreal was contracted by AECL for engineering design, supply of materials, and site and technical supervision. Canatom, in turn, subcontracted the design and technical supervision of the civil works to a company long involved in the nuclear field, Howe International Ltd. The Foundation Company of Canada Ltd. managed the project construction. Furthermore, the TRR project was the only sale Canada would complete with Taiwan. Future sales possibilities were terminated with the estab-lishment of diplomatic relations with the People's Republic of China. This decision was announced by Canada on October 12, 1970, after it had assured Taiwan that the TRR project would not be jeopardized by the shift in Canadian foreign policy.

Thereafter, the Canadian nuclear industry never missed an opportunity to blame the Department of External Affairs for excluding Taiwan from its market possibilities. The fact that Taiwan later ordered six reactors from the USA was used as proof of the lost opportunity in Taiwan. While this possibly was correct, it appears more like an attempt to pass the blame for an inability to market Canadian reactors. Considering the strong economic and military connections between Taiwan and the USA and the success of American nuclear exports in comparison with Canadian efforts, one recognizes that AECL's assumption that contracts were lost—when they may never have materialized—was not based on a strong foundation. Such attempts were more indicative of the Canadian nuclear industry's concern over the future sales prospects. While AECL attempted to gain public support by announcing the TRR as the beginning of a viable export program, it was not oblivious to the lack of sales and the pressure which would ensue from the absence of orders to keep the industry alive. Proof of the internal concern was confirmed in March 1971 when J.J. Greene, Minister of Energy, Mines, and Resources, stated that Canada's nuclear export program had been a dismal failure. The absence of a viable export program was exerting a strong pressure on AECL. To perpetuate the industry, exports were required to maintain corporate involvement. Thus AECL embarked on its most financially disastrous export project in the history of the corporation—the construction of a CANDU reactor in Argentina.[2]

ARGENTINA

The Argentinean nuclear program began in the years immediately after the Second World War with the support of President Juan Domingo Peron. The program's development parallelled the characteristics of the Peronists' economic strategy. The first Peron period, 1946-1955, was typified by a coupling of anti-imperialism with national capitalism. Thus uranium deposits were nationalized to ensure adequate supplies and national control of the resource, while the Argentinean nuclear program was made largely independent of foreign control. In 1950, Peron established the Comision Nacional de Energia Atomica (CNEA). The Commission was to work directly under the President and through the Ministry for Technical Affairs. The publicly stated purpose of the CNEA was to control private and state atomic investigations in Argentina and to recommend a suitable reactor program that would secure domestic energy self-sufficiency. Great emphasis was placed on the Argentinean nuclear program—particularly the Bariloche Atomic Centre on Huemul Island on Lake Nahoel Hoapi in the Andes.

Considerable changes within the Argentinean nuclear program occurred after the September 1955 military coup ousted Peron from power. What ensued was a rapid transition in the Argentine economy that opened the country to foreign investment and particularly American industrial capital. The amount of American investment reflected the rapid change: from 1951-1955 the amount was $750 million; and for 1956-1960, $3.3 billion. This shift parallelled the change in the Argentinean nuclear program, with American assistance largely responsible for the program's expansion.[3]

The first Latin American reactor, the RA-1, was built at the Constituyentes Atomic Centre (CAC) in January 1958. The reactor was based on designs provided by the United States Atomic Energy Commission (USAEC), and its construction was directed by the US Argonaut program. The 10-KW reactor was started up on January 21, 1958, by Argentina's President Pedro Eugenio Aramburu. Two other research reactors, the RA-0 and the RA-2, were also designed and built by the CNEA at the CAC. It is important to note that these specific American contributions preceded the more independently nationalistic economic approach adopted during President Arturo Frondizi's term, 1958-1962.

The March 1962 military coup which ousted Frondizi from power quickly resulted in increased foreign investment. Within three months of the coup, work was begun on the 5,000-KV RA-3 nuclear research reactor at the Ezieza Atomic Centre, located just outside Buenos Aires. The RA-3 was designed and built near the uranium refinery at Ezieza by the CNEA, with assistance from private industry. American assistance was also formidable. The US supplied the plans for the enriched uranium reactor and contributed $350,000. The RA-3 has been used for research in nuclear energy, the commercial production of radioisotopes, and for the development of nuclear fuels and plutonium.

An additional component of the Argentinean nuclear program was the 1968 commissioning of a reprocessing plant built with American and French assistance during the rule of General Juan Carlos Ongania. It was a pilot plant constructed for the reprocessing of irradiated fuel from the RA-1 research reactor. This process results in the production of plutonium. There are two uses for plutonium: first, in a breeder reactor (which Argentina has not acquired), and second, in the production of atomic bombs. A third option is storage for either of the two. The success in the production of plutonium from RA-1 has encouraged the expansion of the reprocessing plant to accommodate irradiated fuel from the RA-3.

Argentina's decision to move from the research reactor stage to large-scale power reactors was made in the late 1960s, during a period of military rule. The choice appears based in the economic climate of the era—favourable supplier terms, easy credit, and a belief in nuclear power. The previous strategy of dependence upon foreign supplies of research reactor technology was repeated at the power reactor stage. In 1967, the CNEA called for bids on a power plant to be located outside Buenos Aires. A British bid, submitted by Nuclear Design and Construction, a coalition effort by English Electric, Babcox and Wilcox, and Taylor Woodrow, was eliminated, presumably in retaliation for a previous British ban on Argentinean beef, mutton, and lamb. Two American bids by Westinghouse and General Electric were reported to be the lowest. But, due to indigenous supplies of uranium, Argentina did not have to select the American-enriched uranium reactor design. This degree of independence from American fuel supplies allowed the choice of a natural uranium-fuelled heavy water reactor. Thus the Argentinean government accepted the West German bid by Siemens AG over that of General Electric (Canada) Ltd., apparently due to the superior financing offered by the West German government. The $70-million contract, awarded to Siemens on February 22, 1968, resulted in the construction of Latin America's first nuclear power plant, the Atucha I. It was built on the Rio Parana de las Palmas at Atucha, about 100 Km northwest of Buenos Aires. Siemens was responsible for the design, construction, and commissioning of the licensed American-designed reactor. While the contract stipulated that the plant be finished by June 15, 1972, the reactor was over a year late in being completed.[4]

Argentina's decision to buy a second power reactor caused a similar flurry of supplier countries bidding on a rare market opportunity. It also resulted in Atomic Energy of Canada Limited's first major foreign reactor sale and a major scandal.[5]

The Canadian Nuclear Establishment Struggles for a Contract

It was no secret that the Canadian nuclear industry needed a reactor contract. Thus in late 1971, when the CNEA, under the Argentine military regime of General Alejandro Lanusse, called for bids on a second power reactor, AECL quickly mobilized itself for the competition. The Canadian corporation was favourably placed, however, for two reasons. Argentina's first power reactor had been a natural uranium heavy water reactor. With this commitment, there was a greater probability they would choose a similar variety for the second reactor. Second, AECL was not an independent bidder. It had entered into a partnership bid for the Argentine contract with an Italian firm, Italimpianti. AECL had an ulterior motive. It hoped that the partnership would allow it to enter the Italian market.* While these hopes did not materialize, the partnership bid later allowed AECL to try to blame Italimpianti when the Canadian public grew irate over the eventual Argentinean reactor scandal.

On May 23, 1972, AECL received Cabinet approval to submit proposals for the Argentinean reactor and, in June 1972, AECL and Italimpianti jointly submitted a bid for a 600-MWe reactor. Italimpianti was to be responsible for the commercial promotion of the reactor and the supply of the plant's conventional components. AECL was to provide the nuclear steam supply system and promote the technical aspect of the sale.

Nearly nine months passed before the Argentinean government made its decision. But, as *The Financial Post* stated, Ottawa expected that Argentina's announcement would be made before the March 11, 1973, Argentinean election. The *Financial Post's* predictions were correct. The CNEA selected the AECL-Italimpianti bid and initiated contract negotiations on the CANDU reactor to be built at Embalse in the province of Cordoba. The CNEA decision was made before the Peronists returned to power.[6]

The elected Peronists re-entered the Argentinean government nearly eighteen years after they had been removed by the 1955 military coup. Their election led to a shift away from Argentina's dependence on Western investment, imports, and technology toward a policy which again promoted independent national development within a capitalist framework. The shift also precipitated a major change in Argentinean science policy. While the Peronists continued the negotiations initiated by the military government, they also launched a debate over the importation of foreign technology and the development of a national science policy.[7]

---

* See Appendix I for a brief review of AECL's marketing attempts in Italy.

Despite the nationalism of the Peron government, on December 20, 1973, a contract approving the reactor sale was signed by CNEA, AECL, and Italimpianti. A second contract was signed between AECL and Italimpianti. It formalized their division of the estimated $420-million Argentine contract. The Italimpianti part of the deal involved approximately $270 million for the conventional generators and plant sections of the nuclear power station. A third contract was a component supply contract, worth approximately $150 million, between AECL and CNEA. It was broken down as follows: $61 million for Canadian goods and services; $56 million for Argentine goods and services; $30 million for the supply of heavy water; and $3 million if Argentina decided to purchase Canadian uranium. Most of the financing for the AECL-CNEA supply contract was made possible through a Canadian Export Development Corporation (EDC) loan of $129.45 million. Yet the $150-million contract could be reduced to a firm $91 million, since $56 million was to be spent in Argentina, and the $3 million for uranium was optional. The contracts came into effect in April 1974.[8]

Canadian government support for the sale was understandable; a reactor contract was desperately needed. But why did the Peronists authorize a reactor import when they were advocating a nationalist science policy? While it was possible that the CNEA was primarily allied with the Argentine military and other segments of society favouring foreign imports, another possible reason was also evident. This related to the favourable financial terms offered by Canada. There appeared to be no other major reason to explain why Argentina accepted Canada's offer. The possibility that Argentina refused the bid by West Germany, the only other heavy water reactor exporter, due to Siemens' lack of a design for a 600-MWe reactor or that Argentina wanted to decrease its dependence on West Germany does not seem likely. Later, in October 1979, Argentina would choose the bid from Kraftwerk Union (which owned Siemens) without a reactor design. It was the Canadian debt financing of the Argentinean reactor and AECL's use of an agent to procure the contract which prompted the CNEA to order a CANDU.

The Conditions for Financing the Argentine Reactor

While the Argentinean contract seemed to promise a beginning to commercial reactor exports for AECL, it soon revealed the corporation's inability to market its product successfully. The greatest blunder involved the original $150-million supply contract between AECL and CNEA. It was backed by a $130-million EDC loan at "a rate of interest somewhat lower than the domestic Crown corporation rate" payable over twenty-five years but did not adequately account for inflationary pressures on the prices of items included. By 1975 it was evident that, unless the contract was renegotiated, AECL would lose over $200 million.[9]

One could conclude that AECL was inept at negotiating a contract. But a more probable conclusion is that the contract revealed AECL's desperation for a reactor export; why else would it negotiate a firm contract price with a 25 percent ceiling on the allowable inflation? The results of this tactic undoubtedly were exacerbated by the 1973-74 inflationary spiral, but it appears that when AECL signed the December 20, 1973, contract it hoped to build its reputation as a low cost nuclear supplier. The Argentinean reactor was considered by the industry as a loss-leader. AECL needed the Argentinean contract to get a large power reactor out on the export market so that other purchasers could recognize the Canadian corporation as a viable reactor exporter and thus ensure the involvement of domestic industries in the supply of nuclear components.[10]

Later, however, AECL became worried that the size of the anticipated loss would be counterproductive for the domestic and international community's perceptions of the corporation. Thus between January and June 1976, the contract was renegotiated. James Casterton, in "The International Dimensions of the Canadian Nuclear Industry," argues that renegotiation was made possible as Argentine law is based, in part, on Roman law which allows for "adjustment if circumstances outside a contract change significantly so that the contract became too onerous for one party or the other." He cites the 1974 oil crisis as the external factor which enabled the contract negotiations. While this may have aided the agreement to renegotiate, a more fundamental reason was offered in the House of Commons by Alastair Gillespie, Minister of Energy, Mines, and Resources: "I believe there was some additional financing... that would cover the escalated costs of the total contract."

Events in Argentina also facilitated the renegotiation process. On March 24, 1976, a bloody military coup ousted Isobel Peron's government. The coup—which did not halt the renegotiation process—seriously altered the Argentinean science community. Immediately after the military take-over, the Navy began killing, kidnapping, and arresting many of Argentina's prominent physicists. Maximo Pedro Victoria, the former head of the metallurgy division of the Argentine Atomic Energy Commission (AAEC) and former director of the National Institute of Industrial Technology, stated that physicists were singled out due to their activity in the discussion of a national science program that began in 1971 and continued until 1975. Victoria stated: "We were defining a policy in Argentina [against] technology that we were importing. This does not go well with a group in the Navy that prefers to obtain technology from outside." The military coup silenced the physicist opposition. Three members were killed; some were missing and assumed dead; others were imprisoned; more than eighty physicists were removed from their positions.

Yet despite the silencing of a segment of Argentinean society that would have opposed the renegotiated sale and the Canadian promise of additional financing, the renegotiations did not remove the deficit to be paid by Canadian taxpayers. Instead, the amount was reduced from $200 million to approximately $130 million in May 1977. Since then, AECL has struggled to halt the rise of the loss. In the fall of 1980 AECL was attempting to ratify the transfer of construction responsibilities to the CNEA. It was part of a continuing effort to diminish the losses for which it was largely responsible due to the original contract terms.[11]

The Argentine Agent

The second aspect of the Argentinean contract which infuriated Canadian domestic opinion was the use of an agent in procuring the reactor deal. The employment of an agent was agreed upon by AECL and its Italian partner, Italimpianti. The contract stated that the agent's payment would be split equally by the two companies. When Italimpianti informed AECL that it had paid its half, the Canadian corporation deposited $2.415 million in the Banca della Suizzera Italiana in Lugano, Switzerland, for the Intercontinental General Trading Establishment (IGT) of Schaan, Liechtenstein. On April 19, 1974, J. Lorne Gray, President of AECL, authorized the money.

Investigations by the Parliamentary Standing Committee on Public Accounts and the Royal Canadian Mounted Police attempted to determine who received $2.4 million of Canadian taxpayers' money. Throughout the investigations, AECL and federal Cabinet officials testified that they did not know the agent's name. While neither investigation revealed the individual(s), both received much public criticism. The opposition parties accused the Government and AECL of withholding information before the Public Accounts Committee investigation. Supporting the opposition's claims, Dr. Marvulli, a federal state prosecutor in Genoa, Italy, stated that the thoroughness of the RCMP investigation left "much to be desired." Actually, it was an investigation in Argentina that named two possible recipients of the Canadian money: Jose Ber Gelband, former Argentinean Minister of Economic Affairs, and Adolfo Mario Savino, former Minister of Defence. But nothing was proven.[12]

It is a matter of speculation whether Canadian officials actively frustrated the full examination of the agent's payment. What is known, however, is that nobody admitted authorizing the agent. The federal Cabinet tried to plead ignorance and stated that they had not specifically approved the use of the agent. Meanwhile, AECL argued that when they had discussed the matter with Cabinet in early 1974, the idea had not been vetoed. AECL later claimed that Cabinet silence meant approval. It seems that from the Cabinet's and AECL's perspective, it was simpler to hide the truth in this fiasco. Without such efforts, it would have been detrimental to all parties involved in the Argentinean deal. AECL was not about to press Italimpianti for the name of the agent, as that could have jeopardized future relations with the Italian company. The Canadian corporation wanted this connection to break into Italy's nuclear market. There also were important personal involvements. Pressuring Italimpianti might have jeopardized the position of J.L. Gray, the former AECL president (he retired January 1, 1975), as a consultant to Finmecanica, Italimpianti's parent company. And pressuring Lucien Secouri, Italimpianti's president, for the agent's name might have made it more difficult for Secouri due to his preoccupation with corruption charges he faced in connection with the Argentine Alvar Aluminum Company.[13]

Summary of the Sale

The total cost of the Cordoba reactor to Canadian taxpayers has not been made public. A crucial fact necessary for such a calculation is the exact subsidized rate of interest on the $130 million EDC loan. An additional amount must be included to cover the cost of the defective boilers installed by Babcox and Wilcox (Canada) Ltd. Large numbers of the boiler tubes were bent and warped due to a heat treatment process applied by the private company. In 1979, AECL estimated the cost of repair between $3.75 million and $15 million plus the additional cost of delaying the project by more than a year. [14]

The Cordoba reactor sale revealed the desperation of the Canadian nuclear industry. To make a sale, AECL used secret agents when GE and Westinghouse had stopped such practices. It also negotiated a subsidized contract to break into the market and had poor quality control on the items it contracted in Canada. But the Cordoba scandal did not stop AECL from attempting to secure a second Argentinean contract. After the CNEA announced its decision to build another natural uranium heavy water reactor, AECL submitted a comprehensive tender in March 1979. Castro Madero, CNEA President, announced in October 1979 the decision to accept the West German bid on a reactor the Germans had yet to design. In Ottawa, the Liberal opposition tried to blame the Conservative government for the lost sale. The Liberals, in accusing Joe Clark's Cabinet of not actively pursuing the Argentine sale, ignored the more likely fact that AECL, due to a multimillion-dollar deficit, was unable to offer a competitive bid for the reactor and that Argentina had probably initially chosen the AECL-Italimpianti offer for the Cordoba plant because of an extremely low bid. [15]

It also appears that the segments of Argentine society that favoured strong dependent ties with international finance capital have profited from the Cordoba reactor. Its placement at Embalse on the Rio Tercero just south of Cordoba in Cordoba province was seen as an important key to Argentinean industrialization. But due to the military's economic policies, the profits from the industrialization will not be equitably distributed. Instead, the CANDU supplies power to the region's foreign-owned automobile plants and fuels the profits of foreign corporations operating in an economy where workers' wages are maintained at an artificially low level. [16]

From the Argentinean example, one can better understand why a country that is extremely dependent upon Western trade and investment is more likely to import nuclear technology. First, due to its receptivity to foreign capital, it is more capable of receiving Western financing for nuclear technology. Second, such a country is more willing to purchase the technology to have an energy source available to attract and fuel foreign-induced industrialization while it receives some of the revenue from this process. Thus the government and ruling elites can gain personally and enable their country to become known in Western finance circles as a good investment area. Since the 1976 coup, the Argentinean government has continued its support for importing technology; witness the 1979 Argentina-Kraftwerk Union contract. The further nuclearization of the Argentine economy has been reduced in the early 1980s by economic constraints. These are largely an outcome of the global economic depression.[17]

For these reasons, the Cordoba reactor contract resulted in a large Canadian public outcry against the way AECL was conducting its business and its impact on other countries. The opposition to the Canadian reactor export to Argentina, however, was increased, as many of AECL's tactics were duplicated in the sale to South Korea.

REPUBLIC OF KOREA

Since the end of the 1950-1953 war, South Korea's development strategy has been relatively consistent. Throughout the period, Korean leaders have tied the country to American and, more recently, Japanese investment centres. Based as it is on repressed wage levels and foreign investment and loans, the South Korean model of development is neo-colonial. But South Korean business also depends on the existence of a strong state.

It is the South Korean state which has created the reciprocal dependency between itself and the Western powers. The American investors require and aid the continuation of a strong South Korean state to secure investment opportunities. The amount of military and economic support provided by the Americans to South Korea—$189 billion between 1945-1976—underlies the importance of the area to American capitalism. As well, the South Korean state requires the foreign capital to perpetuate its existence and receive revenue—not simply in the form of tax revenues but in joint ventures.[19]

The South Korean nuclear program reflects the continuous maintenance of strong foreign connections since the Korean War. American involvement and encouragement have always been evident. In this sense, there is an important distinction between the Argentinean and South Korean nuclear programs, and it is a function of the specific form of economic development dominant at the time of initial nuclear involvement. Whereas the Argentineans, while pursuing a national development strategy under Peron, supported indigenous nuclear research and development and thus later possessed a stratum of society opposed to the importation of foreign technology, in South Korea such a result has not occurred due to the more consistent pursuit of a state-capitalist economic strategy. Indicative of the importance of foreign— specifically American—penetration is a chronology of South Korean atomic energy activities compiled by the South Korean Ministry of Science and Technology. The first item is the February 3, 1956, signing of a nuclear cooperation agreement between the USA and the Republic of Korea.

It was not until after the nuclear agreement had been signed that South Korea began creating the infra-structure necessary to develop and administer the technology. Thus on March 9, 1956, the South Korean government established an Atomic Energy Section in the Ministry of Education; and on August 8, 1957, the country became affiliated with the International Atomic Energy Agency (IAEA), which facilitated the importation of foreign nuclear technology. To coordinate and direct the South Korean nuclear program, the Office of Atomic Energy (OAE) was established, under the direct control of the President on January 21, 1959. To help develop Korean research capabilities, the Atomic Energy Research Institute (AERI) was established within the OAE on March 1, 1959. American assistance and involvement in the South Korean nuclear program was continued throughout the early development stage and enabled the Koreans to build the 100-KW Triga Mark-II research reactor. Construction of the $520,000 research reactor began in July 1959 and was made possible due to the American supply of at least $330,000.[20]

South Korean Use of Nuclear Power Reactors

What is of greater interest and importance, however, was the reason for the South Korean progression from the research reactor stage to the importation of nuclear power reactors. The post-1973 South Korean rationalization for a planned nuclearization totalling 4.2 million kilowatts (which, in 1983, was already far behind schedule) was that rising oil prices necessitated this shift. The Western press accepted and emphasized this argument, as it served to instill an anti-OPEC/pro-nuclear sentiment among the domestic Western populace.[21] While aggravated by the rise in oil prices, the real origin of the South Korean advocacy of a large nuclear power component preceded the 1973 OPEC decision and was a function of an important shift in the South Korean economy that began in the late 1960s.

South Korea has been known for its production of light consumer goods. Foreign industries have profited from the large—primarily non-unionized—South Korean labour force. The export statistics reveal the monumental growth: from $54.8 million in 1962 to over $5 billion in 1975.[22] Fueled by the profits from an export-led light industry economy, the South Korean state and private investors increasingly were interested in diversifying the economy. Such concerns parallelled the needs of Western investors wanting to locate in a cheap (i.e. repressed) labour area. The result was the development (beginning in the late 1960s and thus coinciding with the decision to begin nuclearization) of large-scale, energy-intensive petro-chemical and manu-facturing sectors to augment the profits from consumer goods production. Typical of previous South Korean business practices,

> petroleum is 100 per cent controlled by subsidiaries of US corporations such as Gulf, Caltex, and Union, in joint ventures with the ROK [Republic of Korea] government, while the petro-chemical sector is also dominated by foreign (largely, but not exclusively, American) capital in 50:50 joint ventures with vthe South Korean government.

One can conclude that the decision to implement a program of power reactor construction was caused by the decision to move into highly energy-intensive production.

Once again, American corporations, technology, and financial assistance were prominent. Westinghouse received the contract for South Korea's first nuclear power plant, the 595 MWe KORI I. Construction of the plant, begun on December 31, 1971, was for the Korean Electric Company, the state body responsible for power generation. The South Korean program further expanded with the achievement of criticality at the second 100-KW research reactor, Triga Mark III, on May 19, 1972. Westinghouse also received the contract for South Korea's second power reactor, the KORI II. As before, the US Export-Import Bank was responsible for most of the financing of KORI II which, in 1975, was estimated at approximately $450 million. [23]

The availability of power for industries is essential. But it can result in monumental profit because of a repressed wage area and corruption in the South Korean economy. Kim Chang Soo, in an article examining the effect of the South Korean economic strategy on the workers, states that without committing a cent, $92 million in profits was extracted from joint petrochemical ventures between the South Korean government and a number of US companies including Gulf, International Mineral, Skelly Oil, and Swift Agricultural Chemicals. The US Agency for International Development provided the low interest loans—taxpayers' money. [24] Such examples and others of corruption and kick-backs later generated the suspicion in Canada that AECL, through its vagent, bribed its way to a South Korean reactor contract.

Canada's South Korean Agent

Exactly how Canada was able to break into the American monopoly in South Korea has remained something of a mystery. It also was somewhat peculiar that Canada was chosen, in January 1975, to build a 629-MWe reactor at Wolsung without the normal procedure of the purchasing country's calling first for international bidding. How has Canada's receipt of the contract been explained? The reason most often given by AECL and its publicity agents was that the South Koreans were impressed with the CANDU reactor. However, this failed to explain why, in 1979, Westinghouse was awarded the contract for KORI III and has been considered to be the likely recipient of future South Korean reactor contracts. Obviously, being impressed with the CANDU was insufficient to guarantee future contracts. Actually, this line of reasoning could lead one to conclude that, at some point, the South Koreans became disillusioned by the Canadian system. [25]

A more plausible explanation for Canada's having been awarded the South Korean contract appeared to be a combination of two factors. The South Koreans may have wanted to decrease their dependence on American supplies of enriched uranium and, in turn, by appearing to take a more independent position, force the Americans to increase their military and economic commitment to the region. However, such an approach could only be fulfilled with an economically viable reactor contract to interest the Koreans. This is where Shaul Eisenberg's role in the South Korean contract becomes important.

In late 1968, Shaul Eisenberg, an international wholesaler and financier based in Israel, approached J. Lorne Gray, President of AECL, stating that Canada did not know how to market its technology. Eisenberg committed himself to aiding the Canadian corporation to break into the South Korean market.[26] By 1973, negotiations between AECL and the Korean Electric Company (KECO) were underway. It is not known if, or the extent to which, Eisenberg may have bribed South Korean officials. It is apparent, however, that Gray discussed the potential South Korean reactor sale and the use of an agent at a Cabinet committee meeting on government operations on June 11, 1973. Later, this particular Cabinet meeting caused a lot of confusion. The opposition parties claimed that since the agent had been discussed, the Cabinet had given approval. Prime Minister Trudeau explained that though Gray may have discussed the matter with Cabinet, he had not asked for authorization and, thus, it had not been given. But why was AECL's President addressing a Cabinet committee meeting? Trudeau stated, "because it was a very large budgetary matter which was being dealt with that AECL came before Cabinet to indicate what it was doing." Yet while he refused to concede that there was anything unusual about paying an agent to sell a reactor, an examination of the contract settlements with Shaul Eisenberg suggested an attempt to mask the size of the agent's fee.

On December 30, 1974, J.L. Gray confirmed in a letter to the South Korean officials that an agreement was being negotiated to pay Shaul Eisenberg of Tel Aviv $17 million plus another $3 million at a rate of $500,000 per year for six years. This must have pleased the South Korean officials, for on January 27, 1975, they signed a contract for a $500-million 629-MWe CANDU reactor. The contract came into force on January 26, 1976. However, on January 1, 1975, J.S. Foster became the new president of AECL. Foster immediately took up the issue of the agent in the South Korean contract with Donald Macdonald, Minister of Energy, Mines, and Resources, and Ross Campbell, Chairperson of AECL's Board of Directors. Eventually, by March 1976, AECL was able to reduce Eisenberg's straight 4 percent commission, or $20 million, to $18.5 million. AECL and the Government continually emphasized that they had saved the Canadian taxpayers approximately $1.5 million. (Ironically, it was the attempt to reduce Eisenberg's original fees that caused the Auditor General to investigate the issue, for the bookkeeping was not to his satisfaction.) It is important to recognize, however, that AECL did not renegotiate the contract simply to save money. It was later revealed that Eisenberg accepted the cut in pay after AECL agreed to hire him as the sole agent for negotiating a possible second reactor contract. Thus, as Ed Broadbent, the leader of the New Democratic Party queried, if a second CANDU sale were achieved, could not the renegotiated agreement between AECL and Shaul Eisenberg allow him to "more than recoup his loss"? It appears that the renegotiation of the contract served to cut AECL's costs by $1.5 million but also maintained the services of the man largely responsible for the initial reactor contract.

The renegotiated $18.5-million agent fee appears even more interesting when one examines how it was broken down. The original contract had

Shaul Eisenberg as the recipient of $20 million. The renegotiated settlement, however, went to a number of companies. It was the manner in which the rewritten contract was composed that leads one to question if AECL was attempting to cover up the recipient of the money. The $18,515,574 agent fee was broken down as follows: $5,142,393, or 1 percent of a $514 million reactor; $8,098,500 for expenses; $132,289 in interest for delay of payment; and $5,142,392 for post-contract services. The $8,098,500 for expenses wase divided as follows: $5,400,000 "allocated in accordance with Eisenberg's instructions," and $2,698,500 to three consulting firms. One firm, the Triangular Trading Company of Panama, received $1,285,000 and turned out to be not a firm at all but a lawyer for the United vDevelopment Company, owned by Eisenberg. The two other companies, Industrie Export GmbH. of Frankfurt, Germany, and International Shipping and Shipbuilding Establishment of Hong Kong, received $514,000 and $899,500, respectively. It was later discovered, however, that both companies were owned by Shaul Eisenberg, located in the same office, and used the same telephone.

The $5,142,392 allotted for post-contract services also was noteworthy. Eisenberg was paid $2,000,000 in advance, and the remaining amount was to be paid in quarter annual amounts of $175,000. What was AECL to receive for $5.1 million? Maurice Dupras, Parliamentary Secretary to the Minister of Energy, Mines, and Resources, went to great lengths to specify exactly what Eisenberg was doing for his money:

> first, assistance in getting AECL's office and personnel established in Korea; second, assistance with the entry and handling of all goods imported for the job ... third, assistance, as necessary, with local subcontracts for labour, material and services; fourth, advice on Korean laws and regulations affecting the execution of the main contract; fifth, commercial assistance to AECL in respect of dealing with the customer concerning changes in the scope of the work and the provision of spare parts; sixth, provide experienced staff in Korea and elsewhere as necessary to perform these functions.

Dupras added that other services which could arise would be performed by the agent. While the list appeared rather formidable, it also seemed that many of the duties could have been assigned, for example, to a project manager, a lawyer knowledgeable about South Korean law, and others that would have accomplished the jobs with equivalent efficiency and less cost to the Canadian taxpayer. And Eisenberg's services were for only $5.1 million of the $18.5 million total.

Sung Nack Chung, Vice-President of the Korean Electric Company, provided further support for the contention that what AECL had belatedly called an "agent fee" had been in fact a pay-off for a reactor contract. Sung reportedly stated that an agent was not necessary. Allan MacEachen, speaking as the Acting Prime Minister, retorted that Sung did not hold the position at the time of the contract settlement and therefore was misinformed. Yet one would assume that Sung Nack Chung would know if Eisenberg was fulfilling the required post-contract services. Evasive replies from Canadian government officials, however, were not limited to the use of an agent in South Korea. It also was difficult for Canadians to determine the extent to which the Canadian-supplied Wolsung reactor had been subsidized.[27]

Financing Wolsung

The Canadian government was generous to not only Shaul Eisenberg. The financing of the Wolsung reactor also revealed a generous settlement with the South Korean government. On May 28, 1975, the financial agreements were signed. This finalized the specific contract negotiations, signed in January 1975, that became effective one year later. When the May 1975 financial contracts were settled, the price of the reactor was $576.5 million (up 15 percent from the $500- million figure quoted in January 1975). Possibly due to the long lead time involved in reactor construction and the Canadian desire to save on interest charges, it was agreed to finance the Wolsung reactor in two stages.

The first loans, agreed upon in May 1975, totalled $380 million. Of this, $50 million was provided by a consortium of British banks, headed by Hambros Bank Limited, for the purchase of turbine generators from a British firm, Howard Parsons Limited. The remaining $330 million was arranged by the Canadian Export Development Corporation (EDC). It included: a $250- million loan on the authority of the Canadian government; a $50-million credit extended by the EDC; and a $30-million loan by the Royal Bank of Canada. Three facts about the initial financing deserve attention. First, the $50 million for British goods and services belied the wonders of the Canadian designed and produced CANDU. Second, the $330-million EDC loan was the largest the organization had arranged to date and thus emphasized the extent to which Canadian government agencies were pushing the reactor sale. Third, the terms were extremely favourable; the EDC loan was payable in thirty semi-annual installments commencing not later than six months after the reactor's commissioning or October 1982, whichever came first. Since Wolsung was not commissioned prior to October 1982, the repayment period began at that point and will continue until October 1997. The rate of interest on the loan was not announced. The Canadian federal government argued that to do so publicly would impair future negotiations. Such a stance meant that the Canadian public remained unable to calculate the extent to which their tax money had subsidized the Canadian nuclear export program. It was not a question of whether or not the reactor was subsidized, for even researchers generally sympathetic to the industry admitted it. The issue was the extent of subsidization. Considering AECL's track record in export sales, the revelation of the interest rates probably would have created more domestic repercussions than lost sales.

By late 1978, South Korean and Canadian officials were negotiating the second set of loans for the Wolsung reactor. In May 1975, they settled on an additional $200 million (on the $576.5 million total base price the Canadians were trying hard to maintain). The EDC acted as an agent for a number of

Canadian banks: the Royal Bank of Canada, the Bank of Nova Scotia, the Canadian Imperial Bank of Commerce, the Toronto Dominion Bank, the Banque Nationale du Canada, and the Provincial Bank of Canada. The reasons for the additional funding were easily discernible. First, the loan would aid South Korean financing of the expensive project, the price of which was already increasing due to inflation. The second relates to the timing of the loan; AECL was attempting to negotiate a second reactor contract. The additional loan would serve to increase the image of Canada as a nuclear supplier willing to assist its customers.

The subsequent Canadian loan, however, failed to secure a second reactor sale. Canadian officials had been rather optimistic about the South Korean prospects. In 1974, G.T. Leaist, the manager of nuclear power marketing for AECL, reportedly stated that the South Koreans had decided to purchase a second CANDU. Why did Canada fail to receive the additional contract? Two possible reasons exist. First, American officials exerted pressure on their South Korean counterparts to accept the Westinghouse bids. One must remember that J.L. Gray, President of AECL, had admitted that American pressure may have been responsible for the South Korean cancellation of meetings in 1968 and the awarding of the contract for Kori I and II to Westinghouse. The Americans also had exerted strong pressure on the South Koreans in 1976 not to purchase a French reprocessing plant. At that time, The New York Times stated that unless American desires were heeded, "steps would be taken to block South Korea's acquisition of nuclear reactors for peaceful purposes." And finally, at a critical time when South Korea was making its decision, US President Jimmy Carter and American Treasury Secretary W. Mitchell Blumenthal just happened to be in Seoul urging the South Koren government to buy two reactors from the United States.

Independently, American pressure, while important, appears insufficient to explain the South Korean acceptance of the Westinghouse bids. To understand the dynamics of the South Korean decision, one must examine the second reason for the Canadian loss of a reactor sale—the financial arrangements offered to the South Koreans. When Carter and Blumenthal were in Seoul, South Korean officials admitted to the American press that they intended to borrow $1.4 billion from the United States Export-Import Bank to finance two reactors. When the financial agreement finally was signed in Washington on February 20, 1980, by Lee Hahn-Been, South Korean Deputy Prime Minister, it had been reduced to $1.1 billion. While the amount had been significantly reduced, one must still question whether Canada could have provided equivalent funding for the South Korean deal when it already was under contract to provide $1 billion to Romania.* To understand the relevance

* Canadian marketing attempts in Romania will be examined in Chapter V.

of this question, one must examine the status of the Canadian nuclear program after 1975. [28]

POLITICAL FALLOUT

The Taiwanese, Argentinean, and South Korean reactor deals may have assisted in the perpetuation of the Canadian nuclear program, but they were counterproductive to the industry's attempts to improve its domestic public image. Sectors of the Canadian press and public were critical of the realities of AECL's involvement in the international market. Having to pay known and unknown individuals millions of dollars on reactor contracts which were financial disasters, and subsidizing the sales with interest rates that could not be made public served to create a demand for a public inquiry. However, a full-scale public inquiry did not occur. Later, there were two inquiries, but as we shall see, not all their findings were made public, and their terms of reference were circumscribed. The Canadian nuclear program was not even subjected to the well-known Canadian institutional device for mediating, diminishing, and delaying conflicting interests—a Royal Commission. Joe Clark, as Leader of the Conservative opposition, was insistent upon the need for a Royal Commission, yet curiously delayed its authorization throughout his nine months as Prime Minister in 1979. Such procrastination forces one to question whether there was, as Clark claimed, insufficient time, or were the pressures emanating from the Canadian nuclear establishment too strong to permit an investigation?

The Liberal government was consistent in refusing to admit the need for an investigation. While the 1975 Liberal Party Convention had supported a general review of the Canadian nuclear program, the Government had never responded favourably. Instead, it argued that provincial inquiries were sufficient. In this sense, the provincial governments had been more responsive to public demands for action: in British Columbia, uranium mining and health and safety were examined; in Saskatchewan, the Bayda inquiry investigated the impact of existing and continued uranium mining; in Ontario, the Royal Commission on Hydro Electric Power Planning, or the Porter Commission, examined a deluge of primarily industry-generated material related to the impact of nuclear technology. The provincial investigations, while important in revealing a wealth of information, tended to deal with more specific and provincial matters and within these confines served to mediate—not solve—the problems. But relying on provincial investigations of a federal issue, as Trudeau repeatedly suggested, further fragmented the issue, allowed many questions to remain unanswered, and perpetuated the functional secrecy in which the Canadian nuclear industry operated. From the industry's perspective, it was crucial that a full inquiry be avoided at all costs, as it was more advantageous to have those opposed to nuclear power remain confused and uninformed than to involve itself in a serious public debate.

The issue of debate was crucial, for public propaganda sessions were obviously insufficient. A case in point was the March 1979 conference called

"Nuclear Issues in the Canadian Energy Context." It was organized by the Committee on Nuclear Issues in the Community (CONIC), which was created in early 1978 by the Royal Society of Canada and v the Science Council of Canada, with funding from the Department of Energy, Mines, and Resources and the Department of Fisheries and Environment. Curiously enough, the formation of CONIC coincided with the public outcry against the Argentinean and South Korean reactor contracts. This coincidence was compounded by the grant of $200,000 given to the co- sponsors of the conference, the Royal Society of Canada and the Science Council of Canada, and the Government's rejection of a motion that the Canadian Coalition of Nuclear Responsibility (CCNR) and Energy Probe (two public interest groups critical of the Government's nuclear policies) receive equal funding to balance the CONIC presentation. Nor was there any apparent governmental concern when two CONIC members resigned. David Brooks quit when the committee refused to hold public meetings in three communities—Kingston, Peterborough, and Sault Ste. Marie—which had expressed an interest in making presentations. The City Council of Kingston had even offered to pay for the transportation of interested members to Ottawa for a public hearing but was turned down. Dr. Pierre Dansereau, a committee co-chairperson, distinguished scientist, and Massey Medal winner, also resigned due to the preponderance of pro-nuclear representatives. [29]

It appeared that the Canadian nuclear industry favoured secrecy and biased presentations. The secrecy was particularly important, for as long as it prevailed, the industry could argue that the Canadian public's opposition was based on emotionalism and lack of information. Yet who was responsible for the lack of information? Surely not those without access to it.

The CONIC Conference failed to thwart the growing opposition to the Government's export program. But instead of granting a full public investigation, the Liberals authorized a Royal Canadian Mounted Police inquiry and a review by the Standing Committee on Public Accounts. This was necessitated by AECL's financial irregularities as listed in the Auditor General's 1976 report. Both investigations had extremely limited objectives. The RCMP were to determine the name of the agent in the Argentinean deal and whether there were any contraventions of Canadian law. The Public Accounts Committee examined AECL's inadequate documentation of the money paid to agents and the corporation's financial management. It was indicative of the narrow concerns of the Government that investigations were warranted only when a Crown corporation ran into financial difficulties. Other questions—nuclear weapons proliferation, Canadian aid and Third World poverty, or the creation of long-term radioactive nuclear waste—were not regarded as subjects worthy of investigation.

Not only were the two investigations limited in their objectives but they also failed to answer the questions asked of them. The RCMP investigation, which started in early 1977 and continued for more than a year, apparently could not determine the name of the Argentinean agent or whether Canadian laws were broken by AECL. On the other hand, it is possible that the RCMP did fulfill its objectives, which might explain why a report was never released to the public. The meetings by the Standing Committee on Public Accounts ran from November 30, 1976, to November 22, 1977. It also failed to unravel the intricacies of AECL's export program, for there remained many unanswered questions.

It is important to review some of these AECL mysteries. For example, in the case of Argentina, why did AECL issue a cheque for $2.5 million (U.S.) to the Intercontinental General Trading Establishment, a company of which it knew nothing but the name? Why, when J.L. Gray testified before the Committee that he had discussed the whole matter of the use of agents with AECL's Board of Directors, do not the minutes of the meeting "mention the transaction nor do they contain a resolution appointing an agent and authorizing payment of the $2.5 million (U.S.)"? Who was the recipient of the $2.5 million (U.S.) that AECL deposited into a Swiss bank account? In regard to South Korea, why do the minutes of the AECL Board of Directors not refer to Shaul Eisenberg prior to February 27, 1975, which was nearly one month after the contract had been signed? Why were there no details concerning the fees to an agent, when J.L. Gray testified before the Committee that he had discussed the issue with 15vthe AECL Board? Why did Gray feel that the lack of Cabinet opposition to the use of agents implied approval? Why did Gray state that on December 13, 1974, AECL's Board of Directors gave approval in principle to a 5 percent agent fee when the Board's minutes do not refer to such a discussion? Why is there a discrepancy between the Argentinean agent fee, which approximated 2 percent, and the South Korean agent fee, which was closer to 5 percent? Why do the minutes of the Board of Directors show that saving money was not a criterion in the renegotiation of the South Korean contract? With respect to the renegotiated contract between AECL and Eisenberg that resulted in an approximate $1.5 million reduction in the agent fee, the Committee was particularly perplexed. They asked,

> How did Mr. Campbell know what AECL was saving when the Memorandum of Understanding [March 2 & 3, 1976, between President Campbell and Mr. Laidlaw, the Corporate Secretary, and Eisenberg, in Tel Aviv] provided for an undetermined amount of expenses and overhead? Why did Mr. Eisenberg limit his expenses to $5.4 million when he claims his actual expenses were much higher? Why did Mr. Gray testify that his conscience would not have allowed him to keep the savings and that he would have given a credit note to the client, the Korean Electric Company? What authority did Mr. Campbell have to appoint Mr. Eisenberg as exclusive agent for any future sales? What was to be the fee payable for any future sales?

These questions, and many others, were never adequately answered. The Committee recognized that its inability to complete its investigation was complicated, since "some witnessess, particularly Mr. J. Lorne Gray, failed to answer questions fully and did not display a co-operative attitude." The

Public Accounts Committee report was justifiably critical of AECL's financial activities. While guarded and restrained in its language, the report accused AECL of lacking expertise and misjudging the risks it undertook. It concluded that, though affected by inflation, "the magnitude of the losses clearly indicated fundamental weaknesses in ... [AECL's] procedures."

The Committee's report was accurate in its criticisms but rather reserved in its recommendations. It suggested that when Parliament established a Crown corporation it should require a mandatory parliamentary review if the Crown corporation's activites were to change significantly, as did AECL's from primarily a research to a commercial organization. While important, this recommendation ignored the reason why AECL undertook this transition. The Committee was unable to recognize that AECL became a marketing organization to perpetuate the Canadian nuclear program. It was due to the nature of nuclear technology and its high capital requirements that AECL transformed itself to underwrite some of the costs. Similarly, reactor exports were pursued because the domestic market was insufficient to maintain the Canadian nuclear industry. But AECL's international success was limited due to the competition from larger corporations from other developed countries. To break into the world market, AECL was forced to undertake large agent fees and improperly negotiated contracts, which undercut the competition. The Public Accounts Committee, however, due to a narrow investigative focus, was capable of perceiving AECL's activities only as a function of improper legislative control over the Crown corporation. While this was fundamental in enabling AECL to undertake its international deals, such a conclusion ignored why AECL was forced to initiate such activities. Exports were needed because the domestic market was too small. Hence the Committee's recommendations focussed primarily on increasing Parliamentary control and the reorganization of AECL's upper management. The recommendations were as follows:

The Government should ensure that:

(i)   responsibilities and duties of Crown corporation boards of directors be clearly enunciated;
(ii) senior management be qualified for the tasks assigned;
(iii) its approval be required for contracts that may expose Canada to significant financial risks;
(iv) a code of business ethics be established including guidance on such matters as the use of agents; and
(v)   a central government agency be designavted to monitor financial practices.

In addition,

The Board of Directors of Crown corporations should ensure that:

(i)   the job requirements for senior management be better defined;
(ii)   limits be established on the authority delegated to corporate offices;
(iii)   standards be established defining the quality and nature of information management submits to them;
(iv)   the duties of senior financial officers and others involved in the contractual or payment processes be clearly defined;
(v)   decisions be based on adequate information and be properly recorded in the Minutes of Board meetings; and
(vi)   contracting procedures and codes of business ethics be specified in greater detail than in the guidelines issued by the Government on December 16, 1976.

What effect did the narrowly circumscribed investigation into AECL actually have on the corporation's marketing capabilities? Had the recommendations been completely implemented, the effect could have been substantial. The Trudeau government, however, severely limited such attempts in three ways. First, it accepted the Committee's criticism of AECL's upper management, for this implied that the problems were a result of specific individuals and therefore would not reoccur if those individuals were removed. Alastair Gillespie, Minister of Energy, Mines, and Resources, the minister responsible for AECL, stated that

> the roots of the projected losses lie in management decisions taken a number of years ago and the inflationary international situation that broke upon the world in the early 1970s.

Thus he announced to the House of Commons a number of bureaucratic changes: increased representation by business interests on the board of directors; management consultants to develop new financial control systems; and a vice-president for finance chosen from the private sector. The most symbolic change, apparently at the request of the AECL Board of Directors, was the dismissal of J.S. Foster as AECL president. Foster was not fired from AECL but relegated to a less prominent position. It was somewhat perplexing that Foster was chosen as a major scapegoat, considering that most of AECL's activities had occurred under J.L. Gray. One must wonder if the Canadian nuclear industry held him responsible for the discovery of AECL's marketing techniques. After all, it was Foster who had initiated the renegotiation of Eisenberg's contract. This resulted in a series of bookkeeping alterations of which the Auditor General did not approve.

A second way in which the Government limited the implementation of the Committee's recommendation was the passage of an order-in-council (P.C. 1977-2738) on September 29, 1977. The Government anticipated a critical report. Hence, the order-in-council was issued well before the Committee's findings were released in March 1978. The aim was to appear to be placing AECL under closer scrutiny. Thus the day after the Committee's report was tabled, Gillespie stated that "action on most of the recommendations, if not all of them, [had] substantially advanced." The intent was to decrease the impact of the Committee's recommendations by suggesting that everything was under control. The Government's order-in-council, however, did not seriously endanger AECL's independence. Increased scrutiny of AECL was to be achieved by requiring initial and continuous Treasury Board participation in large contract negotiations. But this control could be rather ineffective. As Gordon Sims, a researcher generally sympathetic to the industry, states,

> The form of scrutiny imposed by the Treasury Board is obviously crucial to the success of this new arrangement. It can vary from a quick look at the contract to a thorough examination of all submissions by AECL describing the details involved in each step of the negotiations. This latter course would impose a considerable workload on the Treasury Board. ... Later on ... the scrutiny will probably become more cursory.

The third change occurred in August 1978. This one, like the others, was primarily internal in origin. It led to the restructuring of AECL and the creation of a number of smaller companies within the corporation. According to AECL's *Annual Report: 1978-1979*, the reorganization was "designed to enable the company to establish firm control of existing projects and to make a reasonable return on investment in all new undertakings." One must question, however, whether the restructuring and increased departmentalization of AECL will only increase the Treasury Board's workload and thus make review more cursory.[30]

It is evident that the Canadian nuclear program, and particularly Atomic Energy of Canada Limited, emerged essentially unscathed from the scandals surrounding the reactor exports. The most serious threat, the Public Accounts Committee investigation, was in itself a severely circumscribed examination. It resulted in a number of recommendations which the Government undercut with the order-in-council of September 1977. The Canadian nuclear industry was able to navigate the public opposition to its activities without a serious threat to its existence, but events served to aggravate its crisis of legitimacy. For this reason, it appeared that while serious impediments to a repeat of earlier practices had not been established within the Canadian parliamentary system, the Argentinean and South Korean contracts had stimulated an extra-parliamentary public opposition which could serve as a domestic brake on AECL's international marketing plans. But, while opponents to Canada's nuclear program were working to have it changed, AECL was busy trying to win a reactor contract from Mexico.

68

MEXICO

It was in the late 1960s that Mexico considered acquiring its first nuclear power reactor. This decision coincided with the Mexican government's planned export diversification and promotion of manufactured goods. As in the case of South Korea, nuclear power was seen as the energy source that could facilitate this process. The uniqueness of the Mexican situation, however, relates to the abundance of indigenous oil reserves. Why did Mexico not use its oil supplies? A number of factors could have encouraged the choice of nuclear power. First, oil revenues were required to pay for other areas of development; second, diversification suggested developing both nuclear and oil power; and third, Mexico may have received promises of an extremely cheap reactor contract.

Whatever the reason(s), in 1969, the Mexicans requested a bid on a 600-MWe reactor to be located at Laguna Verde in the eastern state of Veracruz. From the seven bidders—General Electric, Westinghouse and Combustion Engineering of the USA, Mitsubishi of Japan, Siemens of West Germany, the United Kingdom Atomic Energy Authority, and AECL—the Instituto Nacional de Energia Nuclear (INEN) chose General Electric (GE). The United States Export-Import Bank and the Wells Fargo Bank of San Francisco provided part of the reactor financing with a $54.18-million August 1973 loan. The venture, however, between Mexico and GE experienced monumental price increases. In 1973, it was anticipated that the Laguna Verde plant would be completed in three years, at a cost of $263 million. By May 1982, the tentative completion date was set for some time in 1984, with cost estimates varying between $2 - 2.25 billion.[31]

Even though the Laguna Verde plant's cost escalations had increased to $1.5 billion by March 1980, the INEN issued requests for a second round of bidding. Mexico was embarking upon a crash program of nuclearization, yielding 20,000 MWe by the year 2000 at an estimated $32 billion. The same seven bidders entered their proposals by the June 1982 deadline.

It is interesting to note the extent to which the Canadian nuclear industry rallied to try to win the contract, despite its troubles in Argentina, Taiwan, and South Korea. It seemed that not only did AECL and its affiliated private companies need the contract to help the program's economic survival but a lucrative contract was seen as a possible aid for the industry's beleaguered public image. An initial Canadian offer had been made in January 1979. Alastair Gillespie, Minister of Energy, Mines, and Resources, discussed an energy cooperation agreement with the Mexican government that would eventually result in supplying 100,000 barrels per day of Mexican oil, with deliveries beginning in late 1979 or early 1980. Part of the same agreement required that Mexico study the feasibility of introducing the CANDU reactor into its power grid. AECL even paid for and undertook the implementation of the $2-million feasibility study. Additional support for a CANDU export came from the Prime Minister's office. In January 1982, Pierre Trudeau arrived in Mexico to trumpet the wonders of the CANDU. For the Mexican government, however, this was nothing new, for Trudeau had made similar attempts in 1976 and 1981. But Trudeau was not alone, as sales pitches also were made by federal Cabinet ministers, the Canadian Embassy, the Export Development Corporation, the Atomic Energy Control Board, Ontario Hydro, and various Canadian manufacturers and contractors.

These efforts were in vain. In June 1982, Mexico decided to forgo any additional nuclear construction. But this did not surprise individuals aware of Mexico's economic problems. In 1981 alone, the Mexican economy added $18 billion to its public and $20 billion to its private foreign debts. There appeared little possibility in the interim that Mexico would be purchasing any nuclear reactors.[32]

SUMMARY OF CANADIAN REACTOR EXPORTS TO THE THIRD WORLD

A number of important conclusions follow from the Canadian nuclear industry's post-1968 international marketing record. First, it is apparent that the Canadian government had an extremely difficult time selling its reactors, and when a sale was concluded, it occurred under rather scandalous conditions. The Taiwan research reactor might be seen as an exception, but it also included favourable financing. The Argentinean losses and the use of agents both there and in South Korea revealed the desperation of the Trudeau Cabinet for an export sale to maintain a capacity that the domestic market could not provide.

Second, to perpetuate the Canadian nuclear program, the federal government spent huge sums of taxpayers' money at the expense of developing more viable energy sources and worked to cover up the nuclear industry's operations. The steadfast refusal for a complete public enquiry and the unwillingness to determine or expose the name of the Argentinean agent are but two examples of a suspension of the democratic process to serve the interests of the federal government and the industry. Such activities support Robert Jungk's contention that nuclear technology is incompatible with parliamentary democracy.[33]

Third, AECL's limited ability to compete internationally was a function, in part, of the relative corporate strength of its competitors. It seemed that if a country imported a reactor, there was a strong tendency to deal with the foreign supplier from the country with the largest commercial penetration in the region. Thus, except for Argentina where a West German firm was the main competitor, Canada had to compete with American corporations. To overcome this disadvantage, Ottawa paid various agents.

Fourth, it was not coincidental that right-wing dictatorships tended to import nuclear reactors. The decision to import reactor technology coincided with the specific form of economic development in Third World countries, with the neo-colonial regime the most likely to import nuclear technology. The ready access to foreign capital and the receptivity of a neo-colonial regime to the importation of foreign technology to offer an energy source for foreign-owned companies served to perpetuate the repressive regimes.

Finally, the economic crisis affecting Western countries in the late 1970s and early 1980s also affected the viability of nuclear technology. Even if it were ecologically and technologically safe and not a factor in weapons pro-liferation, what use was a technology if nobody could afford it even when it was highly subsidized by the supplier countries? The Canadian nuclear industry remained optimistic about the long-term international economic climate and the possibility of exports. But what about the interim period? Third World debt would take years to eradicate, even if the world economy improved. And while nuclear power might help conserve petroleum resources, the original question remained: Would anyone be able to afford it?

This chapter has shown that nuclear power has been affordable only under generous supplier terms which, in the early 1980s, still appeared insufficient to guarantee sales. As well, it has been argued that nuclear sales aggravated existing patterns of economic development in many Third World countries. But, in order to answer the question of affordability in the broadest sense (beyond economics), one must also examine how Canadian nuclear exports have contributed to the proliferation of nuclear weapons.[34] This is the focus of the following chapter.

CHAPTER III

CANADIAN CONTRIBUTIONS TO GLOBAL NUCLEAR PROLIFERATION

The intent of this chapter is to examine how Canada contributed to nuclear proliferation. What part did it play in making technology and fissionable material available to countries which were interested in building atomic bombs? Canadian officials—understandably—tend to play down their role in this process, but the facts show that they promoted sales at the expense of safeguards against the diversion of power applications to weapons production. As will become evident from the following examination of export policy, the federal government's occasional anti-proliferation rhetoric did not threaten the nuclear export program but in many ways facilitated its growth.

FOUR TYPES OF PROLIFERATION

To understand Canada's role in disseminating atomic technology and material, it is important first to have a brief understanding of the types of nuclear proliferation. The term "nuclear proliferation" seems clear enough. Yet it is not really very precise and leaves many questions unanswered. For example, does it refer specifically to military technology or to peaceful application as well? Similarly, does it refer to the material or the technology, or both? The failure to distinguish between different types of nuclear proliferation often has needlessly confused the debate. For this reason, researchers have developed more specific categories of nuclear proliferation. The following four types are the most important.

Vertical proliferation is the quantitative and qualitative escalation of nuclear weapons and delivery systems within one country. When it occurs between two or more countries, it is popularly referred to as "the arms race." It has been the primary form of nuclear proliferation within the American and Soviet nuclear programs, though it also occurs in France, Britain, China, and possibly India, Israel, South Africa, South Korea, Argentina, and Pakistan.

Vertical proliferation is the form of military build-up that has resulted in the rapid change from at least three crude nuclear bombs possessed by the Americans in July 1945 to the situation in the early 1980s whereby the USA and the USSR each has perhaps over 40,000 nuclear warheads.[1]

Horizontal proliferation is the spread of nuclear weapons technology and capability to additonal countries, resulting in an increased number of nations with nuclear arsenals. Once it takes place, vertical proliferation can then occur. Horizontal proliferation has been of concern, as the number of nuclear weapon states has increased: the USA, July 1945; the USSR, August 1949; Britain, October 1952; France, February 1960; China, October 1964; and India, May 1974. Horizontal proliferation may result from independent military research, a military transfer from one country to another, or the application of a power reactor to a military program.[2]

Fred Knelman has identified "the acquisition of a nuclear explosive device through an act of malice" as inadvertent proliferation. This form involves the diversion of fissionable material. It takes only about 10 Kgs of plutonium-239 to build a 20-kiloton weapon, the same size as the Hiroshima bomb. Knelman does not limit inadvertent proliferation to governments, as it conceivably might be perpetrated by terrorists. It thus also includes all non-state authorized attempts. Theodre Taylor has written extensively on the issue of non-government proliferation, terrorist threats, the vulnerability of nuclear power plants, and other points in the nuclear fuel cycle. The solutions which have been proposed to safeguard nuclear installations possibly would infringe on many civil liberties—including the public's freedom of information. However, the absence of stricter safeguards appears less the result of concern with civil liberties than of trying to keep down the costs of nuclear power generation.[3]

A fourth type of nuclear proliferation may become the most serious—if we survive the first three. Albert Wohlstetter calls it "overhang." It is an outcome of the promotion of the peaceful atom since the mid-1950s. As successive groups of scientists from different nations have been trained by the nuclear suppliers, the same civilian technology may be used for military purposes in the country of origin. Furthermore, the sale of reactors, reprocessing plants, enrichment facilities, and other forms of nuclear technology have provided the required material with which to initiate a nuclear bomb program.[4]

Horizontal and vertical nuclear proliferation have long received the most public attention. Concern over vertical proliferation was the impetus behind the peace movements of the late 1950s-early 1960s and the early 1980s. Unrestrained vertical proliferation also was used by non-nuclear powers to justify their interest in achieving nuclear weapons capabilities. The opposition to horizontal proliferation has been strongest in the nuclear weapons states, as they tried to maintain their hegemony in the field. Yet vertical and horizontal proliferation were not the only types. As we have noted, inadvertent and overhang proliferation posed equally dangerous risks. Most importantly, the Canadian nuclear export program contributed to all four.

To recognize this, one must examine two periods within the Canadian nuclear export program. The first was from the secret wartime project that eventuated in the bombings of Hiroshima and Nagasaki, through to the early 1970s. It was during this period that Canada moved from simply being a participant in vertical proliferation to being a contributor to the horizontal, inadvertent, and overhang varieties. The second period began with the Indian nuclear explosion of May 18, 1974. The Canadian nuclear program still contributed to the various forms of nuclear proliferation and prioritized sales over safety but required more complex obfuscation due to the rising domestic oppositon. Thus a few changes were implemented during this period to maintain the export program. These were finalized with the December 1976 announcement of a new export policy requirement. Throughout the discussion of the two periods, the emphasis will be on examining the actions of the Canadian government and its nuclear agencies rather than simply reviewing press releases or Canada's declarations and voting patterns at the United Nations. In this manner, the discrepancy between rhetoric and reality will be clarified.

FIRST PERIOD: MID-1940s TO EARLY 1970s

It is not generally recognized that as early as November 1945 the Canadian federal government had committed the country to a future of exporting nuclear technology. This was done in a tripartite declaration with the USA and Britain:

> Representing as we do the three countries which possess the knowledge essential to the use of atomic energy, we declare at the outset our willingness, as a first contribution, to proceed with the exchange of fundamental scientific information and the interchange of scientists and scientific literature for peaceful ends with any nation that will fully reciprocate.

It is important to realize that in the immediate postwar period, the three countries possessing atomic information were intent on disseminating the technology only to selected Western countries.

The Americans were particularly concerned with maintaining and accelerating their lead in atomic technology. This concern in many ways was responsible for the 1946 McMahon Act. It unilaterally terminated technological dissemination and was not repealed until the Americans secured commercial leadership in the power reactor market. The Americans were trying to develop a nuclear power reactor for the US Navy's submarine program. By 1948, Westinghouse had succeeded in developing a prototype thermal reactor. Following the successful full-power demonstration in mid-June 1952 of the USS Nautilus and the signing of the Korean armistice on July 27, 1953, the Americans were prepared to expand the use of nuclear technology. The result was US President Eisenhower's "Atoms for Peace" speech before the United Nations in December 1953. Eisenhower proposed the global use of nuclear technology and the creation of an international agency (eventually the International Atomic Energy Agency) to monitor the use of the technology.

Eisenhower's speech served at least two important functions. First, it assisted the burgeoning American nuclear establishment with large state subsidies and taxpayer-funded research and development information that was given to the private sector as an inducement for its involvement. Second, it was an effective Cold War tool designed to link Western industrial countries to the USA. Equally important, it helped American capitalism penetrate many underdeveloped countries. The free or highly subsidized research reactors and the training of foreign scientists served to create a vested interest in the promotion and expansion of nuclear power in other countries. In retrospect, Eisenhower's "Atoms for Peace" speech was the harbinger of horizontal, inadvertent, and overhang nuclear weapons proliferation.[5]*

The Canadian reaction to Eisenhower's "Atoms for Peace" program was extremely supportive. Enthusiasm was mixed with a concern for profits. As George Drew, leader of the Conservative Opposition, said,

> If the offer extended so open-handedly today by the President of the United States at the United Nations, and so obviously with the support of Great Britain and France, is accepted in that spirit by the nations of the whole world—and I hope, as I believe we all hope, that it will be so accepted—then this northern area of Canada may become the centre of one of the greatest peaceful developments ever known to mankind.

Eisenhower's "Atoms for Peace" program was ideally suited to Canadian interests. The nuclear program offered many promises: increased uranium development and the hope that this area would be opened up for private enterprise; expansion of the Canadian nuclear program; construction and manufacturing contracts for Canadian-owned companies; and the maintenance of good Canada-US relations, which were fundamental for the postwar Canadian economy.

These reasons accounted for the Canadian government's willingness to sign the IAEA statute. This facilitated the export of nuclear technology but did not lead to a safeguard system until 1965. In the 1950s, Canada appeared more concerned with promoting nuclear power than with establishing adequate control mechanisms. Thus on October 26, 1956, with W.J. Bennett (who had been executive assistant to C.D. Howe, president of Atomic Energy of Canada Limited, and later president of Eldorado Mining and Refining Company) as the deputy head of the Canadian delegation, Canada became party to the IAEA statute. It was pushed through the House of Commons by April 12, 1957, amid accusations of a rush job and resentment that the upcoming dissolution of Parliament precluded a committee's examination.

---

* See Appendix III for a review of "Atoms for Peace" and the limitations of the IAEA as a vehicle for non-proliferation.

After signing the statute, the federal government revealed its attitude toward controls during the next session of Parliament. For example, in November 1957, when six Soviet scientists requested an international conference of scientists to discuss the dangers of nuclear war, the Canadian government gave a polite rebuff. While the conference idea was supported by *The Bulletin of the Atomic Scientists* and Cyrus Eaton, one of the founders of Pugwash, an international research group committed to peace, the Canadian government stated it would neither encourage nor discourage the proposed discussions. Evidently, Ottawa did not feel the subject warranted its active support.

The Canadian government's interest in such matters was limited. As with the Americans, it officially wanted a "comprehensive disarmament agreement." And until such an all-encompassing treaty was concluded, Canada often remained uninterested in more narrowly defined treaties. This was the reason used in the late 1950s to justify Canadian opposition to a ban on nuclear tests. In addition, perhaps the Government feared that control mechanisms might limit export opportunities. This was probably why the IAEA was supported by Canada. The Agency's nominal controls were ineffective, while its promotional capabilities promised an expansion in the use of nuclear technology. As Sidney Smith, the Canadian Secretary of State for External Affairs, stated,

> Canada wholeheartedly supports the newly established international atomic energy agency, which is designed to encourage, to complement and to assist the efforts of government, individually or in co-operation on a bilateral or multilateral basis, to develop and apply the peaceful uses of atomic energy.

Yet one should not be overly surprised by the Government's position; after all, Canada was already one of the world's major contributors to vertical proliferation. Vested interests were fearful that their growth and profits would be threatened by serious international control mechanisms. By 1959, Canada would earn $1.5 billion through uranium sales to the American bomb program. AECL had, in April 1957, suspended work on the NPD reactor for a changeover from pressure vessel to pressure tube design, a change that eventually would enable on-line refueling of the CANDU and thus facilitate the extraction of fissionable material. Furthermore, Canada had moved from simply exporting plutonium and uranium and renting reactor loops for US military experiments to exporting nuclear reactors with the 1955 agreement to supply India with a research reactor. The shift to exporter of reactor technology and equipment was part of a developing Canadian contribution to global nuclear proliferation. But due to its singular importance—the CANDU has become the largest research and development project the Government has ever undertaken—it is imperative to examine the specific ways that the Canadian reactor export program has contributed to the four types of nuclear weapon proliferation.[6]

CIRUS

The first Canadian reactor export, the Canada-India Reactor (CIRUS), was achieved through the efforts of Prime Minister Louis St. Laurent's Liberal government. CIRUS was an important component of the Colombo Plan which, in turn, was part of Canada's postwar attempts to stabilize Third World markets by promoting Canadian exports. The plan's main varea of focus—India, Pakistan, and Ceylon (Sri Lanka)—evoked romantic notions of the "white man's burden," but the crux of the relationship was economic. CIRUS was primarily a $9.5-million gift from the Canadian taxpayers to aid the Indian Department of Atomic Energy. The deal was negotiated in April 1955. On September 16, 1955, the Canadian offer was made public, as was India's acceptance. And on April 28, 1956, the details were finalized when Indian Prime Minister Jawaharlal Nehru and Escott Reid, the Canadian High Commissioner in India, signed an intergovernmental agreement on the CIRUS.

The CIRUS reactor was possibly the export that the Canadian nuclear industry would most like to forget. Plutonium created in CIRUS was used to fuel the May 18, 1974, Indian nuclear explosion. The Indian action was facilitated by the absence of effective safeguards on the use of the reactor. The Canadian government, in a hurry to market its first reactor abroad, failed to require adequate inspection or material accountancy. Canadian inspections were allowed only if the reactor used Canadian fuel. These ended, however, once the Indians had built their own fuel fabrication plant to supply the reactor.

How has the absence of effective Canadian safeguards been explained? Later, there were Government excuses about the absence of the IAEA in 1956. This served two functions: first, it diminished the Canadian responsibility; and second, it implied that everything was under control since the IAEA was created. There also has been a tendency to recoil in middle-class shock from Canada's involvement. As Robert Morrison and Edward Wonder state in *Canada's Nuclear Export Policy*, "The 'white knight' of the Western world had contributed to nuclear proliferation and world insecurity, not through cynical arms sales or manipulative power politics, but through sheer naivete." This was wide of the mark, for there was nothing naive about the CIRUS export. AECL's enthusiasm for exporting a reactor coincided with the Department of External Affairs' involvement in aiding Western market expansion in Asia. Moreover, the Canadians knew that CIRUS was an efficient plutonium producer. After all, CIRUS was modelled on the NRX reactor, built at Chalk River, to produce plutonium for the American bomb program. Granted, there were obstacles preventing bomb production: the plutonium-239 used in the bomb had to be separated from the spent fuel; and India had pledged that the program would be restricted to "peaceful" purposes. The first barrier was demolished by the construction of an Indian reprocessing plant, built in late 1964. The second was negated by Edward Teller's concept of "peaceful nuclear explosions" (PNEs)—that is, the use of nuclear bombs to facilitate open pit mining or major earth-moving projects (e.g., for the US, a second

Panama Canal).[7] The potential for the military use of CIRUS existed from the very beginning, yet sufficient safeguards were not required. Purporting naïvete—or even stupidity—absolved the people involved of their responsibility to prevent such an occurrence. It must be remembered that CIRUS, when operated at 75 percent capacity, produces 8.76 kg of plutonium-239 per annum, which would amount to approximately 25 bombs' worth of fissile material as of July 1983.[8] The only plausible reason for exporting a virtually non-safeguarded reactor was that AECL wanted to break into the nuclear export market.

RAPP I

Following the successful start-up of CIRUS in July 1960, the Pearson government secured a second reactor export, once again with India. The agreement signed on December 16, 1963, in New Delhi pertained to the transfer of the RAPP I power reactor, which was modelled on the Douglas Point plant in Ontario. As well, the Indians received free of charge—but conservatively valued at $5 million—the scientific and technical information necessary for designing and constructing a 203-MWe CANDU reactor. Despite giving away the blueprints and heavily subsidizing RAPP I, members of the Canadian program loudly proclaimed that the country had entered the era of power reactor exports (CIRUS was a research reactor).

But, as before, the concern with nuclear sales predominated over safeguards. RAPP I, in operation since the fall of 1972, produced over 133 kg of plutonium-239 per annum when run at 75 percent capacity. This provided enough material for 180 bombs by the fall of 1983, or over 16 bombs per year. Did AECL or the Canadian government require the repatriation of spent fuel? No. Instead, the reactor was placed under bilateral safeguards between Canada and India that were transferred to the IAEA on September 30, 1971, prior to the reactor's start-up in August 1972. While a considerable improvement over those applied to CIRUS, it has become increasingly evident that the IAEA safeguards are far from adequate and ignore the potential use of spent fuel.

It appears that certain segments of the Canadian government, presumably the Atomic Energy Control Board and the Department of External Afffairs, were considering withholding RAPP as a lever to compel India to increase the CIRUS safeguards. But commercial pressures predominated and thus increased the Indian production of weapons grade material without increasing the safeguards on CIRUS. This move revealed, aside from the Canadian prioritization of sales over safeguards, the difficulty of changing old contract obligations. Once the initial CIRUS blunder had occurred and, given that the Canadians wanted a sale, they had little maneuverability to increase the safeguards in light of the Indian opposition. It does not follow, however, that Canada should have sold RAPP to India. While AECL and the Department of Industry probably would have argued that continued involvement might increase monitoring or bargaining possibilities, the Indian atomic explosion in May 1974 proved the irrelevance of this contention. The Canadians were fully aware of the hazards involved in continued development of the Indian nuclear program but considered the hazards of not selling to be greater. Canadian subcontractors might have lost interest in the program. Thus to compensate for an inadequate domestic market, the Canadian nuclear industry concluded its first power reactor export. And as before, RAPP I was a Canadian taxpayer-subsidized reactor export that increased the Indian production of bomb material.[9]

KANUPP

The governments of Pakistan and Canada, after ten months of negotiating, on December 24, 1965, signed an agreement relating to the construction of a CANDU nuclear power station. The Karachi Nuclear Power Plant (KANUPP) was Canadian General Electric's first and last full export contract for a CANDU.

The safeguards on KANUPP initally were between Canada and Pakistan, but contract provisions enabled the safeguarding of the reactor to be transferred to the IAEA, which was accomplished in 1969. On August 1, 1971, the 125-MWe CANDU began operation and was heralded as the first CANDU to operate on foreign soil. Since that date, however, as a by-product of inefficient electrical generation, the KANUPP has been producing approximately 82 Kg of plutonium-239 each year when operated at an annual average capacity of 75 percent. Thus, as of August 1983, the reactor could have produced enough fissionable material for approximately 123 nuclear bombs. Yet the Canadian government required only the standard IAEA safeguards. Even assuming 99 percent accuracy of material unaccounted for (MUF), this would still leave Pakistan with enough plutonium-239 for one bomb.

RAPP II

On December 16, 1966, three years after the RAPP I contract signing, the Indian and Canadian governments concluded another agreement for a power reactor export. While of the same size and capacity as RAPP I, this reactor would take nearly fifteen years to construct. The reason for the delay was the May 18, 1974, Indian detonation of a nuclear bomb. The explosion finally was a sufficient reason for the Canadian government to terminate nuclear cooperation with India—but it took two years for the decision to be made and announced. After the termination, the Indians turned to the Soviet Union for heavy water—which was eventually provided but with strong safeguards—and the Indian nuclear agencies continued the construction of RAPP II, using the information gathered from the 1963 technology transfer and the building of RAPP I.

If RAPP II, like its predecessor, was at any point considered by some members of the Canadian nuclear program as a lever for increasing Indian safeguards, the Canadians did not succeed. Instead, the RAPP II reactor has increased the material accounted for (MAF) or weapon useable material available to the Indians. According to Nucleonics Weekly, the RAPP II has been in commercial operation since April 1981. Thus, assuming a 75 percent capacity for CIRUS, RAPP I and II, the total MAF available to India from Canadian-supplied reactors as of July 1983 was approximately 1,935 Kg of plutonium-239, or sufficient material for over 240 bombs. This amount could be increased on an annual basis by approximately 275 Kg plutonium-239, or 34 bombs. The annual plutonium production will increase considerably with the completion of the independently constructed Indian reactors based upon the 1963 Canadian technology transfer. There were four such 200-MWe reactors under various stages of construction. MAPP I and II at Kalpakham, Tamil Nadu, and NAPP I and II at Narora, Uttar Pradesh. Two additional reactors also were being planned. Due to the lack of effective Canadian safeguard policies in 1963, India had no obligation to place these additional reactors under international monitoring, and it has not done so.

There is a great deal of uncertainty as to whether safeguards are being applied to RAPP II. Originally, the reactor was to be placed under IAEA safeguards. When Canada terminated assistance to India in December 1976, however, the Indians argued that the safeguard requirements were no longer in force, as the contract had been broken. The best available evidence suggests that there was an 80 percent probability that RAPP II was safeguarded by the IAEA, but it is by no means certain, as the AECL is no longer linked to the Indian nuclear program.[10]

Taiwan Research Reactor (TRR)

The TRR was the second and, as of 1983, the last Canadian research (as distinct from power) reactor exported. The September 1969 sale was heralded as an entry into another national market, but the TRR's plutonium-producing capability was underplayed. The TRR was based on the NRX reactor that Canada used to add fuel to the American nuclear arms program of the late 1940s and 1950s. The TRR also paralleled the CIRUS reactor transferred to India in the late 1950s. Another parallel had more ominous implications in the post-Indian explosion period. One member of Parliament argued in 1971 that the NRX's "success and contribution to the Indian atomic energy program undoubtedly influenced the Taiwan decision in favour of a Canadian reactor." One doubts whether such self-congratulatory praise would be heard, since India detonated an atomic bomb from CIRUS-produced material. Nor has AECL advertised that the TRR, when operated at 75 percent capacity, produces approximately 8.76 Kg of plutonium-239 per annum, or enough fissionable material for one bomb per year if Taiwan chose to renounce the IAEA safeguards.[11]

Summary of the First Period: Mid-1940s to Early 1970s

The Canadian government did not seriously concern itself with adequate safeguards in the initial period. While some might argue naivete, such an explanation ignores AECL's and the Canadian government's knowledge of the material and technology, the manner in which they could be used, and the way they had been used earlier by Canada to fuel the American bomb program. The problem was not the Canadian nuclear industry's naivete but rather the need for sales. Among the potential safeguards the Canadian government failed to demand were an effective level of physical security, fuel repatriation, sanctions to discourage potential violations, and an in-house Canadian safeguard inspector.

The next phase in the Canadian nuclear program was exceedingly more difficult for the Government. It slowly recognized the need to revamp its public relations campaign to combat the increased public scrutiny that evolved largely as a result of the Indian nuclear explosion.

SECOND PERIOD: 1974-1976

The Indian Nuclear Explosion

India's May 18, 1974, underground nuclear explosion, equivalent to about 15,000 tons of TNT (about the same size as the Nagasaki bomb), in the Rajasthan Desert, immediately generated considerable international concern over the continued horizontal spread of nuclear weapons. The reasons for the concern were obvious. Three things were needed to construct a crude atomic bomb: competent personnel, a design, and fissionable material. The last was the only relatively difficult component to obtain in a weapons useable form. Thus the pertinent non-proliferation problem had been how to stop the acquisition of weapons grade material. A number of impediments had been advertised as effective by the nuclear suppliers, but the Indian nuclear explosion revealed their limitations.

The International Atomic Energy Agency (IAEA), for example, was unable to monitor the Indian use of CIRUS, the Canadian-supplied research reactor that provided the plutonium, as it was not safeguarded. Yet even if IAEA safeguards had been applied, they were not an adequate guarantee. The IAEA was intended to detect—not prevent—the diversion of fissionable material. It operated on the assumption that no diversion had occurred if the records appeared accurate. Thus the Agency's focus was to detect diversion or material unaccounted for (MUF) and then to work at decreasing the limit of error, which was assumed to be somewhat more than 1 percent. But even if the system were 99.9 percent effective on a global scale, enough plutonium could be diverted without detection to produce more than one bomb per week.

The Indian nuclear explosion also revealed that the technical and economic impediments to nuclear weapons production no longer were sufficient. The technology was extrapolated from the supposedly peaceful nuclear power program, and the bomb was estimated to cost India only $400,000. Thus despite their poverty, Third World countries could pursue the nuclear weapons option.

Finally, the Indian bomb dealt a near fatal blow to the Treaty for the Non-proliferation of Nuclear Weapons (NPT). The Treaty, which became effective March 5, 1970, automatically extended the IAEA system to cover all the non- military nuclear work within a country (under the IAEA, coverage was decided on for each facility). The NPT was an attempt, primarily by the world's nuclear suppliers, to create a political impediment to horizontal proliferation. Due to this bias, the Treaty did not seriously address the issue of vertical proliferation among the nuclear powers. Largely because of this and the implicit attempt to perpetuate the nuclear weapons status quo, the 1970s list of non-NPT signatories read like a "Who's-Who" of actual or potential nuclear weapons states. The list included Argentina, Brazil, Chile, China, France, India, Israel, Pakistan, and South Africa. The Indian nuclear explosion revealed the weaknesses of the NPT and undoubtedly acted as an incentive for other countries to pursue the nuclear weapons route.[12]*

The international implications of India's nuclear explosion shook the Canadian nuclear export program. It was one of the most serious threats to the continued existence of the industry, due to increased public concern and opposition. But while members of the Canadian government and industry publicly appeared shocked and dismayed, the facts were otherwise. There had been many signs coming from a variety of sources, revealing India's desire to produce a nuclear bomb. As Allan Lawrence, MP for Northumberland-Durham in 1976, argued in the House of Commons, the Canadian nuclear industry ignored or dismissed the many warnings. During various disarmament conferences from 1965 to 1970, for example, the Canadian delegation was repeatedly warned by other nations of the use to which CIRUS plutonium was directed. In May 1965 at the United Nations and July 1965 in Geneva, the Indian representatives hinted that India's only alternative to the October 1964 Chinese atomic explosion was to build a bomb. In October 1965, Agha Shahi, Pakistan's Foreign Secretary, argued that the Indians were building a nuclear arsenal from CIRUS-produced plutonium. In April 1967, Mahomedali Chagla, Indian External Affairs Minister, publicly threatened that his country had to develop and explode a nuclear weapon. In 1971, Prime Minister Trudeau travelled to New Delhi to discuss the issue with Indian Prime Minister Indira Gandhi. He returned apparently accepting Indian promises of maintaining a peaceful nuclear energy program.

Rather than inform the Canadian public and work in a manner that could rectify their errors—regardless of its impact on export sales—AECL and various government agencies hid the reality behind a series of hollow promises and declarations. When questioned in 1964 on the Indian comments about the need for a bomb after the Chinese explosion, Paul Martin, Lester Pearson's Secretary of State for External Affairs, gave the standard reply by quoting India's April 1956 pledge to Canada that "the government of India will ensure that the reactor and any products resulting from its use will be employed for peaceful purposes only." Obviously, if Martin had heard of "peaceful nuclear explosions" (PNE), he chose to ignore the possibility of India's arguing that atomic detonations could be peaceful. It was exactly this argument that India used later in 1974. Paul Martin, however, was not the only secretary of state for external affairs who glossed over the problem. In January 1971,

* See Appendix IV for more information on the NPT.

Mitchell Sharp reiterated India's 1956 pledge and added that External Affairs had "no evidence to suggest that the Indian government is not standing firm on the assurances it has given Canada." Sharp's statement was curious, since it was made in 1971, the same year that Pierre Trudeau went to India and discussed the use of CIRUS plutonium with Indira Gandhi. If there was no evidence to suggest concern, why did the two Prime Ministers meet to discuss the issue? One must also question whether Trudeau knew, as the Indian Defence Minister admitted later, that the Indian bomb program began in 1971.[13]

It was only after the atomic explosion that the Canadian government adopted a more cautious position. On May 22, 1974, Mitchell Sharp, Secretary of State for External Affairs, issued the second official statement. It read as follows:

> For all intents and purposes, India has now developed the capability of producing a nuclear weapon. The development of this technology by India is bound to have serious and wide-spread repercussions throughout Asia and the world.
>
> Canada cannot be expected to assist and subsidize, directly or indirectly, a nuclear programme which, in a key respect, undermines the position which Canada has for a long time been firmly convinced is best for world peace and security. The Canadian government has suspended shipments in India of nuclear equipment and material and has instructed the Atomic Energy of Canada Limited, pending clarification of the situation [it took two years to "clarify" the situation], to suspend its cooperation with India regarding nuclear reactor projects and the more general technological exchange arrangements which it has with the Indian Energy Commission.

One might question why such a discrepancy existed between the Government's public statements before and after the Indian explosion. An obvious reason was that both posi- tions reflected the need for markets. In the pre-bomb period, reassuring statements hid the possible misuse of CIRUS plutonium. To have done otherwise might have threatened the export of the RAPP II reactor. After the Indian explosion, the concern was less over the Indian action *per se* than over the impact this would have on RAPP II and particularly the anticipated reactor sales to Argentina and South Korea.

At the time of the May 1974 Indian explosion, the South Korean and Argentinean discussions were well advanced. On May 23, 1974, the Trudeau Cabinet had authorized AECL to submit a bid for the Argentinean project. Nearly ten months later, in March 1973, the Argentine Comision Nacional de Energia Atomica (CNEA) chose the 600-MWe CANDU. On December 10, 1973, the initial contracts were signed between AECL and the CNEA. AECL's receipt of a South Korean letter of intent to purchase a 629-MWe CANDU, with an option for a second, was announced by the Department of Energy, Mines, and Resources on December 7, 1973. Shortly after the announcement, a team of AECL engineers went to South Korea for a series of technical discussions. In January 1974, another team of Canadians travelled to discuss the servicing and pricing aspects of the proposed export.

One could imagine Ottawa's and AECL's concern. Just when two export contracts materialized, an earlier customer exploded a bomb from Canadian-supplied technology. But the Indian nuclear explosion, while compelling the Canadian government to address the question of safeguards, did not much change the manner in which the Canadian nuclear export program was conducted; secrecy and ministerial non- accountability still prevailed. The major difference was the context in which it operated. The media, opposition parties, and ordinary citizens were more vocal and thorough in investigating AECL's atomic transactions. The federal government's response was to issue statements and press releases aimed at deflecting criticism while simultaneously struggling to maintain the Argentinean and South Korean deals. In November 1974, it was announced in the Canadian House of Commons that while the Argentinean contract already had been signed in December 1973, the sale was dependent upon the conclusion of an effective agreement with Canada and the IAEA. As well, the $129-million EDC loan would be withheld until the safeguard negotiations were completed. In the same month, Donald Macdonald, Minister of Energy, Mines, and Resources, informed Parliament that discussions with South Korea similarly had been temporarily halted. The Canadian government operated publicly as if increasing safeguards were its only priority. Yet, when one examined the Government's December 1974 safeguards policy, announced nearly seven months after the Indian explosion, it became evident that safeguards were not their top priority.[14]

The December 1974 Safeguards Policy

Donald Macdonald announced the Government's new safeguards policy in the House of Commons just before the Christmas recess. The declaration was prefaced by a considerable amount of rhetoric explaining, for example, that "Canada's commitment to nuclear power as a peaceful energy source extends back almost 30 years." Macdonald announced three additional safeguard requirements which were intended to close the loopholes that led to the Indian nuclear explosion.

First, all Canadian-supplied nuclear material, equipment, and technology were to require a binding assurance that they not be used to develop a nuclear explosive device, even if such development was stated to be for peaceful purposes. The Government was rejecting peaceful nuclear explosions (PNEs). It recognized that technically nothing differentiated a PNE from a nuclear bomb. This new policy was intended to make continued reactor exports somewhat more palatable to the Canadian public, as it removed a rationale for bomb development prior to the conclusion and implementation of the Argentinean and South Korean contracts.

Two points about the anti-PNE safeguard, however, should be clarified. First, when the Canadian government was supplying plutonium and uranium to the United States and Britain, PNEs were acceptable. Yet, when a Third World country attempted to legitimize its production of nuclear bombs with the term "peaceful nuclear explosive device," the Government recoiled in shock. Thus, while the new policy of the Trudeau government was a welcome shift, it is important to recognize that it occurred less out of a concern over the increasing horizontal proliferation of nuclear weapons than out of a fear that its export program would be threatened. And second, the rejection of the notion of PNEs did not preclude the production of a bomb by a Canadian customer. Unless accompanied by adequate sanctions—which were not included in the December 1974 statement—the recipient country simply was to be warned that Canada would not favour the production of a bomb. Obviously this was insufficient; India knew of Canadian opposition yet produced a bomb anyway. Safeguards could not be effective unless sanctions were so costly as to prevent the manufacturing of a bomb, or if the Indian government did not feel threatened by China or Pakistan, or if India did not see the nuclear weapons states attempting to resolve their security problems by stockpiling nuclear bombs, or if all the fuel had been repatriated to Canada.

Had Canada, the United States, and other Western countries made it clear to Indian leaders that it was not in their interest to develop a bomb program, the situation could have differed considerably. But the West chose not to alienate the Indian government for fear of losing control in an area vital to East-West relations. Thus Canada's belated rejection of the concept of PNEs, while a change, was not an adequate guarantee against the production of nuclear bombs from Canadian-supplied technology.

Many of the same shortcomings were evident in the second requirement of the Canadian government's December 1974 safeguards policy. Often referred to as the "contamination clause," it stated that the

> provisions, to be administered by the International Atomic Energy Agency, or through appropriate alternative procedures meeting requirements of the Treaty on the Non-Proliferation of Nuclear Weapons, will cover all nuclear facilities and equipment supplied by Canada for the life those facilities and equipment...all nuclear facilities and equipment using Canadian supplied technology...all nuclear material—uranium, thorium, plutonium, heavy water—supplied by Canada, and future generations of fissile material produced from or with these materials...all nuclear materials, whatever their origin, produced or processed in facilities supplied by Canada.

It was intended to govern projects designed from Canadian technology, not just Canadian-built facilities. This was primarily a contractual clarification of Canadian opposition to the production of nuclear bombs from Canadian-supplied material, equipment, technology, and their derivatives. It failed to prevent the actual production of nuclear bombs, for it was only a paper promise signed by two parties and was not supported by adequate sanctions. It appeared that the Canadian government was depending upon the IAEA to apply sanctions. Yet many researchers have revealed the inadequacies of the IAEA and the NPT as inhibitors of horizontal proliferation and how both can inadvertently contribute to continued nuclear weapons proliferation by encouraging the spread of material, equipment, and technology.[15]

The third and final safeguard announced in December 1974 stipulated that all Canadian exporters of nuclear material, equipment, or technology must first contact the Department of Industry, Trade, and Commerce and the Atomic Energy Control Board to ensure that there are no safeguards restrictions. While the safeguard limited the ability of private contractors to involve themselves in foreign projects lacking state approval and thus served to punish the Indians, it was not that novel. It appeared that two additional reasons—aimed at decreasing public opposition to reactor exports—were evident for the inclusion of this safeguard requirement. First, it implied that previous exports had not been under stringent controls and that this facilitated the Indian explosion. This was unfounded, as the earlier exports—CIRUS in particular—required Departmental approval prior to implementation. As well, it implied that all future Canadian nuclear exports would be under effective and strict controls. This implication was equally erroneous, as the controls still lacked sanctions. In short, the third agreement requiring bureaucratic approval parallelled the contamination and anti-PNE safeguards. All three seemed to be more concerned with appearances than action.

Yet one must ask why it took the Government seven months to develop three safeguards of debatable effectiveness. And why did Macdonald announce only three safeguards when in fact they were part of an eight-point list approved by the federal Cabinet in December 1974? The remaining safeguards included a binding recognition of Canada's right of prior consent over transfers to third countries, reprocessing of Canadian-origin material, and enrichment beyond 20 percent. As well, Canada maintained the right to apply fall-back safeguards on reprocessing and enrichment should IAEA safeguards cease to be applied for any reason. And finally, a binding commitment required the provision of adequate physical protection for Canadian-origin material.

It was not until 1975 and 1976, however, that the existence of the additional safeguards became public. Was the reason for this, as James Casterton of the Atomic Energy Control Board suggested, "poor drafting...for some reason or other" by Macdonald's speech writers? Or did Canadian officials not want to divulge publicly all eight safeguards until they had negotiated with South Korean and Argentinean officials to determine what was politically feasible? The actual reason is not public. As it turned out, South Korea eagerly signed "almost anything to get the reactor." Argentina, however, preferred to have no strings attached and was less willing to comply with Canadian demands. It appears, therefore, that Ottawa did not want to commit itself domestically to anything that could threaten a reactor export.

Secrecy, while normal, was not the only tactic used by the Canadian government to maintain the export program. The Government did whatever was necessary to protect the Argentinean and South Korean projects.[16]

Cordoba

Reactor export advocates later turned to less tactful ways of guaranteeing the Argentinean sale despite the Indian explosion. One example related to the difficulty Parliament members had trying to determine the exact status of the Argentinean contract negotiations. On June 26, 1975, Mitchell Sharp, as Acting Secretary of State for External Affairs, informed the House of Commons that "we have not yet supplied any nuclear reactor to Argentina." The implication was that construction had not started—but in fact it had. Robert Stanfield, leader of the Conservative opposition party, quickly asked why AECL placed an advertisement in *The Globe and Mail* of June 21, 1975. The ad stated, in part, that AECL,

> in a joint venture, is building a nuclear power station in the province of Cordoba in Argentina and is currently recruiting for professional engineers and engineering support staff.

Sharp backtracked and stated that "the contract is subject to the conclusion of the necessary safeguards." Stanfield later asked Sharp if the Cordoba reactor contract made provisions for the subsequent negotiation of safeguards. Sharp's affirmative reply angered the Leader of the Opposition. Stanfield recognized that the December 1973 contract could not have included the safeguard requirements of the post-Indian nuclear explosion period. But he was dismayed at Sharp's attempts to cover up the retroactive nature of Canadian safeguards on a reactor whose construction had not been halted.

On July 14, 1975, Donald Macdonald tried to clarify Sharp's earlier blunder. Macdonald stated that "the obligation under the financial agreement and the continuance of the [Cordoba] project have been delayed while this [the safeguard agreement] is being negotiated." Robert Stanfield countered by asking Prime Minister Trudeau to explain the press reports from Buenos Aires that revealed the project had continued unabated for the last year under the supervision of AECL. Furthermore, an AECL official in Canada stated that if site work were to be stopped, it was up to the Canadian government, not AECL, to have it terminated. Trudeau replied that it was his understanding that work had been suspended. He was not sure, however, and promised to get back to the House with an answer.

A little more prying by the opposition parties revealed that work on the Cordoba project had not been halted but had continued after the Indian nuclear explosion with site work beginning probably in August 1974. Thus the Canadian government saw fit to begin site construction within three months of the Indian nuclear explosion but waited seven months to announce the first safeguards policy change. Trudeau tried to rationalize the decision:

> We were tied by a contract with Argentina under the previous arrangements, and it is quite possible that AECL had no legal basis under which it could

unilaterally break that contract. It was not its job as an agency to do so. It was relying on the government to do so.

Trudeau was technically correct. AECL's ability to conclude and break contracts required Cabinet approval. Thus the Liberal Cabinet was responsible for authorizing the continuation of the work at Cordoba. But when the Cabinet decision continued to receive strong opposition, Donald Macdonald stated on July 28, 1975, that

> in the view of the government, AECL should meet its obligation but the government of Canada, acting through its agency, the Atomic Energy Control Board, will withhold continuation of the contract, insofar as Canadian component parts are concerned, until they complete the safeguard agreement.

While it sounded as if the project was being halted, the Canadian public's only guarantee was the Government's word. It was possible that only the crucial parts of the reactor would be withheld, which would allow AECL to continue with the preliminary construction phases. This, of course, would increase AECL's stake in completing the project. Furthermore, even if the Liberal Cabinet's limited work stoppage was implemented, it would have had little effect on Italimpianti, AECL's partner in the Cordoba project.

The extent of the government stop work order was revealed in November 1976. While the Government did withhold the EDC loan for the Cordoba project, with the work continuing in Argentina, AECL began experiencing cash shortages. The result was a $15-million loan from the Government of Canada to AECL so that it could "continue to honour the terms of the existing contract."

It seemed likely that the Trudeau Cabinet preferred not to face the obstacles posed by safeguards. To overcome these, however, the Government found it necessary to sidestep sensitive issues. For example, when questioned about the nuclear cooperation agreements between India and Argentina, Allen MacEachen, Secretary of State for External Affairs, replied that the

> government is aware of agreements between India and Argentina on nuclear cooperation, but inasmuch as we have suspended our nuclear aid to India, and that any nuclear supplies to Argentina will be subject to the strictest of safeguards, the government does not anticipate that independent third party transfer of Canadian supplied nuclear material could take place between Argentina and India.

MacEachen ignored the potential transfer or sale of Indian reprocessing capabilities to Argentina. Also avoided was the possible Argentinean abrogation of its IAEA obligations after it had accumulated an adequate stockpile of fissionable material for reprocessing into bomb material. However, for

MacEachen to admit to the very real likelihood of such scenarios would have fueled the critics' argument and threatened the continued existence of the Canadian nuclear export program.[17]

Wolsung

Atomic Energy of Canada's sale to South Korea received less opposition than the Argentinean case. The major reason was that the Treaty for the Non-Proliferation of Nuclear Weapons (NPT)—which South Korea ratified on April 23, 1975, after the USA threatened to withhold an Export-Import Bank credit for the construction of an American reactor—was popularly perceived as an effective method for preventing horizontal nuclear weapons proliferation. But this assumption contained some serious errors which representatives of most national nuclear programs repeatedly attempted to cover up. The NPT's inability to prevent the diversion of fissionable material for bomb production was its major weakness. This was the result of an ineffective accounting system and an absence of effective sanctions. While NPT ratificaton may have calmed certain segments of the Canadian public, the fact remains that the South Korean government bought a 629-MWe CANDU, fueled entirely by Canadian uranium. When operated at 75 percent capacity, it could produce 413 Kg of plutonium-239, or over 50 bombs, per year.

The potential destructiveness of this material was highlighted by Seoul's June 1975 announcement that South Korea intended to purchase a French reprocessing plant. This would enable the easy production of bomb grade material. The reprocessing plant quickly became the focal point of the Wolsung safeguards debate.

Since the issue of the reprocessing plant infuriated the opposition, AECL and the Canadian government worked to calm the public with additional promises and assurances. When Tommy Douglas asked Prime Minister Trudeau if the Government was prepared to suspend the sale until it was certain that Canadian material could not be used for weapons production, Trudeau replied that

> under our type of safeguards we intend to safeguard the material and the technology through the entire life cycle of the supplied fissionable material. Therefore, there is no possibility that the Canadian material would serve in the way the honourable member apprehends.

This was a very bold statement when one considers that the plutonium-239 produced in a reactor has a half-life of 24,000 years. This means that, if stored, one half of the original amount will still exist 24,000 years later, one quarter after 48,000 years, and one eighth after 96,000 years. Trudeau evidently believed that the Canadian state still would be safeguarding the material many millenia into the future. But, according to Trudeau, Canadians could rest assured, as they had a promise in writing which prevented the material from being used in a bomb.[18]

90

One important question by Robert Stanfield, the Leader of the Conservative opposition, was aimed at alleviating the Canadian dependence on a contractual promise for preventing diversion. Stanfield asked if the Government had considered insisting upon the repatriation of all spent fuel produced in the South Korean reactor. Allan MacEachen offered a reply that clearly revealed the Government's priorities. He stated:

> we are not insisting on the repatriation of the spent fuel because of the cost and its environmental implications to Canada, and mainly because such re-patriation would not contribute significantly to the safeguards in the situation we are seeking.

Obviously, the cost of transport and its impact on the commercial viability of the Canadian nuclear program were deemed more important than the prevention of nuclear weapons proliferation. The environmental implicatons to Canada did evoke a rare admission of one of the serious hazards of nuclear technology. Yet it appeared that MacEachen was not concerned with the environmental implications for other parts of the world—at least, when it might threaten to increase the cost of a CANDU reactor. One could conclude that Canada was seeking safeguards which were more cheap than safe.

The Canadian government and AECL were equally uninterested in the high incidence of human rights violations within South Korean society. For example, Douglas Roche, (P.C.: Edmonton-Strathcona) asked if the Government had examined the reports of Amnesty International, the International Commission of Jurists, and the International League for the Rights of Man, which found that the South Korean regime was corrupt, repressive, and relied on torture and false confessions to remain in power. Roche questioned the validity of trusting such a regime. Allan MacEachen's reply was extremely interesting. After admitting that in "the over-all-context" of the sale the Government had considered all the factors mentioned by Roche, MacEachen commented that South Korea was an NPT signatory. Presumably, the Canadian government attributed more importance to a country's international promises to develop nuclear technology for "peaceful purposes" than to its documented violations of human rights. As well, Canadian officials argued that exporting reactors would provide a power source for industrialization and job creation. Thus nuclear power was a means for increasing the equitability of the distribution of goods and services. The critics argued, however, that nuclear power yielded little in the way of a return for many Third World countries. In India, for example, the multimillion-dollar RAPP I and II reactors provided only .25 percent of the energy needed in a country which received most of its energy from firewood and dung. Furthermore, to what degree was the Indian nuclear program maintained at the expense of education, irrigation, soil reclamation, food, and shelter? But India was not unique. The estimated energy contributions by other CANDU exports to the total energy requirements were equally small: Pakistan's KANUPP, .6 percent; Argentina's Cordoba, .9 percent; and South Korea's Wolsung, 1.1 percent.

The Canadian government's approach underestimated the impact of nuclear exports on Third World social structures and how rapid development could aggravate labour repression, pollution, militarization, and urbanization while increasing the economic and social power of state and private elites. But it was extremely functional for the Trudeau government to try to separate economic and political realities. To have done otherwise would have required answering some of the real concerns of Canadian citizens opposed to reactor exports. This might have further threatened the nuclear export program. Instead, the Government chose to rely on more nuclear safeguards.[19]

Safeguard Sanctions in the January 1976 Agreements with South Korea and Argentina

Opposition to the Argentinean and South Korean reactor exports at least forced the Government to make more information available and thus confirmed that the Canadians had conducted business without effective controls. Yet it was precisely the absence of such controls that enabled the Government to continue its export plans even after the May 1974 Indian explosion. Thus the Liberal government signed, on January 26 and 30, 1976, the final nuclear cooperation agreements with South Korea and Argentina, respectively.

The two agreements basically were similar in composition and were signed after the parties had agreed to six conditions. First, the items supplied or produced with the exported material, technology, or information would be used only for peaceful purposes—therefore, no atomic explosions. Second, the IAEA would verify the guarantees. Third, the transfer to third parties of items supplied and items produced with these, including subsequent generations of nuclear material, could occur only with Canada's consent. Fourth, the enrichment and reprocessing of Canadian-supplied material or nuclear material produced required Canadian government consent. Fifth, IAEA safeguards and bilateral verification mechanisms where the IAEA system did not apply were to exist for the life of the item supplied or the material produced. Sixth, adequate physical security measures were to be implemented to prevent terrorist diversion.

The safeguards applied to the Argentinean and South Korean reactors were not a big improvement over those applied before the Indian explosion. Canada still relied on the contractual promise of the recipient country and the IAEA verification system. This was insufficient, as the IAEA's bureaucratic impediments and imperfect accounting systems were far from effective. Of equal gravity was the IAEA's disregard of the material accounted for (MAF)— the spent radioactive fuel that could be used to develop a national arsenal or pollute the environment. It was incorrect to base Canadian exports on the assumption that the IAEA still would be safeguarding CANDU-generated material after 24,000 years. Nor was it wise to assume that at some point in the near future Argentina or South Korea would not choose to renounce the international safeguard system and begin producing bombs if its government perceived such an action to be in its interests.

While the safeguards in the January 1976 agreements were of limited effectiveness, the sanctions were worse. For Argentina, in "the event of non-compliance the receiving Party shall, at the request of the supplying Party, immediately cease to use material, nuclear material, equipment, facilities and information." How absurd to think that Argentina would stop using the material after it had chosen to produce a bomb. Thus the only Canadian sanction was the threat of terminating nuclear cooperation. But since the reactor was completed in May 1983, the threat would have ended.

The sanctions on the South Korean contract were more specific but equally futile. In the event of a violation, the primary sanction enabled Canada "to require the cessation of use and the immediate return to the supplying Party of any or all" material or information used or generated. The sanction was unenforceable. Even Allen MacEachen recognized that while the agreement technically could require the return of the reactor in the event of a violation, "there are practical obstacles in the way" of entering South Korea and bringing home the CANDU.

Thus the sanctions applied to the South Korean and Argentinean reactor exports were a travesty. These, and the simultaneous announcement that the contracts were already signed, infuriated many Canadians. In many ways, the January 1976 contracts fueled the demands for a moratorium on nuclear exports.[20]

The Push for a Moratorium

To many Canadians, their government's nuclear program revealed that the existing system could not prevent nuclear weapons production from Canadian material or technology. Yet instead of complying with public demands for a moratorium, at least until international safeguards had been strengthened, pro-nuclear representatives often derided their opponents. Members of the anti-nuclear/peace movement in particular were portrayed as twentieth-century Luddites. British historian Edward P. Thompson has shown, however, that the original Luddites were not intent on stopping change but were concerned about having an input in their future existence. In the same way, the opponents of the Canadian nuclear program recognized the ecological, financial, democratic, and genocidal threats emanating from the nuclear industry and tried to change these real possibilities.[21]

The Government, however, continued its paternalistic, reassuring statements. In June 1975, Pierre Trudeau stated

> that we have the moral obligation not to keep our technology to ourselves and refuse to share it with other countries if we can find ways of sharing it and avoiding any destabilizing effect on nuclear explosions. We are trying to do both.

But the January 1976 announcements had made it clear that the Government was interested more in "sharing" than in safeguarding nuclear technology and material. In the House of Commons, Tommy Douglas, former leader of the New Democratic Party, summed up the critics' mood by saying that "many Canadians will be saddened today by the announcement the minister has just made." The two major national opposition parties resented the Government's insistence on continuing the CANDU exports to Argentina and South Korea. Both parties opposed the Government's unwillingness to implement a moratorium.

Allan MacEachen rejected the idea by arguing

> that it would not be useful if Canada withheld its sale of these reactors at this stage in the expectation that this would bring pressure to bear on other nuclear suppliers, as it would result in Canada losing sales to other nuclear suppliers, and we would also lose whatever influence we are exercising—and I believe it is considerable—with other suppliers in upgrading the general level of international safeguards.... We believe it would not have any visible, obvious effect in this situation. It might even have a negative effect.

Three points require attention. First, the Canadian government refused to withhold the reactor exports, as it recognized the impact this would have throughout the international nuclear community. It could have increased the domestic opposition to other national export programs. Second, MacEachen's fear of losing reactor sales was grounded in a concern over the impact a moratorium would have on the Canadian nuclear program. A state-imposed moratorium would have been perceived as a critical recognition of, and restriction on, the nuclear industry's relative political and economic freedom to add to global nuclear weapons proliferation. It also would have implied non-confidence in international safeguards, particularly the emphasis on diverted nuclear material rather than spent fuel stockpiles. As well, it would challenge the emphasis on the promotion of nuclear power. Third, MacEachen was incorrect in assuming that a moratorium would end Canada's influence with other nuclear suppliers. A case could be made that it might well be increased.

MacEachen's pronouncements, however, failed to convince his critics. Many people were opposed to the subsidized sale of ineffectively safeguarded reactors. And the knowledge that the $500-million Wolsung and $600-million Cordoba reactors would not contribute substantially to South Korean and Argentinean energy needs only heightened Canadian fears that the reactors were scheduled to play an important military role.

In March 1976, these concerns were expressed by the federal opposition parties in a seven-hour debate on a motion by Allan Lawrence (P.C.: Durham-Northumberland):

> This House condemns the government for increasing the threat posed to mankind by the proliferation of nuclear weapons, and in particular by its present negotiations to resume nuclear assistance with India.

94

The debate really did not shed anything new on the situation but allowed opposition members to exercise their right to debate the issue and appear opposed to nuclear proliferation. The system remained intact, for when the vote was called—98 members in favour of the motion and 125 opposed—the division primarily was along party lines.

The debate and other extra-parliamentary forms of opposition did not alter the Canadian nuclear export program. But this does not imply that the Trudeau government was unaware of the call for a moratorium until the international safeguards system was effectively increased. These demands may have encouraged Canadian government involvement in the Nuclear Suppliers Group's (NSG) secret meetings in London. The NSG, or "the London Club" as it came to be known, was a supplier's cartel presumably formed on the initiative of the United States (the record is unclear). While initially rumoured to be an effective vehicle for bolstering the Non- Proliferation Treaty, eventually it was an ineffective attempt by the world's major nuclear suppliers to halt horizontal proliferation. It was implicit in the tidbits of information leaked to the press during the London Club's meetings in 1975-76 that something would be done to halt horizontal nuclear proliferation. But due to the weaknesses of the London Club's guidelines, one could argue that the Club was more effective at reducing domestic pressure for an end to nuclear exports.*

In Canada, however, the opposition continued. Critics recognized that the existing safeguards could at some future point be seen as lax. And an obvious lesson had emerged from the Indian renegotiation process. It was virtually impossible to induce a country to agree to additional safeguards after the fact. From the Indian government's perspective, why should they: CIRUS already was built and producing plutonium.

Due to the persistence of the export opponents, the Trudeau government recognized that the December 1974 safeguards announcement had been insufficient to deflect criticism and protect the export program. After January 1976, with the conclusion of the Argentinean and South Korean contracts, the Trudeau government was free to refurbish its image as a bulwark against the increasing tide of horizontal proliferation. The best way to accomplish this was to focus on the less vital areas of the export program and to increase the level of contractual commitments required of recipient states. This was accomplished by terminating nuclear cooperation with India and Pakistan and announcing the December 22, 1976, policy on safeguards.[22]

Termination of Nuclear Cooperation with India

One will remember that on May 22, 1974, Mitchell Sharp, Secretary of State for External Affairs, issued a statement which reflected the Canadian reaction to the Indian explosion. It stated, in part, that the "Canadian government has suspended shipments to India of nuclear equipment and material and has instructed the Atomic Energy of Canada Limited, pending

---

*   See Appendix V for a review of the London Club's guidelines.

clarification of the situation, to suspend its [nuclear] cooperatin with India."
For nearly two years, the situation remained unsettled.

The main issues were: first, that India made a commitment not to construct nuclear explosive devices or conduct PNEs; second, that the reprocessing and enrichment of Canadian-supplied uranium or material produced in Canadian-supplied reactors required Canadian government approval; and third, that the transfer of items supplied and produced and their subsequent output could occur only with Canadian authorization. The Trudeau government demanded that these safeguards, as well as those announced in December 1974, be applied to the Canadian-supplied CIRUS research reactor, RAPP I and II, and the two MADRAS reactors which were under construction using the information provided free of charge in the 1963 technology transfer. Agreement on these safeguards was the prerequisite to the resumption of Canadian assistance on the RAPP II reactor.

One can assume that when the Canadian negotiating team, led by Michel Dupuy (the Assistant Under-Secretary of State for External Affairs) and Ivan Head (of the Prime Minister's Office), began their secret discussion, they hoped that the Indian government would agree to the new contractual promises. This would have been the easiest route for the Trudeau government. But when India refused to accept these demands, what choices were available to the federal Cabinet? There were basically two options: they could continue or terminate the negotiations. One must then ask what were the economic and political costs of each alternative. AECL would have opposed terminating nuclear cooperation, fearing the economic impact of any lost contracts. But this was not the only factor. As Allan MacEachen argued, Canada's reputation as a nuclear supplier also was an issue. On the other hand, trying to continue negotiations to revive cooperation probably would have had a negligible economic impact beyond RAPP II. Aside from the sale of spare parts and heavy water, future Indian reactor contracts were rather unlikely. The Indian nuclear program was relatively well developed and autonomous, as exemplified by the utilization of the CANDU-supplied technology for MADRAS I and II. Therefore, Ottawa faced Indian opposition to additional safeguards, a relatively negligible economic loss if cooperation were terminated with India as compared to Argentina or South Korea, and domestic opposition to the entire reactor export program. The Trudeau government would have recognized that it could reap valuable domestic political benefits by terminating cooperation with India and appearing tough with customers that did not agree with the new safeguards. Such a move also would have diverted attention from the more important South Korean and Argentinean contracts. Thus on May 18, 1976, on the second anniversary of the Indian nuclear explosion, Canada terminated nuclear cooperation on the premise that India had agreed to safeguard only the RAPP reactors.[23]

96

Termination of Nuclear Cooperation with Pakistan

After the May 18, 1974, Indian nuclear explosion, the Canadian government began concerning itself with other reactor exports that could contribute to the fissionable material needed for another country to enter the nuclear club; KANUPP was an obvious candidate. Concern over various reports that the Pakistani government was intent on producing a nuclear bomb from the plutonium derived from KANUPP (Pakistan's only power reactor) increased in 1972. Pakistan's Prime Minister, Zulfikar Ali Bhutto, argued that there was already a Hindu bomb, a Jewish bomb, a Christian bomb, and a Communist bomb. Bhutto asked why there should not be an Islamic bomb. What was not publicly known at the time—or was conveniently covered up by various international agencies—was that Bhutto was apparently undertaking a bomb program financed through a pact with Libyan leader Colonel Moammar Khadafy.

After the Canadian government announced its December 1974 safeguards policy, an attempt was made to increase the contractual promises on the KANUPP reactor. Cognizant of the effect the Indian nuclear explosion would have on the intense Indo-Pakistan state rivalry, the Canadian government worked to conclude a safeguard agreement with Pakistan similar to the ones being negotiated with Argentina, South Korea, and India. The major safeguards under discussion included a Pakistani commitment to not develop a nuclear explosive device or conduct a PNE, Canadian government approval of the reprocessing and enrichment of Canadian-supplied uranium or material produced in the KANUPP, and an increase in the number of IAEA safeguards applicable to the Pakistani reactor.

The negotiations did not go well. In February 1976, Pierre Trudeau succinctly summarized the problem, stating that the Pakistani government had argued "that our safeguards are in a sense being applied retroactively since they are being heightened in the process of an exchange which began some years ago." The Canadian government was interested in maintaining the uranium export and spare parts contracts. But when faced with Pakistani opposition, the Trudeau government concluded that it could reap valuable political benefits by appearing tough with potential violators. Hence, Trudeau decided to terminate nuclear cooperation. As in the Indian case, it served to divert attention from the South Korean and Argentinean contracts. Furthermore, the termination of nuclear cooperation with Pakistan on January 1, 1977, conveniently coincided with the December 22, 1976, announcement of another "new" federal safeguard policy, and thus each served to increase the political impact of the other.[24]

The December 22, 1976, Safeguard Announcement

Late in the afternoon and just before the House broke for Christmas, Donald Jamieson, Secretary of State for External Affairs, announced one major change in Canada's nuclear export policy. Henceforth,

> Shipments to non-nuclear weapon states under future contracts will be restricted to those which ratify the Non-Proliferation Treaty or otherwise accept international

safeguards on their entire nuclear program. It follows from this policy that Canada will terminate nuclear shipments to any non-nuclear weapons state which explodes a nuclear device.

Jamieson acknowledged that this requirement was in addition to the safeguards announced in December 1974.

Requiring NPT ratification was a positive step. However, the Treaty contained a number of contradictory and discriminating assumptions which reduced its effectiveness. The NPT did not prohibit proliferation outright but allowed the dissemination of nuclear technology. The problem of overhang proliferation remained, and nothing was done about vertical proliferation. The NPT allowed supervised PNEs and relied upon the IAEA's safeguard system, with its primary dependence on material accountancy. But weak as it was, the NPT was the best safeguard mechanism available internationally. It resulted in full-scope coverage of a country's non-clandestine nuclear power program.

Yet there were problems with requiring NPT ratification. First, it revealed that the Canadian government was not concerned with halting vertical proliferation. As Jamieson stated, the Government's new policy was required only of non-nuclear weapon states and that the Canadian government would terminate nuclear shipments should such a country explode a nuclear device. This policy thus enabled the Canadian government and nuclear industries to conclude nuclear transfers with voracious vertical proliferators such as the United States, the United Kingdom, and France. The 1976 safeguard requirement also allowed uranium sales to West Germany even though it was concluding a full nuclear fuel cycle sale to Brazil which would enable the latter to develop a nuclear bomb. Canada's only requirement for nuclear weapon states and NPT signatories was that they accept Canada's post-1974 safeguard requirements.

Requiring NPT ratification only on future contracts was a second shortcoming of the 1976 safeguard announcement. Thus the December 1976 policy change did not stop the Argentinean or South Korean reactor exports. The Trudeau government therefore acted only in areas where the economic loss was negligible.[25]

As with the termination of nuclear cooperation with India and Pakistan, the Canadian government's requirement of NPT ratification prior to nuclear cooperation, while an important step, was also a very important public relations tool. At relatively little cost, the Trudeau government was able to reap considerable political benefits and maintain the nuclear export program. After the December 1976 announcement, when the critics demanded a moratorium on reactor exports, government officials simply could retort that Canada had the strictest safeguards and was "charting a course which we hope will serve as a compelling example for other nuclear suppliers."[26] The implication was that in having the strictest safeguards, Canada's nuclear exports were in some way "safe" from contributing to nuclear proliferation.

After the Indian nuclear explosion, however, fewer Canadians were so certain of their government's assurances.

SUMMARY

It is evident that the Canadian nuclear export program had not changed significantly since its inception during the Second World War. Had it done so, one could conclude that the program could not directly or indirectly contribute to vertical, horizontal, inadvertent, or overhang proliferation. The above discussion reveals that such a conclusion would be incorrect. The major difference was the level of anti-proliferation rhetoric. And while there was an increase in the number and type of commitments required of recipients of Canadian-supplied nuclear material and technology, the system was not altered.

The Canadian nuclear export program still operated without public input. Federal Cabinet control remained intact. And, aside from the interests vested in the Canadian Cabinet, there were large bureaucratic and corporate impediments within the Canadian nuclear industry that would have opposed structural changes or even threats of change.* Evidently, the house that C.D. Howe built was built to withstand intrusions but not alterations. Even the Indian nuclear explosion was unable to change the structure of the Canadian nuclear export program.

The Indian explosion, however, was not the only event that revealed state and private maneuvering to protect vested interests. The Canadian government's involvement in an international uranium price-fixing cartel posed an equally threatening public relations problem for the Canadian nuclear export program. The significance of this undertaking will be examined in the next chapter.

---

* For a breakdown of these vested interests, see Appendix VI.

CHAPTER IV

URANIUM SALES

The preceding chapters examined how the Canadian government promoted the export of nuclear reactors. Canada's stake in foreign sales, however, went beyond the marketing of technology. The export of uranium was also important. Uranium mining was not as capital intensive as the reactor industry, but a similarity did exist between the two. Both were dependent on federal money and support. This chapter will focus on how Ottawa facilitated the growth of uranium production and the marketing of uranium abroad.

There were four phases in the rise of the uranium industry. The first, or developmental, phase extended from the early 1930s to 1959. It was during this period that uranium deposits were discovered and, in due course, committed to the American bomb program. This phase ended with the 1959 American decision not to renew its contract options on Canadian uranium, due to the discovery of sufficient domestic supplies. Throughout the second phase, the Canadian program languished. And a 1963 American embargo on all foreign uranium only cast further doubt on the mineral's future in Canada. But in the same year, a third phase began with the announcement of a federal uranium stockpiling program. Between 1963 and 1970, the Canadian government announced two additional uranium stockpiling programs to help support the mining corporations. The Government also attempted to diversify the purchasers of Canadian uranium. But the level of federal assistance for Canadian uranium industries reached new heights during the fourth phase. The involvement of the Canadian government in the international uranium cartel of the early 1970s revealed rather formidable attempts at increasing uranium profits. The Canadian industry possibly had entered a fifth phase during the late 1970s and early 1980s. It seemed that the industry, fueled by the profits of the uranium cartel, had geared up for a major expansion anticipated for the 1990s. But to understand the industry's confidence, it would help to recognize the degree of its dependency on federal assistance. This was a tradition established from the very first.

PHASE ONE: ORIGINAL DEVELOPMENT AND EXPANSION FOR WAR (1930-1959)

Activities Before 1939

Before the Second World War, there were no commercial uses for uranium. It was pitchblende that was valued in the pre-atomic era. Through a refining process, radium was extracted from the pitchblende, while the uranium remained in the waste. Radium was used for medical purposes and the production of luminous paints, mainly for wristwatches. As war approached, it became increasingly valuable for illuminating airplane guages.

During this formative period, the international radium market was controlled by Union Miniere du Haut-Katanga, a Belgian company that operated in the Congo. In 1921, its radium sold at about $70,000 per gram. This was considerably less than the $170,000 per gram asked by a Colorado company between 1912-1918. While the price difference reflected the greater concentration of the Congo area, it also reflected the international radium market's boom and bust cycles.

Canadian involvement in the international radium market did not begin until May 1930, when Gilbert Labine discovered pitchblende on the southeast shore of Great Bear Lake (later known as Port Radium). Labine was the director of Eldorado Gold Mines Limited, a company incorporated in 1926 for the development of a gold property in Manitoba. This property was closed in 1929 and the surplus money used to finance exploration in the Northwest Territories. Mining began at Port Radium in 1932, and the following year a refinery was built at Port Hope, Ontario. However, the effects of opening a new mine during the global depression, plus the price-setting schemes undertaken by Union Minière to protect its position, resulted in an oversupply—further decreasing the price of radium. By 1940, the bleak economic future forced Eldorado to close its Port Radium mine. The company simply tried to sell its inventory. Yet even these attempts failed. Throughout the period when radium was its principal product, Eldorado did not earn a profit. It was not until the onset of the Second World War and the accompanying interest in the military uses of uranium that the fortunes of Eldorado Gold Mines accumulated.

Wartime Expansion

It was Otto Frisch's discovery of uranium fission in 1938-39 in Berlin that accelerated the growing interest in the potential uses of uranium. With the onset of war in September 1939, experiments continued in England, France, Germany, and the United States. But the German invasion of the Low Countries and most of France in 1940 disrupted Union Minière's operations, threatened Western Allied access to uranium supplies, and restricted most atomic experiments to Britain and, increasingly, the United States and Canada.

As noted in Chapter I, the Americans in particular were concerned with securing a supply of uranium for their atomic pile experiments. By December

1942, they controlled most of Union Minière's uranium stockpiles. More important for Canada, however, the United States Atomic Energy Commission (USAEC) in July 1942 ordered 350 tons of uranium concentrate from Eldorado, or nearly all of its stockpile. The large order sparked the interest of C.D. Howe, Canada's Minister of Munitions and Supply. He wanted Eldorado's Port Radium mine back in production. To facilitate this goal, Howe gave the company clearance for obtaining all materials needed to resume operations. By August 1942, the Port Radium mine was producing uranium ore for the American nuclear bomb program.

But simply having the mine back in production was insufficient to guarantee Canadian control of the mineral, particularly when the Americans and the British were clamouring for more uranium. Thus Prime Minister Mackenzie King's Cabinet implemented the War Measures Act and expropriated Eldorado Mining and Refining Limited (its name had been changed from Eldorado Gold Mines Ltd. in July 1943). On January 28, 1944, for a total payment of nearly $5.3 million, the Canadian federal government claimed technical control of the second most important uranium mine in the non-Axis world. Of similar importance, in turning Eldorado into a Crown corporation, the Government had the only refining mill in North America.

The nationalization of Eldorado was a major step. It came at a time when the Americans had secretly contracted virtually all of Eldorado's production. Why was it taken? Two reasons are evident. First, by establishing a base price, it allayed American fears that the company might rapidly inflate uranium prices. And second, the Canadian federal government profited from the uranium exports. The inital profits were made by funnelling the uranium into the Manhattan Project, the code name for the US bomb program. The exact amounts of Canadian uranium contributed to and the direct revenues received from the bomb program are not public. But it can be assumed that uranium from the Great Bear Lake mine contributed to the deaths of thousands of Japanese civilians in Hiroshima and Nagasaki.[1]

Postwar Development

The end of the Second World War in August 1945 did not halt the export of Canadian uranium to the American bomb program. Instead, deliveries were increased and augmented with supplies of plutonium after ZEEP, Canada's first nuclear reactor, went critical on September 5, 1945. In 1947, the plutonium deliveries to the US were increased when the NRX reactor, also at Chalk River, Ontario, went critical. The cultivation of the American military connection served a number of functions for the real and perceived objectives of Canadian policy makers. It offered considerable revenue to the federal treasury, encouraged the continentalist economic strategy increasingly adopted in the post-1945 period, and aided the Western opposition to the Soviet Union.

In 1948, however, Canadian uranium production was linked even closer to American needs. Two days after the United States Senate endorsed the multibillion-dollar European Recovery Program (or Marshall Plan), on March

16, 1948, C.D. Howe, the Minister of Reconstruction and Supply, announced to the Canadian House of Commons a new and expanded uranium program. A minimum price of $2.75 per pound, guaranteed for five years, was established in conjunction with a policy which allowed private exploration and mining of uranium ore. Despite this shift, Eldorado's position was secure; it was declared Canada's sole purchasing agent. Thus while private participation increased, all sales went through the Crown corporation.

The new policy served a number of important functions. Most notably, it ended American pressure for more uranium and for private mining. The USA, in many ways, was able to force Canada to change its uranium policy. As Lester Pearson stated in 1959,

> I know the pressure that was brought to bear on the Canadian government to make every possible effort to get this field going.... We were told that in doing so it was not only important for the point of view of commercial development in Canada, but it was a great servvice to the defence of the free world.

The pressure was increased in early 1948 when the United States Atomic Energy Commission (USAEC)—Canada's sole uranium customer (supplies to Britain at this time were insignificant)—announced a new policy. It stated:

> In general it will be Commission policy to purchase ores for its program for private sources and limit direct government production vas far as possible.

The American pressure, however, was unnecessary. Mackenzie King's Cabinet recognized that it was in their interest to make the policy change. It decreased government exploration costs and led to a US commitment to buy Canadian uranium until 1962-63. The result was a decade-long uranium boom.

Between March 1948 and February 1958, Eldorado entered into purchasing contracts with sixteen companies and made matching sales contracts. The total value of these agreements was approximately $1,425,723,000. Throughout the 1950s, as uranium production rates skyrocketed, it seemed that a new Canadian staple was emerging. In 1954, production was valued at $26 million. By 1956, uranium production had increased 800 percent since the end of the Second World War. In 1957, the output yielded $136 million and in 1958, the 14,120 tons of uranium oxide earned $290,228,356. In 1958, the value of uranium exports equalled 5 percent of all Canadian commodity exports. And in 1959, twenty-five operating mines produced 15,000 tons of uranium oxide, valued at over $331 million. The 1959 production ranked the Canadian uranium industry first among Canadian-based metal and ore producers in terms of dollar value of exports and made uranium the fourth largest of all Canadian exports.

Yet despite the investment mania, massive private and state profits, and the discovery of more and more uranium for the American bomb program, the industry had been built on a shaky foundation. It basically had only one customer. Granted, in March 1957, Britain agreed to purchase $115 million of uranium, with deliveries running to March 31, 1962. There also was a $105-million contract under consideration for 1962-63. But while some diversification had occurred, 99 percent of all the uranium mined in Canada had been across the border and made into an estimated 15,000 nuclear bombs. As was to be expected, disaster struck when that customer stopped buying.[2]

PHASE TWO: AN UNCERTAIN FUTURE (1960-1963)

The US Decision to Forego Contract Renewals

Beneath the frenzy of the 1950s Canadian uranium fever was a concern about the instability of the boom. And by the end of the decade, members of the Canadian uranium industry had reason to worry. American production, largely from Colorado, had been undergoing a meteoric increase. From 1956-1959, American production of U_3O_8 (the refined uranium oxide, or "yellowcake") had more than tripled, rising from under 5,000 tons to over 15,000 tons. By 1959, the American production of 15,198 tons surpassed the 13,730 tons imported from Canada. The Americans were, as Lester Pearson stated in the House of Commons, "in a position to supply nearly all the world's requirements for uranium."

Thus, in August 1959, the United States Atomic Energy Commission (USAEC), which had until March 31, 1961, to exercise its renewal options, sent a letter to Ottawa saying that the contracts due to expire in 1963 would not be renewed. Fearing the political repercussions, John Diefenbaker's Conservative government did not inform the country. Instead, the American decision was not disclosed until November 6, 1959, when the Government simultaneously announced that the existing contracts with the USAEC and the United Kingdom Atomic Energy Authority (UKAEA) would be stretched out until December 31, 1966. Evidently, Diefenbaker waited until his government could sweeten the bad news. Delaying the announcement, however, made little difference. With the American decision, disaster had struck the Canadian uranium industry. It also was a serious blow to the Conservative government. Diefenbaker needed to be wary of the risks of merging Canadian national interests with those of the United States.

By July 1959, the speculation that the US would not renew its contract options led to a 55 percent decrease in the value of uranium capital equity shares from the 1957 peak. In an attempt to soften the crash, there were several suggestions for other uses of Canadian uranium. *The Financial Post*, for example, hinted that the Canadian production of large quantities of nuclear bombs would aid the domestic nuclear industry. While this suggestion was not adopted, the Diefenbaker government watched as the industry withered. In 1960, uranium production and profits were down 21 percent from 1959. Furthermore, the loss of the American military market rapidly accelerated the process of consolidation. Through a series of mine closures and company amalgamations, the 1959 peak of twenty-three producing mines was reduced to ten by 1960.

The decision to not renew its contract options, vhowever, was not the only blow that the Americans delivered to the Canadian uranium industry. By pursuing their own interests, the Americans blocked Canadian attempts at increasing uranium export diversification. As of July 1956, the US already had concluded seventeen bilateral uranium contracts. But in April 1959, the US announced that within the next four years it would build one million kilowatts of nuclear generating power in six Euratom countries—the Federal Republic of Germany, France, Italy, Belgium, Luxemburg, and the Netherlands (Euratom, or the European Atomic Energy Community, was established on January 1, 1958, and served, in essence, as a regional IAEA). Included in the 1959 US-Euratom agreement was a long-term loan of $135 million and a ten-year guaranteed supply of enriched uranium. American light water reactors used enriched uranium fuel which was not produced in Canada or compatible with the natural uranium-fueled Canadian reactors. It became evident that the burgeoning American nuclear industry quickly was relegating the Canadian reactor and uranium programs to positions of insignificance.

These factors undoubtedly contributed to the Diefenbaker government's rushing of the Canadian reactor program, despite insufficient information from the NRU and NPD prototype models. It was an attempt to bring the Canadian natural uranium reactor onto the domestic and international market. Officials anticipated this would ensure the Canadian reactor program's future and provide markets for Canadian uranium. But while the action offered long-term hope, it was a symbolic move with negligible immediate effects. It was not until after the 1963 federal election that the industry received substantial federal assistance. With the return to power of the Liberal party began the era of federally funded uranium stockpiling.[3]

PHASE THREE: FEDERAL STOCKPILING (1963-1970)

Pearson's 1963 Program

The 1963 federal election was a landmark in Canada's nuclear history, best remembered for the debate on the placement of nuclear missiles in Canada. Earlier, the opposition Liberal party had been against the idea, but in a January 12, 1963, speech at a York-Scarborough Liberal Association meeting, Lester Pearson reversed his policy and committed the party to the acquisition of nuclear arms. Canadian corporate interests actively supported Pearson's new position. John Warnock states in *Partner to Behemoth* that the President of the Royal Bank of Canada sent his employees a letter urging them to vote for the Liberal party. Warnock argues that the Canadian industries engaged in armament production "feared the adverse results of the re-election of John Diefenbaker" and supported Pearson's January 1963 *volte face*. Warnock also cites incidents of American intervention in an attempt to increase the likelihood of Pearson Liberals' victory.[4]

The placement of nuclear missiles in Canada, however, was not the only issue of the 1963 election. Throughout the campaign, the Liberals blamed the Conservatives for losing the American uranium contracts. While the US decision probably was an independent action taken by the USAEC in response to American corporate interests, the Liberal charge denigrated the Diefenbaker government. But the Conservatives did not have many alternatives with which to repair the damage. They succeeded in negotiating a stretch-out of uranium deliveries; but this was not a major accomplishment, as the USAEC did the same with many American mining companies. Likewise, the European market was limited, and the British contracts did not compensate for the drastic drop in demand. Pearson insisted that action be taken and made uranium sales into an election issue. Three weeks prior to the April 8, 1963, federal election, full-page advertisements appeared stating Pearson's guarantee to keep the mines open if he were elected.

The April 1963 Liberal victory recommitted Canada to a policy advocating the continued state expansion of the Canadian uranium industry. Within six weeks of the new session of Parliament, Pearson announced a federal uranium stockpiling program to a selected group of influential people working on uranium revitalization. Mitchell Sharp, the new Minister of Trade and Commerce, later explained Pearson's policy to the House of Commons:

> The government... is prepared to buy, and to stockpile, the quantities of uranium that will enable certain mines to maintain present employment until July 1, 1964, at prices that will cover the operating costs of the mines to vthat date.

The Liberals committed the country to investing $20 million (eventually, close to $25 million was spent) over a one-year period to perpetuate the exploitation of a mineral which, up until that point, was primarily for the production of nuclear weapons. While the amount invested did not fill the void left from the loss of the American contracts, it was an important precedent and a symbolic act that had more immediate effects than the Conservative government's rushing of the reactor program.

Pearson limited his stockpiling program to one year not because of a shortage of taxpayers' money. Rather, a longer program would exert "a depressing influence on the price of uranium for many years." Thus "extended stockpiling would not be in the national interest." Yet one must question the "national interest" of a $25-million program that involved only the Milliken and Denison mines in Elliot Lake—which, incidentally, was in Pearson's Algoma East constituency—and the Faraday mine in Bancroft, Ontario.

The Liberals recognized, however, that the stockpiling program, while a considerable handout, was not going to solve the industry's problems. Without American cooperation, which was unlikely after the 1963 US embargo on foreign uranium, Canada's industry could be left out in the cold. Even Jean Luc Pepin, speaking for the Government, admitted that they did not expect the uranium industry to produce at capacity before the early 1970s. Pearson recognized that this would be too late for large segments of the industry; if it were to be maintained, new sales would be needed immediately. But in the wake of the rhetoric surrounding "Atoms for Peace," the International Atomic Energy Agency's promotion of "peaceful" nuclear power, and the late 1950s and early 1960s groundswell of public opposition to nuclear weapons tests, the Government was hard pressed to ensure its citizens that Canadian uranium would no longer contribute to more nuclear bombs. Thus the contradictory objectives of trying to increase uranium production while promising peaceful purposes were embodied in the Liberals' 1965 federal uranium policy.[5]

Canada's Uranium Proclaimed Peaceful

Prime Minister Pearson announced the Government's new uranium policies to the House of Commons on June 3, 1965. The first part of the program pertained to the uses of Canadian uranium. Henceforth,

> export permits will be granted, or commitments to issue permits will be given, with respect to sales of uranium covered by contracts entered into from now on, only if the uranium is vto be used for peaceful purposes.

Before such sales were authorized, the recipient country must already have concluded a verification and control agreement with the International Atomic Energy Agency. But the emphasis on peaceful applications was a public relations tool that hid the weapons potential from Canadian citizens; Pearson's clause could not stop the production of nuclear bombs from Canadian uranium.

Gordon Edwards, in an article in *Transitions*, has argued that the commitment to peaceful uses can exist only on paper. The reason is a functon of nuclear technology. To make a nuclear bomb, usually one needs to enrich the naturally occurring 0.7 percent level of U-235 in natural uranium to over 90 percent. To fuel a light water power reactor (most Canadian uranium exports are used for US-derived technology), the 0.7 percent level of U-235 must be raised to 3 percent (American-supplied light water reactors use slightly enriched fuel). In the enrichment facilities of the nuclear weapons states, uranium from a variety of countries may be used simultaneously. At the 3 percent stage, the required amount is removed for the nuclear power program. The remaining uranium then can be enriched to over 90 percent. This enriched material can be used for nuclear weapons production.

The paper promise that Canadian uranium would be used for peaceful purposes simply required a little juggling of the books. The recipient was obliged to ensure that the amount removed at the 3 percent stage was equivalent to or greater than the amount of Canadian uranium used at the beginning. There was no physical guarantee that Canadian uranium would not remain for enrichment to weapons-grade material, only a degree of calculation on paper.

Yet most of the members of Parliament listening to Pearson's promise that Canadian uranium would not be used for military purposes did not realize that the prohibition existed only on paper. On this the Government was silent. Rather than address the issue of Canadian uranium facilitating the production of nuclear weapons, the Government preferred to emphasize the promotional component of Pearson's 1965 uranium policy. This pertained to the three ways the Liberals planned to increase uranium sales. First, the Government was prepared to authorize contract commitments "for the average anticipated life of each reactor," estimated to be thirty years. Such exports did not have to be used in Canadian reactors. Second, Pearson announced the Government's willingness to authorize exports for up to a five-year period during which time the recipient country could simply stockpile the Canadian uranium. This would allow the purchasers to accumulate uranium supplies for reactors not yet under construction or in operation. And as part of this program, Pearson stated that "the Canadian government will actively encourage and assist the Canadian uranium industry in seeking export markets." The Government's third point was an important tidbit saved for the end. Pearson stated that prevent any further reduction in uranium production and to compensate for insufficient sales, the Government was undertaking another stockpiling program. This plan, limited to companies that already had produced uranium, resulted in the federal government's buying uranium oxide at $4.90 per pound and in quantities that maintained employment and corporate profits.

It was an important policy announcement. Yet two points should be made about this major new program. First, not surprisingly, the new peaceful-use requirement did not affect the existing contracts with the United States and Britain, even though the two countries had been consulted before the program was announced in the House of Commons. This leads one to suspect that both refused to comply with the new demands. And second, admirable as it was to increase the safeguards on Canadian uranium exports, there was something peculiar in the timing of the policy change. It coincided with French attempts to obtain Canadian uranium.[6]

Canadian Uranium in French Bombs?

In February 1960, France had detonated its first nuclear bomb and in the years immediately following was struggling to develop its own nuclear force. It also was undertaking the first phase of its nuclear power program. Thus, to meet the needs of the two programs, the Commissariat d'Energie Atomique (CEA), the state body that managed the French power and military nuclear programs, wanted to purchase considerable supplies of uranium to augment the country's domestic production. Denison Mines, a private Canadian mining company, was interested in providing the uranium. In February 1965, the company was negotiating with Euratom and France for a rumoured 50,000 tons, or $700-million contract.

It was during the Denison-CEA negotiations, in June 1965, that Ottawa announced its peaceful-use requirement. The French were offended. They resented the sudden and, from their perspective, discriminatory change in the Canadian uranium policy. From the Canadian producers' viewpoint, while the change in policy possibly legitimized uranium exports in the eyes of the domestic population, it made it increasingly difficult to conclude a sale with France. Despite the Paris meeting of influential Canadian uranium figures such as Pearson's Minister of Trade and Commerce, Robert Winters, who was opposed to Pearson's peaceful-use policy, and the French Minister of Scientific Research, Alain Peyrefitte, in February 1966, a settlement was not reached. The two simply agreed that it would be good to "meet from time to time," which was Ottawa's diplomatic description of the breakdown in discussions.

France's refusal to accept Canadian safeguards seemed to imply that France wanted the uranium for military purposes. As well, it appeared that the Liberal government's policies, in this instance, had been effective in limiting the use of Canadian uranium for nuclear weapons. But why, in June 1965, did Pearson implement a policy that essentially halted the French uranium sale and instead encouraged a taxpayer-funded stockpiling program to compensate Dension Mines for some of its potential losses? Was it that Pearson suddenly felt Canadian uranium had contributed to enough nuclear bombs and that June 1965 was the appropriate time to end this tradition? While possible, it seems simplistic, particularly when one remembers the dismal status of Canada's uranium mines in 1965 and the over $75 million required to implement the 1965 stockpiling program. Or was Pearson's policy, as some speculated at the time, implemented after the US had brought pressure to bear on the Canadians not to go ahead with the proposed deal? After all, the Americans resented Charles De Gaulle's insistence on an independent French nuclear *force du frappe*. While the public record of the issue has been unclear, it seems that both reasons may have influenced Pearson's actions. Yet one must ask if Pearson also was attempting to achieve a third objective. Was Pearson's 1965 uranium policy aimed at divorcing the entire Canadian nuclear program from its military roots, thus facilitating the expansion of the Canadian nuclear power reactor program? The strength of this supposition is increased when one examines the nuclear market of the 1960s.[7]

The Anticipated Arrival of the Nuclear Power Market

As the 1960s passed, nuclear officials around the world stated that power reactor technology finally had reached the "take-off stage." Such seemed to occur with the Canadian nuclear program. It was developing rapidly. On December 16, 1963, the RAPP I agreement with India was announced. On August 20, 1964, the federal and Ontario provincial governments released their plans to build Pickering I and II. On December 24, 1965, an agreement with Pakistan was signed for the KANUPP reactor. On September 2, 1966, the Gentilly I reactor for Quebec was publicized. On November 15, 1966, the Douglas Point reactor was started up, and negotiations were underway for RAPP II and Pickering III and IV. It appeared that the Diefenbaker gamble might pay off. Maybe the Canadian reactor program could support the uranium industry.

A contract settlement in late December 1966 appeared to prove that it could. Ontario Hydro agreed to buy 6,500 tons of uranium concentrates. Rio Algom Mines Ltd. supplied 80 percent, with the remainder provided by Eldorado Mining and Refining Ltd. Deliveries were to begin in 1970 and continue into the 1980s. The undisclosed price was estimated to be above $5 per pound. The Canadian mining community was jubilant, as the order heralded a significant domestic market. But they recognized that to maintain profits, they still needed export contracts. They were not disappointed.

On October 18, 1966, Ottawa approved an estimated $100-million sale for 8,000 short tons of uranium oxide to Britain. The contract was negotiated between Rio Algom Mines Ltd., a subsidiary of Britain's international mining conglomerate Rio Tinto Zinc, and the United Kingdom Atomic Energy Authority (UKAEA). The contract allowed for continuation of agreements expiring in 1971 to run to the end of 1980 with an option to buy up to 11,500 tons. The Pearson government and the mining community were ecstatic: the IAEA stated there were adequate safeguard mechanisms for proper accounting; the British were willing to negotiate the detailed aspects of verification; and the contract, being filled by Rio Algom's Elliot Lake properties, was expected to keep the company's mine and the community going until at least 1980.

The British contract, however, was not an isolated event. Large deals also were signed with Japan and West Germany. In 1967, Denison Mines Ltd. obtained an order to supply at least 21 million pounds of uranium oxide over ten years starting in 1969 to the Tokyo Electric Power Company. Stephen Roman, President of Denison Mines, stated that this was the largest private commercial sale in the history of the uranium industry. Also in 1967, Rio Algom Mines obtained a contract to supply the Tokyo Electric Power Company with over 10 million pounds of uranium oxide over ten years commencing in 1969. In 1968, Denison mines obtained two contracts to deliver over 800,000 pounds of uranium oxide to West Germany. These two contracts and the one to Japan in 1967 were largely responsible for Denison's $12.7 million profit in 1968. But the mining companies received money not only for uranium sold. In 1969, for example, the Japanese contributed at least $5 million to Denison Mines and to the Kerr-McGee Corporation, a US-based company operating in Elliot Lake. The money reportedly was to aid the companies' prospecting endeavours.[8]

The Expectation Fades

By 1969-1970, however, the undercurrent of uncertainty that existed throughout the mid-1960s "micro-boom" became increasingly dominant. Canadian uranium producers were anxious, once again. Four reasons accounted for the return of the international uranium market's sluggishness. First, the take-off in nuclear power was delayed by lengthened construction periods, technical problems, and considerable cost increases. Second, the mid-1960s forecasts of international reactor sales had been overly optimistic. Third, Canadian uranium companies were unable to break into other large uranium markets. The success of US reactor sales strategies that included long-term low-cost enriched uranium contracts made it difficult for Canadian producers. And fourth, there were more countries selling uranium. South Africa's Nuclear Fuel Corporation, for example, was increasing the competition for the Japanese market. The cumulative effect of these factors accelerated the shakedown and consolidation of the Canadian uranium industry.

The remaining companies worked to ensure their longevity. During this period, they used their previous profits to improve operations and diversify into other fields. Dension Mines, for example, moved into cement and other building materials, as well as increasing its investment in oil. Rio Algom branched into steel production and copper and zinc mining. The companies also encouraged the ending of the US embargo, formally declared in 1963, and re-entering the US market. This time, however, rather than contribute directly to bomb production, Canadian producers hoped to gain access to the developing US fast breeder program, a large consumer of uranium.

Canadian producers also supported the decision by the Crown-owned Eldorado Company to construct a $10.4-million natural uranium hexafluoride plant in Port Hope, Ontario. (Hexafluoride is a gaseous form in which uranium is put into uranium enrichment facilities.) By building this plant, the Canadian federal government was increasing the marketability of Canadian uranium. Producers then could ship hexafluoride directly to European customers, for example, without first having the uranium processed to hexafluoride in the United States. The hexafluoride plant, while a fundamental step revealing the federal government's interest in aiding Canadian uranium producers, also implied an increased concern about the independence of Canadian uranium production from American control. Such concern was further highlighted by Ottawa's reaction to the 1970 attempt by Denison Mines to sell a controlling interest to a US company.[9]

The Ottawa-Denison Deal

Near the end of February 1970, the Roman Corporation, headed by Stephen Roman, planned to sell its controlling 26 percent interest in Denison Mines, the largest Canadian producer, to the American-controlled Hudson's Bay Oil and Gas Company, Calgary. There was not any publicity of American pressure or payoffs for Roman to sell; he simply stated that the mining company could not operate at one-third to two-thirds capacity. Be that as it may, it was extremely curious that in 1968, Denison recorded a $12.7-million profit and in 1969 began its contracted deliveries of over two million pounds of uranium oxide per year, for ten years, to Japan. Nevertheless, Roman was interested in selling and negotiations were underway.

On March 2, 1970, however, Prime Minister Pierre Trudeau announced to the House of Commons that the Government had learned of a proposed Denison-Hudson's Bay deal. Trudeau stated that "if necessary, the government will introduce an amendment to the Atomic Energy Control Act to take effect as of today to prevent such a transaction." Within days, a government representative met with Stephen Roman, who evidently refused to stop the sale to the US-controlled Hudson's Bay Oil and Gas Company. Therefore, the Government implemented its threat.

On March 19, 1970, John Greene, Minister of Energy, Mines, and Resources, announced the Government's new regulations on foreign ownership of uranium-producing companies. The new law limited ownership in the aggregate as well as on the part of any individual or group of foreign investors. Thenceforth, the aggregate foreign ownership of any established productive uranium property was limited to 33 percent with a 10 percent limit on the ownership of such a property by any one foreign investor or group of associated investors. However, the strictness of this regulation was softened. For any new mine brought through the exploration and development phase, the Government would allow a 33 percent ownership to be held by a single foreign investor or group of associated investors. Thus the regulations on foreign ownership encouraged foreign companies to develop new mine production. As well, the regulations encouraged Canadian mining companies to develop new capacity, knowing that they could have access to foreign capital.

The final part of the regulations pertained to the degree of foreign ownership of developed mines. Foreign owners were allowed to retain their holdings, but if they reduced them by selling to Canadians, the new level of ownership was to work its way down to 10 percent and 33 percent. For ownership by a foreign individual or group of associated investors of 50 percent or higher, such holdings could be maintained, but any transfer could be only to Canadians down to the 33 percent aggregate foreign ownership limit. If a non-Canadian owned less than 50 percent, the person was allowed to transfer to other foreign investors. Thus there was no real threat of ousting foreign uranium interests from Canada. Rather, it was an attempt to secure domestic control of the Canadian uranium industry.

The new regulations caused considerable confusion, particularly among members of Parliament. While they generally favoured the Government's actions, they were curious as to why the limits on foreign ownership had been implemented. On this question, the Government was silent. The members recognized that the new regulations, while halting the sale of the controlling interest of Denison Mines to the US-controlled Hudson's Bay Oil and Gas Company, would stimulate foreign and domestic uranium development under Canadian control. But the MPs were perplexed as to why the regulations seemed particularly harsh on Denison's plans.

The confusion increased in December 1970 when the federal government negotiated another stockpiling agreement with Denison Mines. The company had threatened to close down its Elliot Lake operations—which supplied 40 percent of the town's payroll—in mid-1971 unless it received federal assistance. Thus a stockpiling program was negotiated—the third since 1963. Between January 1, 1971, and December 31, 1974, an estimated 6,467,000 pounds of uranium oxide from Denison's Elliot Lake operation was to be stockpiled. The $38.8-million deal was comprised of 75 percent federal money, with Denison providing the remaining 25 percent. The price was $6 per pound, one dollar less than Stephen Roman's original request earlier in the year.

The deal required Denison to produce a minimum of four million pounds yearly between 1971-74. Thus the operation was to maintain the two-third capacity considered necessary to remain economic.

Many analysts, while happy to see the Elliot Lake operations continuing, were puzzled. Why did Denison continue to profit from federal assistance? Nearly $80 million of the total $100 million cost for the 1963 and 1965 government stockpiling programs had gone to Denison Mines. Furthermore, the company had yet to pay taxes even though profits allowed the company to pay dividends to its shareholders. In December 1970, the rate was $1.40 per share. On the surface, the Ottawa-Denison stockpiling deal appeared to be a compensation for halting the controlling interest sale to the American company. Yet this brought one back to asking why the Government implemented its foreign ownership regulations for uranium. It was possible that Ottawa was concerned only with maintaining Canadian control of the mineral. But while admirable from a nationalist perspective, the Government was showing little interest in similar actions for other minerals or sectors of the economy. Publicly, few answers were provided. In March 1970, however, just after John Greene announced the new regulations, Max Saltsman (NDP: Waterloo- Cambridge) offered a very insightful comment. He stated that the foreign ownership

> measure would be a way to escape the extraterritorial conditions which might be imposed upon our industry if United States investors who would be subject to United States law came in at a time when the government might have in mind exporting uranium to a country of which *v*the United States might disapprove.

While not the whole story, Saltsman may have discovered something very important. Was Ottawa attempting to protect Canadian uranium producers from American extraterritorial laws? To better understand why Ottawa's foreign ownership regulations may have been established to block US laws, one must first examine Canada's involvement in the international uranium cartel.[10]

PHASE FOUR: THE URANIUM CARTEL

The Origins of the Cartel

To increase the international price of uranium, which in many cases was below the cost of production, and challenge American control of the world uranium market, a number of suppliers formed a uranium cartel. An excellent analysis of much of the available information relating to the international uranium cartel is contained in June H. Taylor and Michael D. Yokell's *Yellowcake: The International Uranium Cartel*. Their work is based on original documents. In the summer of 1976, a large package of stolen confidential files from the Mary Kathleen Uranium Company of Australia was dropped off at the Melbourne office of Friends of the Earth, an international environmental group. The documents

> included detailed minutes of cartel meetings; letters between cartel companies on rigging bidding or uranium contracts; tables outlining the Club's price-fixing policies; including especially high prices for Asian producers; policy statements on dealing with competitors and middlemen such as Westinghouse and General Electric which supply uranium for their reactor customers; and a host of lesser tidbits.

It was the delivery of these documents that broke the secret of the cartel.

Taylor and Yokell assert that international support for a uranium suppliers' club existed by the beginning of 1970. American domination of the world uranium market had threatened other production countries. The Australian, Canadian, and French governments had engaged in uranium stockpiling to protect their domestic industries and already had significant control of some mines. The organizational process started in 1971 when the three governments began announcing the need for a "'common marketing policy' or a 'world supplier-price minimum.'" Taylor and Yokell, while admitting that the record is somewhat unclear, implicate the Canadian government as the initiator of this concern for establishing a suppliers' union. Meetings between the governments led to a February 1972 Paris gathering attended by government representatives and the majority of the world's uranium-producing companies, including US-based multinationals. Many US companies also objected to American government restrictions.* Canadian representatives included Gordon MacNabb, Assistant Deputy Minister for Energy, Mines, and Resources, and a repesentative from the Ministry of Industry, Trade, and Commerce. Taylor and Yokell state that

> what resulted from these meetings was not simply a floor price, but a full blown cartel to control prices and amounts of production, and to assign the available contracts to the various cartel members at steadily increasing prices. An elaborate organizaton known as the Uranium Club was formed to effect the cartel.[11]

The cartel was dominated by four countries—Canada, South Africa, France, and Australia. Sweden's uranium was low-grade, thus making extraction economically difficult which, when coupled with domestic political opposition to its exportation, ensured it would not be on the international market. The other nations possessing commercial-sized deposits were controlled by the leading organizers. Gabon and Niger were former French colonies, and the perpetuation of imperial control over certain sectors of their economies resulted

---

* See Appendix VII for a list of the corporations with ties to the uranium cartel.

in French control and marketing of their uranium. Zambia's uranium, as the rest of its economy, was dominated by South African capital.

After the February Paris meetings, the countries involved carried on negotiations with their respective producers and coordinated state and private actions for the next meeting, held in Paris in March 1972. But it was not until the meetings in Johannesburg, South Africa, in late May and early June 1972 that a number of agreements were finalized. First, the Western world's uranium market was divided among the cartel members (see Table 1).

The reason for the inclusion and relatively large percentage to new mines, particularly in Australia, was to prevent their exclusion from the cartel and to inhibit them from underselling cartel members. Second, the May-June 1972 Johannesburg meetings established an initial agreement on a minimum price schedule ranging from $5.75 to $7.50 a pound for delivery between 1973 and 1978. Third, the countries agreed to charge more to East Asian members (Japan, Korea, and Taiwan). Uranium oxide was to sell for $0.20 per pound higher, and uranium hexafluoride $0.25 per pound higher. Ostensibly, the reasons were that East Asian markets were extremely vulnerable, due to their higher dependency on nuclear power and their lack of alternative energy sources. Aware of the earlier contracts to Japan, one wonders if Canadian representatives encouraged this discriminatory agreement. And finally, with the fourth Johannesburg agreement, cartel members promised to exclude from the arrangement their domestic markets and the American market. The position was undertaken for two reasons: first, the US embargo on foreign uranium was still in effect; second, and of greater concern, the members feared US anti-trust legislation. Due to the transnational corporations involved in the cartel, many had either parent or subsidiary offices in the USA that would be vulnerabale to legislation. Thus one can recognize why Trudeau would want to stop the sale of the controlling interest in Denison Mines at a time when the cartel concept was being studied. The problem was the US anti-trust laws. This would also explain the subsequent federal subsidies for Denison's uranium production.

Table 1:   Division of the Western World's Uranium Market Among Cartel Members.

GROUP	1972-77	1978-80
Canada	33.50%	23.22%
Nufcor (South Africa)	23.75%	19.26%
Uranex (France)	21.75%	19.26%
Australia	17.00%	24.44%
Rio Tinto Zinc (Britain)	4.00%	13.82%

Source: June Taylor, Michael Yokell, *Yellowcake: The International Uranium Cartel* (New York: Pergamon Press, 1979), p. 81.

The establishment in Johannesburg of a uranium price-fixing scheme secured and stabilized the world market. While many factors outside the cartel's control contributed to the uranium price spirals of 1974-76, it was apparent that without the previous cartelization of the market, the spiral would not have been as strong (see Figure 1). The cartel was well prepared for the following three events. First, the October 1973 OPEC price escalation. While the Western world has tried to blame the OPEC move for many economic problems in the post-1973 period, the coordinated escalation in the price of oil contributed to—but did not cause —the entire inflationary trend in the West. Some Canadian officials even tried to blame the uranium price hike on OPEC. A direct and immediate relationship did not exist due to the long lead times required for the construction of the nuclear reactor. A more important event which aided the uranium price rise was the 1973 relaxation of the US embargo on foreign uranium. The 1963 embargo had created a protected market for American domestic production. It originally was seen as a temporary measure to block less expensive international uranium, particularly South Africa's, which is mined as a by-product of gold extraction. But the embargo also limited the ability of US producers to export. This appears to be the reason why it was ended. Yet one cannot rule out pressure from US multinationals involved in the cartel. Removing the embargo would increase their freedom to market abroad. When American markets were suddenly opened in 1973, a lack of supply triggered the price spiral of 1974-75. A direct result of the increased price was a third event, which forced the world uranium price to unprecedented levels— Westinghouse defaulted on contracts to deliver between 70 and 80 million pounds of uranium to 27 domestic and international utilities. The official announcement of default occurred in September 1975, but earlier rumours of this had sufficed to escalate the price to $20 a pound by August 1975, up $4 in four months.

Westinghouse claimed it was not obligated to fulfill the contracts

> citing the 'commercial impracticability' section of the American Uniform Commercial Code which allows the breaking of contracts when 'unforseeable' events create a situation which makes completion of the contract so damaging to the supplier that fulfillment is 'commercially impracticable.'

Looking for a way out was to be expected. At the time of the default, Westinghouse stood to lose $1.2 billion, but the effect of the corporation's default quickly esclated the price and moved the loss closer to $2 billion. Taylor and Yokell put the default in perspective by comparing the 32,500 tons Westinghouse owed to various utilities with the total American production capacity, which ranged from 13,000 tons per year (actual 1975 US production) to 18,000 tons per year (the potential maximum capacity). Thus the Westinghouse default was twice the entire US production.

It was during the suits and countersuits between American utilities and uranium producers that the Mary Kathleen documents were delivered to John E. Moss, Chairperson of the House Subcommittee on Oversight and

Figure 1: Uranium Prices, 1969-1976

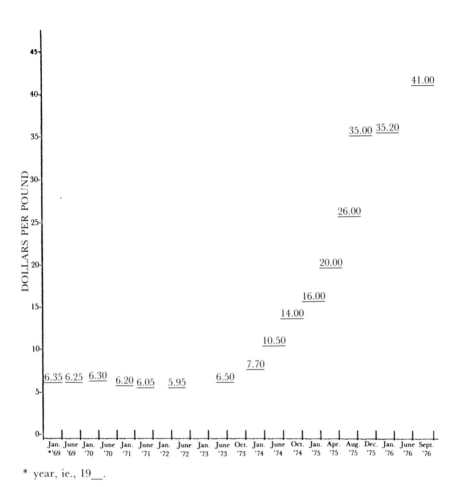

* year, ie., 19__.

Source: June Taylor, Michael Yokell, *Yellowcake: The International Uranium Cartel* (New York: Pergamon Press, 1979), p. 102.

118

Investigation of the Interstate and Foreign Commerce Committee. The Moss Committee launched an immediate investigation.[12]

Ottawa Responds to the Discovery

To protect the interests of the Canadian uranium industry, the Canadian federal government passed Order-in-Council 76-644 on September 21, 1976, which read as follows:

> No person who has in [their] possession or under [their] control any note, document or other written or printed material in any way related to conversations, discussions, or meetings that took place between January 1, 1972, and December 31, 1975, involving that person or any other person or any government, crown corporation, agency or other organization in respect of the production, import, export, transportation, refining, possession, ownership, use or sale of uranium or its derivatives or compounds, shall
> a) release any such note, document or material, or disclose or communicate the contents thereof to any person, government, crown corporation, agency or other organization unless
>   (i) [they are] required to do so by or under a law of Canada, or
>   (ii) [they do] so with the consent of the Minister of Energy, Mines, and Resources; or
> b) fail to guard against or take reasonable care to prevent the unauthorized release of any such note, document or material or the disclosure or communication of the contents thereof.

Aside from the "gag law" on November 8, 1976, Alastair Gillespie, Minister of Energy, Mines, and Resources, wrote to Gulf Minerals of Canada Limited for all documents relating to the cartel. While many documents were already in the possession of the US corporate office, Gillespie's action further dried up Canadian sources of information. This move, while seemingly meant to protect the Government from further implication, was part of a promise to Gulf Minerals of Canada to "prevent any action under Canada law... at least as long as the present government is in power." Yet, as Taylor and Yokell state, the order-in-council and subsequent refusal by the Canadian government "to cooperate with efforts by the United States courts to secure more information create speculation on what aspects of the cartel's activities remain to be revealed."

The federal government suppressed evidence and legislated that open debate on the matter be punishable by imprisonment, revealing the extent to which it demanded the issue be covered up. While Trudeau admitted that the cartel "was deliberately encouraged by the government," the Canadian public, press, and opposition parties were denied the facts. In 1977, when the Government did relax somewhat its order-in-council, this enabled only those involved in the cartel access to the material. Instead of providing documents, Canadians were informed, for example, that Steve Roman, President of Denison Mines Ltd., liked the cartel. Could one expect any different from a company which, aside from profiting from the inflated world price, was able to meet some of its new contract obligations by buying back from the federal stockpile—at the original $6 per pound price—the uranium it had sold to the Government in 1970 and re-selling it at 1976 prices, which were over $30 a pound higher?

The Government's pronouncements and actions implied that what was good for uranium producers was good for the country. This was debatable. Contrary to the Government's statements, the cartel did affect domestic uranium prices. But when it was revealed that a Gulf Minerals (Canada) Ltd. contract with Ontario Hydro was negotiated in the spring of 1974 at world prices and resulted in a $51-million profit on a $98-million sale and that a March 8, 1974, Gulf memo stated that the Department of Energy, Mines, and Resources knew Canadian prices parallelled the export price, the Government simply replied that it was up to the producers to make their own deals.

Even the request for investigations was thwarted. The opposition parties requested one under the Inquiries Act, which would open the matter to greater public scrutiny. For obvious reasons, however, if an investigation were to occur, Trudeau wanted it under the Combines Investigation Act (CIA). He favoured this course, as the CIA could not investigate when criminal offences may be involved. As well, it limited access to documents and their publication, limited the freedom of the investigative director, and in sum left ultimate power with the Government.[13]

The Effect of the Cartel

While further examples of the flouting of the Canadian democratic process could be documented, it must be recognized that the cartel was functional for Canadian corporate purposes. Thus the federal government was willing to usurp the democratic rights of Canadians in order to protect the domestic uranium industry. It was apparent that a guaranteed rise in the international price of uranium would increase the general revenue and profit of uranium corporations. In this sense, the cartel was a huge success. Within the first six months of 1974, Canadian uranium companies contracted for export in future years a total of 45,000 tons of uranium oxide, or approximately ten times the then Canadian annual production rate. On September 5, 1974, the Government announced a Uranium Export Policy, allegedly to secure domestic supplies. More importantly, however, the new policy required a government review of a contract prior to export. This ensured that cartel prices—and therefore profits—were maintained. The statistics reveal a 26 percent increase in yellowcake production between 1971 and 1977. Couple the production increase with the over 600 percent increase in the world uranium price between 1972 and 1976, and it is clear why, for example, Stephen Roman liked the cartel.

Large profits, however, were not the only outcome. The cartel helped increase national exploration and federal revenue. In the early 1970s less than $4 million per annum was expended nationally on uranium exploration;

yet in 1978 alone, $70 million was spent. The profits by Canadian Crown corporations experienced equally dramatic increases. Uranium Canada Ltd., the Crown corporation formed to manage the federal uranium stockpile, reported a $5.1-million and $6.7- million profit in 1975 and 1976, respectively. A large portion of the profit resulted from sales to Japanese utilities. But it was the statistics for Eldorado Nuclear Ltd. (its name was changed from Eldorado Mining and Refining in 1968) that revealed the most startling results. In December 1972, Eldorado's income was $9.7 million and was operating with a net loss of $3.6 million. But by December 1978, Eldorado's income exceeded $124 million, and its net earnings were over $17.6 million (see Table 2 and Figure 2).[14]

PHASE FIVE: AFTER THE CARTEL

The Cartel Comes "Out of the Closet"

The desire to generate private and state profits among all the members was the prime motive for creating the cartel. The members recognized, however, that in the long term, the high price of uranium would be counterproductive

Table 2: Eldorado Nuclear Limited's Products and Services Income 1969-1978

December 31, 1969	Income:	$ 3,760,781
	Net Loss:	$ 1,218,786
December 31, 1970	Income:	$ 5,637,284
	Net Loss:	$ 2,608,493
December 31, 1971	Income:	$ 11,095,320
	Net Loss:	$ 2,329,355
December 31, 1972	Income:	$ 9,730,486
	Net Loss:	$ 3,640,832
December 31, 1973	Income:	$ 14,715,981
	Net Loss:	$ 2,941,867
December 31, 1974	Income:	$ 34,130,485
	Net Income:	$ 2,638,060
December 31, 1975	Income:	$ 48,499,229
	Net Earnings:	$ 9,873,789
December 31, 1976	Income:	$ 47,707,734
	Net Earnings:	$ 4,045,160
December 31, 1977	Income:	$ 68,622,704
	Net Earnings:	$ 6,933,172
December 31, 1978	Income:	$124,046,000
	Net Earnings:	$ 17,618,000

Source: Eldorado Nuclear Limited, *Annual Reports*, 1969-1978. The distinction, if any exists, between "income" in 1974 and "earnings" in subsequent years is not contained in the original reports.

**Figure 2:   Eldorado Nuclear Limited's Income and
Net Loss/Income (1969-1978)**

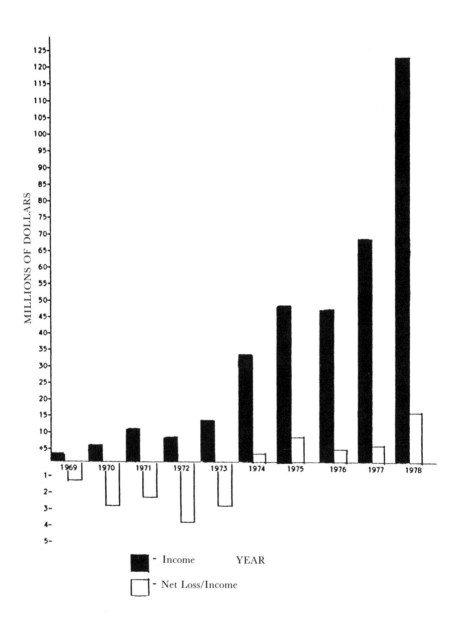

to increasing the use of nuclear power. But they also did not want to return to the pre-cartel American-dominated buyer's market. Thus, instead of disbanding the cartel, it was transformed into the Uranium Institute. Taylor and Yokell state that the decision to establish a more formal organization was made at the last recorded cartel meeting in Johannesburg in 1974. Having fulfilled its function of radically increasing the price of uranium and obtaining the market control formerly handled by the Americans, the cartel attempted to legitimize its existence. Or, as Taylor and Yokell put it, "the cartel was coming out of the closet." The Uranium Institute was formed in 1975 and held its first annual meeting in London in June 1976. The Institute further justified itself by stating that it also served a research function and was willing to admit uranium consumers. Interestingly, the Americans were noticeably absent at the Uranium Institute's inaugural London meeting. A Canadian, John Kostuik, President of Denison Mines Ltd., was the Institute's first chairperson. And the market price was still artificially high. Thus, while the Institute purported to be a legitimate research organization, little had changed.[15]

What's Next?

Despite the maintenance of some form of a suppliers' union, by the end of the 1970s, the international and Canadian uranium markets entered into another slow period. While not comparable to the downturn of the early 1960s, uranium mines were not producing at capacity. And, by May 1982, uranium was down to $22.50 per pound. Granted, the price still seemed high compared to the $4 to $5 paid per pound in the pre-cartel period, but a number of factors militated against the industry's continued prosperity. Foremost among these were the Western world's massive economic depression and the accompanying decrease in energy consumption. Combine this with an increasingly energy-conscious domestic population, massive escalations in nuclear reactor plant and construction costs, high interest rates, and tight money markets and one can understand the virtual halt in new reactor orders around the world. As well, the growing crosssection of people opposed to nuclear power struggled to publicize the waste disposal crisis and the nuclear weapons links, thus making it increasingly difficult for utilities to follow the nuclear route. And there was the March 1979 disaster at Three Mile Island which further galvanized international public opposition. By the early 1980s, the cumulative effect of these factors resulted in a relatively fixed amount of uranium required for the international power market. American producers undoubtedly profited from President Reagan's accelerated build-up of nuclear bombs (and some Canadian producers probably clamoured for a relaxation of Canadian safeguards to allow access to that market), but the Canadian struggle for international power contracts continued amidst numerous mine closures.[16]

While the industry was in a slump during the early 1980s, it would be incorrect to assume that Canadian uranium mining—for power or war—was coming to an end. In May 1981, for example, the world's largest uranium mine opened at Key Lake, Saskatchewan, about 550 Km north of Saskatoon. Despite setting international records for the amount of radioactive liquid spills—between September 1983 and January 1984 there were eight spills involving 1,508,675 litres of radioactive waste—uranium mining continued with approval from provincial and federal governments that ignored widespread public opposition. As before, Canadian uranium interests were protected by various state bureaucracies. Largely due to this support, in 1982, Canada regained its position as the world's largest producer of uranium and second in exports only to the USA.[17]

As this chapter has demonstrated, the uranium industry had setbacks before, but due to the assistance of the Canadian federal government, it also had resilience. In the early 1980s, with its new mine capacity, the industry appeared to be waiting for the next upswing in sales. Whether these will be generated by another cartel, a fourth stockpiling program, or the relaxation of Canadian safeguards remains to be seen. Then again, the next form of federal assistance could be entirely different. In fact, Ottawa's proposed plan to rescue the Canadian nuclear reactor program also could help revive the domestic uranium industry. The next chapter will examine the Ottawa plan.

CHAPTER V
REVIVING THE SALE OF REACTORS: THE LATE 1980s AND BEYOND

By the late 1970s, the Canadian reactor export program was still in grave difficulty. It had failed to make up for the small domestic market. The export program's links to nuclear weapons production, particularly in India, had served to publicize its implicit hazards. AECL's $350-million deficit for 1977-1978 and the cartel scandal also caused serious public relations problems. But by the end of the decade, public awareness had decreased, while the industry continued its self-confident struggle for sales. In 1980, the Department of Energy, Mines, and Resources stated that

> there are reasonable opportunities for CANDU exports, especially in the mid-to-late 1980s. Such sales could be of great benefit to Canada and could do much to sustain the domestic nuclear industry.

But it was not only future sales that were promising. As the Canadian nuclear industry rested upon the supposed laurels of the Government's 1974 and 1976 safeguards requirements— Canada's being "among the most strigent"— the implication was that the public should not fear additional Canadian contributions to nuclear weapons proliferation. In short, the industry promised sales and no bombs—the same rhetoric to which Canadians had been subjected since the early 1950s.

It is important to recognize that both promises were incorrect, dangerous, and costly. This requires examining four areas: first, the remarkably different international setting within which AECL attempted to operate; second, the large-scale, expensive plan that Ottawa appeared to be following in the post-1976 period to maintain the industry; third, AECL's marketing attempts to Romania; and finally, some of the industry's other self-perpetuating projects.

It will be evident that the nuclear export program was not going to disappear but would continue due to the Canadian federal government's steady support.[1]

THE DECLINE OF THE INTERNATIONAL NON-PROLIFERATION INFRASTRUCTURE

Judging by its public pronouncements, the Trudeau government hoped that the December 1976 safeguard announcement, whereby NPT ratification was required of future customers, would encourage other nuclear suppliers to increase their safeguard requirements. Admirable as this was, it reflected a considerable change in the international non-proliferation—or, more correctly, regulated proliferation— infrastructure. The need for unilateral Canadian action signalled that the post-1945 non-proliferation attempts had failed. It was not something that happened suddenly but had evolved during the twenty-three-year promotion of the "peaceful atom." To understand why this occurred, one must examine briefly the structure of the international nuclear market.

According to *Nuclear News*, as of June 30, 1981, there were 535 power reactors (30 MWe and over) that were operable, under construction, or on order. Of this total, the USSR's forty-one domestic and thirty-three export power reactors (primarily to Eastern Europe) represented 3.83 percent. The remaining 86.17 percent of the world's reactors were primarily in the Western bloc—the exceptions being a proposed Canadian sale to Romania and the Westinghouse sale to Yugoslavia. Within the Western world, the American nuclear industry was by far the largest, with the US market alone accounting for 37.3 percent of the Western total. The major American competitors in the international market were the European American licensees; the French Framatome and West German-based Kraftwerk Union were created by Westinghouse and General Electric, respectively. But one question remains: How did the American hegemony affect the strength of non-proliferation strategies? This requires reviewing three periods of nuclear exports.[2]

During the first period, from the early 1950s to the mid-1960s, there was relatively little control, as nuclear information and technology were disseminated primarily to the non-communist countries. Under Eisenhower's "Atoms for Peace," America's concern for promotion before control was entrenched at the international level and facilitated the launching of the export industry with gift reactors and technical instruction. Nuclear power was packaged and sold like most other commodities: in effect, free samples were provided; expensive product promotion campaigns were launched; and once the customers started appearing, the prices were raised.

It was during the second period, from the mid- 1960s to the early 1970s, that an increase in control was allowed. Nuclear reactor sales were numerous and the future was considered very promising. Thus the industry as a whole appeared capable of accepting the International Atomic Energy Agency's (IAEA) 1965 safeguard system and, in 1968, the Treaty for the Non-Proliferation of Nuclear Weapons (NPT). But the controls were not onerous. For example, the crucial issue of MAF (material accounted for, or the spent fuel that could be used in bomb production) was not considered important. To have done otherwise would have increased the cost of nuclear power. Likewise, the opposition to the NPT by major nuclear importers such as India and Argentina was allowable. NPT ratificaton was not required and other markets existed.

But starting in the early 1970s and roughly coinciding with the Indian nuclear explosion, the international nuclear industry entered a third phase that lasted well into the 1980s. While public concern for effective control escalated dramatically, this was not transformed into a workable international mechanism for halting all forms of nuclear weapons proliferation. The need for sales in a declining market explained the decrease in state and corporate concern for the potential military uses of nuclear power programs. With the early 1970s and the onset of the Western world's worst economic crisis since the 1930s, the nuclear market disappeared. It was a sad comment on the international nonproliferation infrastructure that while the Chinese atomic explosion in 1964 was an important catalyst urging the creation of the NPT in 1968, the Indian nuclear explosion led only to the London Club's suggestions in 1976 which, given the economic depression, proved unenforceable.

Did this mean, as Amory Lovins states in *Foreign Affairs*, that the contemporary demise of the international nuclear market reflected the end of the American-led nuclear age? It seemed unlikely. Instead, as Mark Hertzgaard argues in *Le Monde Diplomatique*, due to the deep financial commitment involved, the American government and corporations were prepared to absorb the losses and revive the industry through increased subsidies and decreased environmental and regulatory controls. Hertzgaard recognizes the importance of nuclear power to American and Western capitalism and criticises Lovins for underestimating corporate resiliency when backed by state capital. Hertzgaard offers an example. To revive the power industry, attempts were made in the early 1980s to increase its links with the nuclear weapons program. The power program possessed a large quantity of plutonium, stored in the spent fuel, required by the Pentagon. Thus, as the Reagan administration undertook its massive nuclear weapons escalation, it appeared that an original function of Eisenhower's "Atoms for Peace" would be revived. The military would aid the power program.[3]

At the international level, the collapse of the export market resulted in similar attempts to decrease controls. India's bomb did not strengthen the NPT but rather led to the London Club suggestions—which were not followed by actions—that the IAEA, rather than the NPT (which was considerably more stringent), should be strengthened. In effect, the London Club was attempting to return to the pre-NPT status quo. But while attempts to by-pass controls during a market slump have been a typical Western industrial strategy, they no longer suited the nuclear market. Weakened controls facilitated the continued increase of international spent fuel stockpiles and mobilized the anti-nuclear forces.

As Albert Wohlstetter *et al.* argued in "The Military Potential of Civilian Nuclear Energy," to prevent horizontal proliferation, the crucial issue is not the 1 percent of material unaccounted for (MUF) with which the IAEA and the NPT are concerned. Instead, it is the 99 percent of material accounted for (MAF) in the spent fuel stockpiles which is "likely to be decisive." By 1985, approximately forty countries will have enough fissionable material to yield three or more bombs, and almost as many countries will have enough fissile material for more than thirty to sixty bombs (see Figure 3 and Table 3).[4]

Nevertheless, from the mid-1970s into the 1980s, various governments and nuclear agencies acted as if the issue of materials accountd for (MAF) were unimportant and that the IAEA and NPT would prevent diversion. As well, they claimed that the London Club guidelines—assuming members abided by them—would restrict the exportation of "sensitive" materials, particularly enrichment and reprocessing technologies. These were dangerous short-term gambles. The advances in laser technology, for example, could make it difficult to restrain widespread construction of enrichment facilities.[5] And an American experiment showed that reprocessing capability was easy to obtain. The

Table 3: World plutonium production and accumulated stocks even if safeguards are 99.9 percent effective, in 1980 enough plutonium could be diverted without detection to produce nuclear weapons at the rate of one a week.

Year	Total world nuclear generating capacity GWe	Approx. annual commercial plutonium production tons	Approx. accumulated commercial plutonium stock tons
1970	20	4	20
1971	26	5	25
1972	35	7	30
1973	47	9	40
1974	72	18	60
1975	100	25	85
1976	150	35	120
1977	180	45	165
1978	210	50	215
1979	260	65	280
1980	300	80	360
1981	470	125	385
1982	570	160	545
1983	670	180	725
1984	770	210	935
1985	870	240	1175
1986	1030	270	1445
1987	1190	300	1775
1988	1350	360	2135
1989	1510	400	2535
1990	1700	450	3000

Source: Frank Barnaby, *The Nuclear Age*, Stockholm International Peace Research Institute (Cambridge, Mass.: The MIT Press, 1974), p. 81.

Figure 3: Countries with Enough Separable Plutonium for Primitive or Small Military Forces

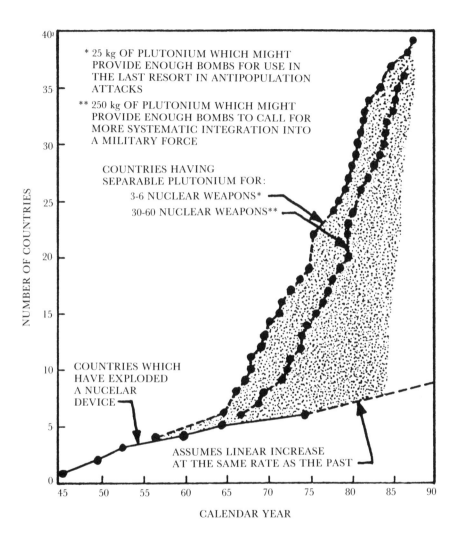

Source: Albert Wohlstetter, Thomas A. Brown, Gregory Jones, David McGarvey, Henry Rowen, Vincent Taylor, and Roberta Wohlstetter, "The Military Potential of Civilian Nuclear Energy Moving Towards Life in a Nuclear Armed Crowd," *Minerva*, Vol. 15, Nos. 3-4, Autumn-Winter, 1977, p. 403.

Oak Ridge scientists developed a conceptual design for a "quick-and-dirty" reprocessing plant which could allegedly separate a bomb's worth of plutonium per week, with only a modest risk of detection during the relatively short construction time (of the order of a year).[6]

Thus, in a very real sense, the international community may have already passed a point of no return. But seldom has one heard representatives of the nuclear industry voice concern over the issue of MAF or admit the likelihood that sensitive technologies will proliferate globally. To do so would admit that the international safeguard system was incapable of preventing weapons proliferation. This, in turn, could spark a domestic outcry that would threaten the state and corporate exports of uranium, reactors, and other nuclear material and technology just when sales were at an all-time low. Not surprisingly, Canadian nuclear officials duplicated the actions of their international counterparts.

THE CANADIAN NUCLEAR INDUSTRY'S INTERNAL REVIEW

In the early 1980s, the Canadian nuclear program's future appeared secure. This was despite the decline in the international non-proliferation infrastructure, the lack of sales (the January 1976 South Korean contract was the last firm order), and the myriad of technical, political, ecological, and economic problems associated with the industry. Though a reverse trend had begun, nuclear power—which provided less than 5 percent of Canada's total energy requirements—still received a disproportionate amount of funding (see Table 4). Rather than develop alternative energy sources and effective conservation programs, the historic pattern of state support for the Canadian nuclear program was maintained. In fact, it appeared that the program's expansion, rather than contraction, was being planned. This was evident from the policies suggested by the "Inter-Agency Review of the Nuclear Power Industry in

Table 4:   The Federal Energy Research and Development Expenditures (in $ millions)

Year	1976-77	1977-78	1978-79	1979-80	1980-81	1981-82
Total	120.5	118.2	150.7	157.9	173.9	205.9
Nuclear	90.3	87.9	105.8	106.4	117.2	118.4
% Nuclear	**75%**	**74%**	**70%**	**67%**	**67%**	**57.5%**

Source: Office of Energy R & D, EMR, Ottawa. Cited in Gordon Edwards, "Canada's Nuclear Dilemma," *Journal of Business Administration*, Vol. 13, Nos. 1 & 2, 1982.

Canada," an internal government review conducted under the direction of Reiner Hollbach of the Department of Energy, Mines, and Resources.

The decision to conduct an internal review was announced by Pierre Trudeau to the House of Commons on May 1, 1980, after Rear Admiral Castro Madero, head of the Argentinean Comision Nacional de Energia Atomica (CNEA), visited Ottawa to placate Canadian concerns about price escalations on the Cordoba reactor. Trudeau announced that the Department of Energy, Mines, and Resources would be conducting an in-depth review of the Canadian nuclear industry to determine what was needed to keep it intact. Upon demands that the Government launch a public inquiry, Trudeau argued that while the intent was not to ignore public opinion, "we cannot wait for a long inquiry to decide whether we stay in the game or get out of the game." Not surprisingly, the internal review —leaked to the Ottawa press in June 1981— supported staying "in the game."[7]

The review recognized that "consumption of electricity will continue to grow for the rest of the century at rates which will likely remain well below recent historical averages." This, in turn, could "cause severe disruption within the Canadian nuclear industry." Yet the review anticipated that the low point would be reached by the mid-to late 1980s because "options for meeting projected load growth will be limited to coal, hydro, and nuclear." The review disregarded soft energy forms such as conservation, solar, biomasss, or wind in an equitable energy mix, and forgot that high electricity use is often not efficient. As well, it argued that the economic and environmental costs of coal and hydro had increased (conveniently ignoring similar difficulties with nuclear power). Such tactics, however, were important. They enabled the industry's reviewers to reach a second conclusion; mainly, that there "is a good economic argument for maintaining the nuclear option to the 1990s" when it assumed electricity demand would increase. The review, while circular, was intended to legitimize the numerous policy suggestions for expanding the Canadian nuclear program and, indirectly, the domestic uranium program. The EMR report examined three major areas: the domestic market, reactors for power exports, and reactors for the export market. Each of these will be discussed, as they affect the direction of the Canadian nuclear program in the early 1980s.[8]

The Domestic Market

Prefacing the domestic market policy options, the internal review argued that the "underlying determinant" of the domestic demand for nuclear reactors was the growth rate of electricity demand. It was important, therefore, "to promote the rate of growth of electricity demand over and above market determined levels." While the review recognized the limitations on electricity end use and the problems of increased national electricity consumption, evidently it supported electrical heating and provincially directed electricity promotion campaigns. These plans were being implemented in the early 1980s. The federal government, for example, adopted an oil substitution program which served to increase electricity consumption, while Ontario

Hydro resurrected its "Live Better Electrically" campaign of the 1950s and 1960s.

The review argued that increased electricity use— in a country that had the world's largest per capita energy consumption rate—was an underlying determinant of increasing the domestic nuclear market. Thus there were at least three major areas which "directly determine the demand for reactors and which the government can influence." These included increasing public acceptability, improving nuclear incentives to the provinces, and rationalizing Canadian heavy water production.

Public acceptability

The review cited three major areas of public concern: "The long-term management of radioactive wastes, the safety of reactor operation, and the possible impact of nuclear energy on human health and the natural environment." Evidently, Reiner Hollbach, the review's director, felt the Government's multimillion-dollar glossy propaganda pamphlet program was insufficient. Instead, he preferred more "positive action." With radioactive wastes, for example, one option was

> to issue a clear indication of confidence by the government that the waste management question is on its way to solution, and at the same time providing increased funding of the waste disposal program to allow it to proceed at the technologically determined pace.

It seems that the policy option was acted upon. On August 4, 1981, Marc Lalonde (Federal Minister of Energy, Mines, and Resources) and Robert Welch (Ontario Minister of Energy) released the "Canada-Ontario Joint Statement on the Nuclear Fuel Waste Management Program." The release stated in part that

> the program is expected to demonstrate that the concept of deep geological disposal in stable rock formations is a fully acceptable method of disposing permanently of high-level radioactive wastes from the nuclear fuel cycle.

The statement announced the expansion of the $20 million program started in 1977. Thenceforth, East Bull Lake, 35 km east of Elliot Lake, and Overflow Bay-Denmark Lake, 75 km southeast of Kenora, would be drilling sites to complement the work at Atikocan, Chalk River, White Lake, and Pinawa. It was at AECL's Whiteshell Nuclear Research Establishment in Pinawa that a major test construction of an underground radioactive garbage vault was under construction. Manitobans had no guarantee—AECL's promise to the contrary was insufficient—that the test site would not create a vested interest and turn the project into an actual dumping site. But in the early 1980s, even AECL did not publicly indicate how or where the program would

132

unfold. While southern Canadian sites were being considered, Dr. Bruce Goodwin, the director of the transportation section in the environmental and safety assessment branch at the Whiteshell Research Establishment, stated, at a February 1984 University of Winnipeg seminar, he would recommend that Canadian politicians turn northern Canada into a nuclear waste disposal site for the world.[9]

As of early 1984, the Canadian government had not implemented similar "positive action" programs in the other areas suggested by the review. But while pamphlets such as "Living with Radiation" temporarily may have sufficed to placate some public concern over the impact of nuclear energy on human health and the environment, it appeared that the industry had to coordinate its press releases to deal with the reactor safety issue. This was particularly important after the August 1, 1983, pressure tube rupture in the Pickering II reactor. By rupturing without warning, the tube dissolved one of the Canadian nuclear industry's fundamental tenets of reactor safety. Previously it was argued that pressure tubes inside the CANDU reactor would leak before rupturing, thus allowing detection by the reactor operators. Supposedly, this would have allowed the implementation of the necessary safety precautions. While Ontario Hydro tried to mask the problem's severity and lay blame on human error rather than admit a problem existed with the design of the CANDU system, the safety issue once again was recognized publicly as fundamentally important.

Norman Rubin, of Energy Probe (a non-aligned energy analysis foundation), states that the Pickering pressure tube rupture possibly was a function of the reactor's advancing age—something Ontario Hydro had anticipated would not cause problems until the end of the century. But Hydro previously had experienced difficulties with the zirconium alloy pressure tubes' tendency to stretch. Possibly, this rupture was a prelude to many others. It will be important to observe how the nuclear industry struggles to bury this accident— after the public has paid for the tube replacements. Nevertheless, the rupture re-exposed the inherent difficulties of nuclear technology and made it increasingly difficult for the industry to improve its public acceptability.[10]

Improving nuclear incentives to the provinces

The review recognized that Ontario was experiencing a serious oversupply of electrical generating capacity and thus intended the incentives for New Brunswick and Quebec. Among others, these included federal financing to 75 percent of the delivered or actual reactor costs as compared to the existing 50 percent of the estimated costs; decreasing and lengthening the already favourable interest rates and repayment terms, respectively; and considering federal equity participation in reactor projects. Hollbach argued that such policies would result in increased domestic sales and "demonstrate to foreign customers a clear Canadian commitment to the nuclear option." What he ignored, however, was the cost to the Canadian taxpayer and economy for capital- intensive radioactive generating stations that were not required for energy needs but for the perpetuation of the Canadian nuclear industry.

Rationalization of Canadian heavy water production

The heavy water section of the Canadian nuclear program was an embarrassment. As Hollbach stated, "there does not appear to be any plausible scenario in which the output of all Canada's heavy water plants will be required." "Rationalization" was an industry term intended to cover its monumental planning blunder that led to a major oversupply of heavy water. Without access to the American military market and depressed domestic and export sales, the heavy water was accumulating. The review stated that even "with the most optimistic sales scenario, AECL and Ontario Hydro inventories could total 15 reactor loads by 1990 at a cost of about $2 billion ($1980)."

While the heavy water oversupply was costly, Hollbach felt it was "difficult to foresee any gains from a rationalization decision in terms of the problems facing the industry as a whole." Thus, while closing a plant would not solve the industry's problems, it would help cut costs. He offered the advantages and drawbacks of closing either an AECL or an Ontario Hydro heavy water plant. Hollbach argued that while Ontario Hydro's plants were more efficient than AECL's and large enough to saturate domestic and foreign markets, the closure of AECL's Maritime plants would "generate adverse socio-economic impacts" and might affect Canada's reputation as a reliable supplier.

Evidently, the federal Liberal Cabinet recognized the dire situation of heavy water oversupply and the potential impact a plant closure would have on the local Maritime economy. In June 1983 it was announced that one of Ontario Hydro's heavy water plants would be shut down. One also could question whether the federal Liberal Cabinet wanted to avoid aggravating their party's decreased popularity at the polls when Brian Mulroney, the new leader of the Conservative opposition, was seeking election in the Maritime riding of Central Nova.

The review's conclusion for domestic market policy options

The conclusions were quite simple: the industry's policies should be directed toward "achieving an early commitment by Quebec and New Brunswick to Gentilly III and Lepreau II, respectively." Considering how the review's policy options were pursued regarding the radioactive waste crisis and the heavy water shutdown, one can conclude that considerable pressure existed for a provincial commitment to construct the increasingly subsidized CANDU reactors.[11]

Reactors for Power Exports

The second major area for which the leaked internal review offered policy options was the construction of CANDU reactors on the northern side of the Canada-US border for electricity exports to the northeastern American states. The EMR review placed considerable emphasis on this option and threatened that a decision soon had to be made to take advantage of the opportunity.

Haste was encouraged, since reactor construction required a long lead time, and the openings into the American market were expected to last only between 1990 and the early twenty-first century. EMR argued that constructing up to five or six 630-MWe CANDUs in New Brunswick and five to seven 850-MWe CANDUs in Ontario would provide the contracts required to maintain the Canadian nuclear industry.

This scenario demands public criticism for a number of reasons. First, the market study for the proposed reactors was conducted by the Department of Energy, Mines, and Resources, which had a vested bureaucratic interest (and some corporate links through its staff) in expanding the Canadian nuclear program. Second, it ignored the tremendous strain on the Canadian economy caused by a project that would cost at least $10 billion. Third, if there were promising power markets in the northeastern US states, would not American utilities attempt to reap the profits? If not, to what extent did Ottawa plan to underwrite the program? Was it possible that the 75 percent federal financing at "more favourable interest rates" than before (suggested earlier in the review as an incentive to increase provincial nuclearization) would apply to the reactors built for electricity exports? If so, this suggested that the American market possibilities were less important than the perpetuation of the Canadian nuclear industry. Fourth, the reactors for power export section mentioned radioactive waste disposal but ignored the specific economics of trying to control the spent fuel from ten to thirteen reactors over the next 24,000 years. But then again, some AECL officials wanted to turn northern Canada into the world's radioactive dustbin; so one knows where waste would be sent. Fifth, the EMR review ignored the cost of decommissioning the proposed reactors. The Canadian government did not know the cost, as it had never attempted to decommission a CANDU. This was another issue kept from the public. While AECL's public affairs office published glossy, colourful, expensive brochures for the interested citizen, the technology was untried and the economic estimates were industry favourable guesses. Sixth, the review also ignored the large amount of plutonium that would be generated in five 630-MWe and five 850-MWe CANDUs (the review's lower estimate) over thirty years (a reactor's estimated lifetime). The ten reactors, if operated at 75 percent capacity, would produce approximately 145,850 kg of plutonium-239, or enough material for over 18,230 bombs. And finally, assuming that AECL received the power export contracts to the USA for the anticipated ten, possibly twenty, year period, what of the remaining life of the reactors? It seemed unlikely that the excess capacity could be channelled into the Canadian market: Hydro-Quebec was expected to have a 20 percent over-capacity by 1990 without any more nuclear power plants due to its planned hydro-electric expansion; Ontario Hydro experienced a 45 percent overcapacity in 1980 and was expected to have at least a 30 percent overcapacity to the end of the decade; and New Brunswick's Point Lepreau was providing a 50 percent overcapacity which the provincial utility was trying to export to the US. Considering EMR's ability to inaccurately forecast anticipated demand (see Figure 4), it was not surprising that critics were opposed to EMR's planned, but taxpayer-funded, bail-out of the Canadian nuclear industry.

Despite these problems, Ottawa appeared to favour the idea of building reactors for power exports. What was not public in early 1984, however, was how many reactors were part of this program. AECL had only admitted that New Brunswick's Point Lepreau II was slated for power export. Yet with Point Lepreau I's 50 percent overcapacity, one could question if its power also has been originally intended for export. As well, considering Ontario Hydro's overcapacity, one also could ask if the anticipated Darlington I through IV were intended for power export. If so, the industry was silent.[12]

Reactors for the Export Market

The leaked internal review argued that while customers considered the CANDU technology to be a strong selling point, there were a number of areas where the Canadian nuclear industry was considered to be weak. Thus the review examined ways to streamline government machinery, reduce safeguards, open up formerly closed markets, improve the already favourable financing, and correct the CANDU marketing strategies. All policy options reflected the industry's nagging concern with expanding the CANDU market.

Government machinery

The review wanted to further remove the Canadian nuclear program from public scrutiny. While it stated that the maintenance of "adequate controls" was desired, the examples offered reflected a desire to return to the freedom experienced before the Argentinean and South Korean contract fiascos forced the Canadian government to nominally increase the controls on the export program. The review offered three examples. First, "maintaining overall approval for nuclear cooperation with a potential foreign government as required by current non-proliferation policies." While apparently concerned with preventing nuclear proliferation, the request appeared to be based on the industry's recognition that it was easier to collect from a government, regardless of the number of military coups, than a business or government department. The second option simply was stated as "modifying contract approval processes." While not specific, one can conclude that the industry would not favour additional controls. The third option was the most revealing. It suggested

> instituting a reporting process by which AECL, at the time a contract is concluded, reports details of terms and conditions to the Treasury Board. Further, the corporation would be required to provide to the Board an update of progress with each contract every six months.

Such a situation would be after the fact. With the contract concluded, AECL would be informing only the Treasury Board. Yet, even if Treasury Board

Figure 4: Canadian Nuclear Capacity Projected to 2000 A.D.

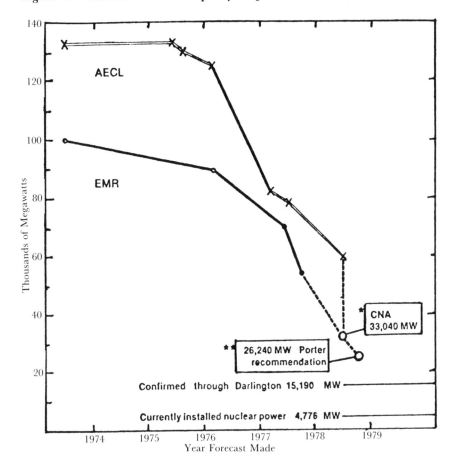

Each point on this graph represents an official published projection of estimated nuclear capacity by the year 2000. The great expectations of 1973 had all but disappeared by 1979. In 1981, the EMR Internal Review estimated less than 22,000 MW installed by the year 2000.

* Leonard & Partners, *Economic Impact of the Nuclear Energy Industry in Canada.* Prepared for the Canadian Nuclear Association. (Toronto: CNA, September, 1981).

** Porter *et al., A Race Against Time,* Interim Report on Nuclear Power, Royal Commission on Electric Power Planning, September, 1978. (Toronto: Government of Ontario, 1978).

Source: *Canadian Renewable Energy News,* Vol. 1, No. 11, November, 1978. Adapted from Exhibit SES-196-V, Cluff Lake Board of Inquiry into Uranium Mining in Saskatchewan, 1977. Cited in Gordon Edwards, "Canada's Nuclear Dilemma," *Journal of Business Administration,* Vol. 13, Nos. 1 & 2, 1982.

approval were required, it likely would not take long before the Board simply rubber stamped AECL's independent activities.

It is interesting, however, that while the review reflected the industry's resentment of controls, one statement implied that they were considered unimportant. Hollbach argued that even if his suggested controls were implemented, these

> may not affect AECL's probability of success in foreign markets to an appreciable degree. It is likely that much more controversial policy changes would be required to signifivcantly enhance sales prospects.

Safeguards

A number of options were included: (1) Leave Canadian safeguards intact but attempt to upgrade the safeguards of other suppliers; (2) Leave safeguards unchanged but apply them more flexibly; (3) alter the 1974 policy by limiting bilateral agreements to those specified in the 1978 nuclear suppliers' agreement (London Club); (4) eliminate the existing bilateral agreement and maintain the December 1976 full-scope NPT safeguards requirement; (5) abandon full-scope safeguards and limit safeguards to those required by the nuclear suppliers' agreement. The review considered options 1 and 2 to be of limited effectiveness and 3, 4, and 5 as varying in their potential usefulness. While a conclusion was not offered for this specific section, it was evident that pressure was developing to revert, in some way, to the pre-1974 status quo. This was a typical industry response during a sales crisis. Rather than recognize that the technology was largely unaffordable—unless a country was intent on producing a nuclear arsenal and was thus less concerned with cost effectiveness—the review argued that "safeguards policies do limit the ability of the Canadian nuclear industry to sell abroad." It seemed that the ineffectual safeguards applied between 1974 and 1976 to relegitimize the industry were being used as an excuse for the industry's inability to remain viable in the post-1976 period.

Opening formerly closed markets

South Africa, Middle East countries, and Taiwan were listed as target areas for new markets. While encouraging sales efforts in these areas, the review omitted noting that the Canadian exclusion policy was neither long-standing nor inflexible. For example, Canada cooperated with, and thus encouraged, the South African regime's exploitation of Namibian uranium during the period of the uranium cartel. AECL salespersons also tried to solicit reactor contracts in Egypt and Iraq. Seven months after the Indian nuclear explosion and days before Donald Macdonald announced to the Canadian public the Government's December 1974 safeguards policy, a CANDU sales team reached Baghdad. As Steve Weissman and Herbert Krosney state in *The Islamic Bomb*,

138

They sat around their hotel puffing the virtues of the CANDU natural uranium reactor to their potential clients, hinting broadly at its excellence in producing the deadly substance [plutonium] and even more broadly at the possibilities of keeping safeguards at a minimum. What bothered Cirard [at the time an advisor on nuclear affairs at the French Department of Energy] most about them was not that they had tried to sell the CANDU that way. It was their later hypocrisy in pointing to the French sale as a danger for nuclear proliferation when actually they had desperately wanted the sale for themselves, and had indicated no concern whatsoever whether Iraq got the bomb or not.

These factors conveniently were ignored by the internal review. Instead, it emphasized ways in which the Taiwanese market, for example, could be developed. These included sounding out the Chinese reaction to a Canadian marketing attempt in Taiwan, not requiring a bilateral agreement with Taiwan (using instead the "US-Taiwan agreement as an umbrella"), or a revision of the 1970 Canada-China agreement. While the review did not conclude which option was superior, once again it was evident that the industry wanted all limitations, no matter how small, removed from its export program— even if such an action could contribute to global nuclear weapons proliferation.

Financing

The review suggested increasing taxpayer subsidization by having the Canadian federal government "guarantee financing at concessional rates for foreign sales" and make available "'credit-mixte' for reactor exports to countries qualifying for Canadian aid which have been offered credit mixte financing by competitors." The review supported improved taxpayer subsidization, as it would not structurally change the export program and could improve immediate sales possibilities in South Korea and Mexico. Actually, the subsidization would have to be very high, as both countries had deferred nuclear development due to their economic problems in the early 1980s. But EMR recognized that even with increased subsidization

the main drawback is expense. EDC (the Canadian Export Development Corporation) estimates that a 1% reduction in interest rates is equivalent to roughly a $30 million reduction selling price. Thus, meeting 'credit-mixte' terms (5 to 6% per annum to countries which qualify) offered by competitors may involve subsidies equivalent to 25 to 30% of the cost of a reactor sale. The implicit subsidy involved in competing with concessional financing (as opposed to credit-mixte, which involves a foreign aid component [a different form of subsidization]), would be somewhat less costly.

To detract from this expensive drawback, however, EMR offered a profound insight. It stated that "while the costs of concessional financing are large, such expenses are only incurred if sales are successfully completed."

139

CANDU marketing

The review's authors recognized the obvious: from the industry's viewpoint, Canadian marketing efforts were inadequate. To improve this, two options were suggested. First, AECL's marketing activities should receive additional funding. But this would only "increase the probability of a sale" while the possibility of no return at all would remain. The second option was considerably more extreme. It suggested the use and payment of agents in marketing the CANDU. EMR admitted that the 1976 policy statement required that subsequent use of agents necessitated comprehensive written agreements and prohibited practices which would be illegal in Canada or in the importing country but argued that the "use of agents and payments of agents' fees is a prerequisite to success in some important markets." The review offered a clear threat: "observe the 1976 policy to the letter and lose a sale; or modify the 1976 policy (or interpret it more flexibly) and conclude a sale." Between the review's suggestions for increased financial subsidies and agent payments, one must question exactly what percentage would be left for the CANDU customer to pay for a reactor with limited safeguards. In short, to what extent did EMR expect the Canadian public to pay for a foreign country's potential bomb program while resuscitating the Canadian nuclear export program?[13]

Implications of Not Implementing the "Suggestions"

For readers of the internal review who felt some of the policy recommendations were too drastic or expensive, Reiner Hollbach included a discussion on a "laissez-faire option." Such an approach was "attractive, as it avoided the economic, financial, and public acceptability costs of an active policy." It implied that not adopting many of the active options would cause the Canadian nuclear industry to fall apart when private contractors turned to other areas. Hollbach argued that if this were to occur prior to the load growth, which he expected to appear in the 1990s, Canada would have to do without nuclear technology, import technology, or reassemble the Canadian nuclear industry.

From Hollbach's perspective, all these alternatives were fraught with serious problems. To do without nuclear power would "include higher costs in economic, social, and environmental terms of resorting to less efficient alternatives, as well as lost industrial and technological benefits." This conclusion was based on the assumption that the only alternatives to CANDU-generated electricity were hydro, coal, and imported nuclear reactors. Hollbach ignored the growing recognition that Canada already used too much electricity—primarily due to inefficiency—when other energy sources, such as solar technology and conservation, could achieve a more equitable energy mix that would decrease Canada's dependency on specific energy forms (hydro, oil, and gas).

Hollbach argued that the second alternative, importing reactor technology from abroad, not only would critically threaten large segments of the Canadian

140

nuclear industry but would decrease energy security. He did not expand on the latter point, as the main thrust of his criticism was to elaborate on how the Canadian nuclear program would further reduce its Canadian content and irrevocably become altered.

The third alternative was called "exit and reassembly." Hollbach stated that this was possible, but only in principle, for it ignored the interim technological advances, the cost of reconstructing the Canadian nuclear industry, and the difficulty of getting people and companies with investment capital interested in an industry "which had floundered once before." Aside from ignoring that the industry already had been floundering for a number of years—despite massive state assistance since the 1940s* (estimated total: $3 billion)—the scenario was based on the debatable assumption that nuclear power was necessary. [14]

It seems that the inclusion of these threats in the international review was to increase, or at least maintain, the Trudeau Cabinet's economic and ideological support. Those directly involved in the nuclear program did not question the need for continued help and urgent action. Witness the number of programs already implemented that appeared to parallel the review's suggestions. Equally important, while Energy, Mines, and Resources was conducting the internal review, Atomic Energy Canada Limited was busy trying to make a sale in Romania.

ROMANIA

Canada has been trying to conclude a Romanian deal since 1967. It tried first between 1967 and 1969. [15] Evidence of a second attempt was provided when Donald Macdonald, Minister of Energy, Mines, and Resources, announced the Government's December 1974 safeguards policy to the House of Commons. For two reasons, this round was considerably different. First, AECL gave up on achieving a direct reactor sale and instead worked to conclude a reactor licensing agreement. And second, the Romanian government actually agreed to purchase at least one CANDU reactor. But as the following review of the second round of negotiations explains, as of early 1984, the project was not guaranteed.

After two years of negotiations, Canadian and Romanian officials completed, in November 1976, a preliminary joint examination of the division of responsibilities, scheduling, and financing of a proposed CANDU reactor to be located at Cernavoda, approximately 150 km from Bucharest. On October 24, 1977, the two countries signed a nuclear safeguards and cooperation agreement in accordance with the Canadian government's December 1974 safeguards policy. These prerequisites led to a November 1977 initialling of a licensing agreement between AECL and Romanergo, the Romanian state trading company. The licensing agreement, upon conclusion of the procurement and engineering services agreements, provided Romania with the design of

---

* See Appendix I for federal expenditures on nuclear R & D, 1947-1979.

141

a 629-MWe CANDU. The Canadian licensing fee was estimated at $5 million per reactor for the first four and, should AECL and Romanergo renegotiate the contract for additional reactors, it was anticipated that the licensing fee would drop steadily to about $2 million for the last of Romania's sixteen anticipated reactors.

The November 1977 Licensing Agreement led to the exchange of the draft reactor procurement and engineering services agreements. By July 1978, AECL and Romanergo officials had initialled the engineering services agreement which covered the first reactor—additional reactors required renegotiations. This agreement enabled AECL to transfer some of the costs of reactor design to Romania. Instead of redesigning the reactor to fit the Romanian conditions, the licensing agreement provided Romanergo with an "off-the- shelf" reactor design and required AECL to be reimbursed for any additional costs incurred in constructing the reactor according to Romanian site and regulatory requirements. The engineering services agreement also reflected a compromise, as it included fixed price and cost escalation clauses to accommodate the demands of the Romanians and Canadians, respectively.

The third accord which enabled an AECL-Romanergo contract was the October 8, 1978, initialling of the procurement agreement. It stipulated the degree of Canadian content in the Romanian project. For the first reactor— the only one covered by this contract—Canadian content was to be approximately $100 million on an $800-million CANDU, or 12.5 percent. It was estimated that Canadian content would be reduced considerably should a second, third, or fourth reactor be negotiated, the percentages being 6, 4, and 4, respectively.

With the three stages of contract negotiations completed, all that remained were official approval by the respective governments and completion of the financial arrangements. These actions would allow construction to begin at Cernavoda. Government approval was expected as a rubber stamp to an agreement that both governments supported. It was the financial arrangements which were more complicated.[16]

Financing Cernavoda

In November 1978, the Export Development Corporation (EDC), the federal export financing institution, announced that it was negotiating a $1 billion line of credit to allow Romania to purchase four CANDU reactors under a licensing agreement. The financing of EDC's loan to the Romanian Bank of Foreign Trade was broken down as follows: half in American and half in Canadian dollars; and of the $500 million in Canadian funds, a consortium of Canadian banks, led by the Bank of Montreal, lent $320 million. The rate of interest, however, was kept secret. When the financing was completed in December 1978, the three earlier agreements were signed and the EDC loan approved.

Yet one question remained unanswered. Why was the EDC offering $1 billion for four reactors? Granted, the licensing agreement covered the first four of an anticipated sixteen reactors. The procurement agreement, however, covered one reactor with an option for a second, and the engineering services agreement covered only one reactor. Canadian government officials stated that the amount would provide the "additional incentive" to expand the Romanian order from one to four reactors. But was $1 billion sufficient to interest Romania in an estimated $3.2 billion project? It appears the EDC loan was an insufficient incentive for four CANDUs but was a generous amount of credit for one reactor—the only one that Romania was under contract to purchase. A breakdown of the costs can better explain this supposition. First, in 1978, the 629-MWe CANDU was priced at an estimated $800 million. Second, *The Globe and Mail* assumed that the licensing fee for the first reactor was $5 million. Third, *The Globe and Mail* also reported that heavy water and uranium fuel were "not covered in agreements already signed or under negotiation." Romania had an insufficient heavy water production capacity and lacked the refinery necessary to produce CANDU fuel. The price of 600-MWe CANDU initial fuel supply for one year at the December 1978 price of $176/kg was $21,964,800. The heavy water costs for one reactor were estimated at $60 million. Thus the remaining $113 million from the proposed $1 billion EDC loan would seem to provide an avenue of safety for probable cost escalations on the Canadian portion of the plant. The publicity of "additional incentive" appears to have been a domestic promotional trick to hide the removal of $1 billion from the Canadian capital market in order to provide a far from equivalent return. It was easier to sell to the Canadian public a $1 billion line of credit for four reactors than to admit that the subsidized loan was for one licensed CANDU with an estimated Canadian content of 12.5 percent.[17]

The Deal Falls Through

On May 11, 1978, the Canadian and Romanian agreements went into effect. But, as of early 1984, the project had yet to get seriously underway. And it appeared that the contract negotiations, reopened due to Romania's inability to meet the original terms, would take years to complete. The reason was simple: Romania could not afford nuclear technology. Signs of this possibility were evident in September 1980. Romanian President Nicolae Ceausescu planned a trip to Canada to negotiate a "contratrade agreement" which would allow the Romanians to export goods rather than cash for the licensed CANDU. But the Canadians refused. In an attempt to increase the probability of a contratrade agreement that could help solve their foreign-exchange shortage, the Romanians agreed in August 1981 (over two and one-half years after the orginal EDC loan) to construct a second reactor at Cernavoda. It did not help; the Canadians remained uninterested in the contratrade agreement. And with Romania's mounting international debt, Bucharest was unable to continue with its nuclear plans.

In June 1982 the Export Development Corporation stopped all further payments for goods and services, and the Cernavoda project was halted. The $320 million loaned by the Canadian banks (half of which was guaranteed by the EDC) already had been issued and used by Canadian sources for site preparation and other preliminary work. Despite this vested interest, Richard Hegan, a spokesperson for the EDC, stated that no further payments would be granted until Romania negotiated its foreign debt.

A review of Romania's economic situation offered little optimism for a CANDU sale. Throughout the second half of 1982, Romania struggled to meet its foreign debt by renegotiating with various Western banks and the International Monetary Fund; yet, by December 1982, its foreign debt was still $11 billion. In January 1983, Romania announced a cut-off of interest and principal payments totalling more than $1 billion. The low probability of a CANDU licensing sale to Romania was compounded by the September 9, 1982, Soviet-Romanian nuclear agreement which provided for the supply of Russian nuclear power plants.

Possibly because of this agreement, in August 1983, the Canadian government made another proposal. A $2 billion credit line was established for two reactors. Half of this amount was an EDC loan that would remain in Canada. The money was to be available for domestic companies to buy Romanian goods. The negotiations came to a standstill, however, as the two parties could not agree on the type of goods to be purchased. The Canadians insisted upon equipment only or, at worst, primarily. They did not want to include consumer goods. But the Romanian proposal included footwear, textiles, farm implements, wine, and frozen strawberries. In early 1984, the outcome of the negotiations was uncertain. While Jean Chretien, Federal Energy Minister, stated that "we are not bartering CANDUs against strawberries," all were aware—particularly the Romanians—that the Canadian nuclear industry needed the sale.

Undoubtedly it was rather embarrassing for Canadian officials to admit the possible loss of a contract that included such favourable terms to the purchaser. Thus it was not surprising that the "International" section of AECL's *Annual Report*, issued in July 1982, only mentioned Bucharest when discussing a trade fair and was silent on the failed contract. While the corporation might disclaim responsibility for the loss by arguing that external economic factors were at fault, the Romanian deal revealed the problems of marketing an expensive energy source and the unviability of nuclear technology in the contemporary world.[18]

SOME OF THE INDUSTRY'S OTHER SELF-PERPETUATION PROJECTS

It was evident from the leaked "Policy Review of the Nuclear Power Industry in Canada" that the Canadian government was not lacking ideas about how to maintain the nuclear program. Two of the most important strategies were inceased taxpayer subsidization and decreased safeguards. But as the Romanian negotiations revealed, increased concessions often were insufficient. There were, however, two additional ways to maintain the program: diversification and deception. Both had been used before, but during the post-1976 sales crisis, they assumed a new importance.

144

Product Diversification

AECL's food irradiation technology, for example, received additional pro-motion. AECL argued that exposing food to gamma radiation could stop potatoes from sprouting, inhibit mould growth on fruit, impede the ripening of soft fruit, stimulate plant growth, eliminate parasites, control infestations, and eliminate pathogens such as salmonella.

In Canada, AECL was behind the seemingly unnoticed increase in the use of food irradiation techniques. Legally, any food could be irradiated with one megarad. Potatoes, for example, have been irradiated since 1964. But AECL had some help. Consumer and Corporate Affairs did not require irradiated Canadian food to be identifiable as such to the consumer; this was unique among international food irradiators. Consumer and Corporate Affairs reportedly was waiting for the food industry's advice on the matter. With this support, AECL worked to expand its operations. In 1983, it began irradiating fish and deboned chicken, hoping to commercialize the process.

AECL also was interested in the international market where food irradiation use had undergone a similar increase. It had been used on over forty foodstuffs in over twenty-five countries, due largely to its acceptance by the United Nation's Joint Expert Committee on Food Irradiation which was sponsored by the World Health Organization (WHO) and, not surprisingly, the International Atomic Energy Agency.

Despite the promising market possibilities, questions remained unanswered. For example, what were the long-term effects of eating irradiated foods? Nobody knew for sure. Somewhat easier to determine, however, was AECL's interest. Joan Havemann, in a *Briarpatch* article, "Food Irradiation—Brought to You by Atomic Energy of Canada Limited," states that

> faced with the collapse of the nuclear market....the beleaguered AECL is making another bid for soulful corporation status by claiming that radioactive cobalt 60—a by-product of CANDU reactors—can help solve the problem of world hunger.

But this time, it seemed AECL was in a stronger bargaining position; it controlled 90 percent of the world's cobalt 60 supply. Thus the Crown cor-poration "stipulated in its contract with prospective buyers that all the spent cobalt 60 rods must be returned to Canada for reprocessing." How convenient; fuel repatriation was enforced when it benefited the Canadian nuclear industry. Yet, in 1975, when asked if Canada would repatriate all spent fuel to prevent nuclear weapons proliferation, Allan MacEachen, Secretary of State for External Affairs, stated that it would not be required due to the cost, the environmental implications to Canada, and his belief that such a policy would not be a major impediment to weapons proliferation. With such support, AECl's future seemed secure as an international supplier of irradiating equipment.

But Havemann argues that the Third World did not require another technical fix. Changes that were needed included a more equitable global food distribution system, a return of much of their land to domestic consumption production rather than the cash crop system for export to the First World, and an end to the standard First World tactic of destroying food or paying farmers not to plant their crops rather than allowing the artificially inflated retail price to fall. While AECL officials claimed that gamma reprocessing would help eliminate hunger, its application, in most cases, would be combined with other modern methods of packaging and storage (i.e., electrical refrigeration). Havemann states that for the Third World, food irradiation

> is an inappropriate capital-intensive technology, dependent on Canadian supplies and reprocessing of cobalt 60, and requiring substantial infranstructure requirements (roads, transport vehicles, storage and packaging facilities, etc.). It is another form of technological colonization.

Furthermore, only the transnational corporate food plantations would have the volume and the capital to use gamma radiation. Thus Havemann contends that the industrialized countries would profit the most from gamma processing. The technology could not "do anything to alter the political and economic conditions which are the real causes of world hunger and underdevelopment."

Havemann also notes that this second generation spin-off from military weapon technology, in turn, could be used for military purposes. She cites J.M. Beddoes, Executive Vice-President of AECL Radiochemical Company (Commercial Products), in his "Review of the Present Status of Food Irradiation." Beddoes lists two advantages of radiation processing as "'the modification of the physical properties of food...' and 'sterilization of meals for hospitals, or of foods, to allow long-term storage for military applications.'" This was not surprising. As Havemann points out, the Joint Expert Committee on Food Irradiation, which endorsed gamma food processing, included representatives from AECL and the US military. Havemann concludes that the technology

> is not the panacea to world hunger that AECL would have us believe. Rather the irradiation of food with cobalt 60 provides the AECL with a commercial rationale for recycling the by-products of the CANDU reactor.

Public Deception

Product diversification was not the only way the Canadian nuclear industry attempted to maintain itself. While there were numerous examples available of continued public deception in the post-1976 period, it was most evident in the implementation of the Argentinean Cordoba reactor contract.

In November 1978, the *Washington Post* quoted Rear Admiral Castro Madero, the director of Argentina's Comision Nacional de Energia Atomica (CNEA), as saying that his country was planning to build a reprocessing plant which could separate the plutonium necessary for an atomic bomb. When Tommy

Douglas, former New Democratic Party Leader, asked Donald Jamieson, Canadian Secretary of State for External Affairs, if this was true, he replied that Madero was "related to atomic energy development but may not be necessarily a formal spokesman for the government." And, as far as Jamieson was concerned, there was no need for concern, as Canada "would have a veto, in effect, over the use of Canadian materials for any reprocessing undertaking." A few weeks later, upon further questioning, Jamieson argued that he had been assured that Madero was not a government spokesperson. Thus, on both occasions, Jamieson avoided the implications for non-proliferation of Madero's statements and instead emphasized he was not a formal government spokesperson. The opposition parties, unimpressed with Jamieson's evasion of the issue, continued their questioning. On December 19, 1978, Jamieson tried to calm them by quoting Article V of the nuclear cooperation agreement between Canada and Argentina which stated, in part, that "in the event of non-compliance, Canada may suspend cooperation and may request that Argentina immediately cease to use any Canadian supplies." Jamieson's statements only revealed that the Government would protect the Canadian nuclear export program—even if this meant aiding another country into the nuclear club. But then again, this was done with India to protect the completion of RAPP I and II—until the May 1974 Indian nuclear explosion compelled the Canadian state to react.

In the spring of 1982, the Argentinean invasion of the Malvinas/Falkland Islands further revealed how the Canadian government protected its nuclear export program; witness the contents of the federal Cabinet briefing document leaked to Margaret Munro at *The Ottawa Citizen*. The Trudeau Cabinet recognized that the Cordoba reactor was an exception, as it was not bound to the existing Canadian safeguards policy (Argentina refused to sign the Non-Proliferation Treaty and, therefore, was not required to safeguard all its nuclear facilities). As well, the Cabinet was well aware that

> the President of the CNEA, Rear Admiral Castro Madero, has in recent statements been unequivocal in rejecting the NPT and fullscope safeguards, while reaffirming his country's desire to retain a nuclear explosive option. Argentina is well on the way to developing an indigenous fuel cycle that is completely free of safeguards. Fuel fabrication, heavy water production and reprocessing facilties are all nearing completion. Argentinean officials have recently suggested they intend to close the unsafeguarded cycle by constructing a 40-60 MWt NRX-type research reactor. [India's CIRUS was modelled on the NRX.]

The briefing stated that during the Falkland crisis, the media and public attention would focus on the Cordoba reactor. Should it deteriorate further, Cabinet would be faced with the decision to "continue with business as usual, suspend cooperation, or terminate the relationship."

The business-as-usual option argued that work at the reactor was almost completed. It recognized that

> AECL is counting heavily on completing the reactor by the end date agreed [April 1983] during the last renegotiations of the contract in 1980, both to stay within the book loss of $130 million and to show potential customers (Mexico, Yugoslavia, South Korea) it can do it.

But aside from AECL, the federal Cabinet was also concerned about protecting the $4-million fuel fabrication contract that Combustion Engineering Ltd. had with Argentina's CNEA. The company was manufacturing CANDU fuel bundles from 64 tons of Argentinean uranium brought into Canada for this purpose in October 1981.

The document stated that the business-as-usual option would not result in serious international contractual difficulties or blackmail. The only foreseen risks were domestic and political, as the

> media has already begun to focus on the nuclear dimension to our relationship with Argentina and if the situation drags on, a highly visible anti-CANDU lobby can be expected. Finally, the fact that Combustion Engineering plans to ship fuel bundles to Argentina may become public knowledge.

The contract did become public, and attempts were made to thwart the deal. In a heroic show of solidarity with non-nuclear proponents, the Saint John, New Brunswick, longshore workers announced that they would refuse to load the fuel bundles and were willing to go to jail for their convictions. Their position was supported by the Canadian Labour Congress and thousands of Canadians. The Trudeau Cabinet quickly worked to head off the publicity that was developing. With Cabinet approval, the fuel bundles were secretly transported to Montreal's Mirabel Airport and flown to Argentina.

From the rapid action to protect Combustion Engineering Ltd., it was obvious that of the three options included in the Cabinet briefing document, business as usual was chosen. While it implied a potential domestic problem, the temporary suspension and termination options threatened that "AECL's reputation as a reliable supplier...might be irretrievably damaged." As before, AECL's image, rather than its contribution to nuclear weapons proliferation, was a more important priority to the Canadian government and nuclear industry. [19]

SUMMARY OF THE POST-1976 PERIOD

The Cabinet decision protecting the Cordoba reactor, the Romanian negotiations, the leaked internal review, and AECL's plans for diversification and waste management clearly demonstrated two points. First, the Canadian nuclear establishment was not disappearing. Second, the Canadian taxpayer could not expect the federal government and nuclear industry to resolve the myriad of political, technological, ecological, financial, and military dilemmas besieging the Canadian nuclear export program which, in turn, was intended to perpetuate the domestic nuclear program. If anything, new government policies appeared directed only at increasing the vested interests of, and taxpayer indebtedness to, the nuclear program. And, to top it off, Canada was attempting to export in an increasingly "nuclear armed crowd."[20] In the early 1980s, it seemed that as long as government bureaucrats and private profit-makers remained in control of Canadian energy strategies, nuclear power would continue to receive a disproportionate amount of state and private support, regardless of its international ramifications.

FOOTNOTES

NB: To avoid an unduly large number of footnotes, citations have been consolidated so that usually each note lists sources for the preceding paragraph or section.

Introduction

1. The Canadian decision not to produce nuclear weapons was announced to the House of Commons in June 1946. Fred Knelman, *Nuclear Energy: Unforgiving Technology* (Edmonton: Hurtig Publishers, 1976), p. 148; L.S. Stavrianos, in *Global Rift: The Third World Comes of Age* (New York: William Morrow and Co., Inc., 1981), pp. 31-34, provides an excellent working definition of "Third World." The term "connotes those countries or regions that participated on unequal terms in what eventually became the global market economy." Thus the Third World's relationship to the First World has been defined by economic and political factors, and the term is not meant to imply cultural or social inferiority. The Third World was born in the fifteenth century when Eastern Europe was linked to Western Europe's expanding economy, but on unequal terms. The second area to be dominated by the West was the New World. By the early 1980s, the Third World included "all of Latin America, all of Africa except South Africa, and all of Asia except Japan and Israel," and also excepting socialist countries or the Second World.

CHAPTER I: CANADA AS A NUCLEAR POWER

1. Canada, Parliament, *Debates of the House of Commons* [henceforth, *Debates*], 1st Session, 20th Parliament, 1945, p. 3633; Wilfred Eggleston, *Canada's Nuclear Story* (Toronto: Clarke Irwin & Co., Ltd., 1965), p. 16. For accounts of the early work in Europe, see Margaret Gowing, *Britain and Atomic Energy: 1939-45* (London: Macmillan & Co. Ltd., 1965), pp. 3-30; and Brian Easlea, *Fathering the Unthinkable: Masculinity, Scientists, and the Nuclear Arms Race* (London: Pluto Press Ltd., 1983), pp. 40-80.

2. The Committee for the Scientific Survey of Air Warfare (CSSAW), a British defense group chaired by Sir Henry Tizard. It was originally concerned with radar but, in April 1940, it was decided to establish a sub-committee to examine the possibilities of building an atomic bomb. Thus was born the code name MAUD Committee. In June 1940, the CSSAW ceased to exist and the MAUD Committee achieved independent existence under the Ministry of Aircraft Production. Gowing, *Britain and Atomic Energy*, pp. 44-90; Eggleston, *Canada's Nuclear Story*, pp. 32,37,53; Martin J. Sherwin, *A World Destroyed: The Atomic Bomb and*

the Grand Alliance (New York: Alfred A. Knopf, Inc., 1975; reprint ed., New York Random House, Inc., 1977), pp. 35-36; *Debates*, 1st Session, 20th Parliament, 1945, p. 3633.

3. Canada, Eldorado Nuclear Ltd., *Annual Report: 1970* (Ottawa: Department of Energy, Mines, and Resources, 1971), pp. 19-20; Canada, Parliament *House of Commons 1952-1953 Special Committee on the Operations of the Government in the Field of Atomic Energy*, No. 3, pp. 47-48; Eggleston, *Canada's Nuclear Story*, p. 44; Robert Bothwell, "Radium and Uranium: Evolution of a Company and a Policy," *Canadian Historical Review*, Vol. LXIV, No. 2, June 1983, pp. 127-146.

4. Eggleston, *Canada's Nuclear Story*, pp. 44-45, Dr. James B. Conant to Dr. Mackenzie, 2 January, 1943, quoted in Eggleston, *Canada's Nuclear Story*, p. 65; Gowing, *Britain and Atomic Energy*, p. 156; James Eayrs, *In Defence of Canada: Peacemaking and Deterrence* (Toronto: University of Toronto Press, 1972), pp. 258-266; C.P. Stacy, *Arms, Men and Governments: The War Policies of Canada, 1939-1945* (Ottawa: The Queen's Printer for Canada, 1970), pp. 514-521; Bothwell, "Radium and Uranium", *CHR*, pp. 127- 141. On June 15, 1942, a British delegation that included Malcolm MacDonald, the British High Commissioner, was actually the first to inform Mackenzie King of the importance of uranium and the British requirements. The delegation suggested Canadian nationalization of Eldorado Gold Mines. Despite this and other British requests, the Canadians would only supply the British when it did not threaten American demands.

5. Eggleston, *Canada's Nuclear Story*, pp. 54-83.

6. Sherwin, *A World Destroyed*, p. 72.

7. Eggleston, *Canada's Nuclear Story*, pp. 121-124. Eggleston provides this information but fails to recognize this as a major factor in the American opposition to aiding the work in Canada.

8. Dr. Wallace Akers to Dr. Chalmers Mackenzie, January 30, 1943, quoted in Eggleston, *Canada's Nuclear Story*, p. 74, 81; Bothwell, "Radium and Uranium", *Canadian Historical Review*, p. 81.

9. Eggleston, *Canada's Nuclear Story*, p. 82; Francis L. Lowenheim, Harold D. Langley and Manfred Jonas, eds., *Roosevelt and Churchill: Their Secret Wartime Correspondence*, (New York: E.P. Dutton & Co. Inc., 1975), pp. 32-33; Gowing, *Britain and Atomic Energy*, p. 159; *Debates*, 1st Session, 20th Parliament, 1945, pp. 757- 758. The original members of the Combined Policy Committee were as follows: H.L. Stimson (USA), Vannevar Bush (USA), James B. Conant (USA), Field Marshall John Dill (UK), Colonel J.J. Llewellin (UK), and C.D. Howe (Canada).

10. Ibid.; The Quebec agreement is reproduced in Gowing, *Britain and Atomic Energy*, pp. 439-440, Appendix 4; Fernando Claudin, *The Communist Movement: From Comintern to Cominform* (Harmondworth, England: Penguin Books, Ltd., 1975), p. 408. By August 1943, many people in the British program were already worried that the bomb program would not be finished before the war in Europe. One could assume that such concerns also existed in the United States. The Americans, however, also were anxious to complete the project before the war ended. It would facilitate explaining to Congress the vast sums of money already spent. Gowing, *Britain and Atomic Energy*, p. 167; Sherwin, *The World Destroyed*, p. 88.

11. Stacy, *Arms, Men and Governments*, p. 521; Eggleston, *Canada's Nuclear Story*, pp. 84-102. Eggleston discusses the American opposition to the multinational composition of the Montreal group and the resultant concern about maintaining secrecy.

12. Ibid., pp. 90-102. Eggleston offers little rationale for the shift in American policy other than pressure by British and Canadian officials. Obviously, C.D. Howe,

as a member of the CPC, could have exerted a degree of influence. But this fails to explain why he did not succeed considerably earlier; Canada, *1952-1953 Special Committee on Atomic Energy*, No. 3, pp. 54, 58.

13. Eggleston, *Canada's Nuclear Story*, p. 131.

14. The Americans were increasingly concerned about the Western control of nuclear technology. Two months after the CPC decision, Roosevelt and Churchill signed an "Agreement and Declaration of Trust." The agreement specified US and UK control of available uranium and thorium ore supplies during and after the war. See Sherwin, *A World Destroyed*, p. 104. Claudin, *The Communist Movement*, p. 412.

15. Eggleston, *Canada's Nuclear Story*, p. 117.

16. The difficulty in obtaining the heavy water and uranium metal from the United States was indicative of some of the problems of a continentalist defence and economic strategy. The heavy water was produced in British Columbia, and the original uranium used in the uranium metal was mined in Canada. Eggleston, *Canada's Nuclear Story*, pp. 124-133. The site specifications included isolation for safety and security reasons, a large water supply to cool the reactor and dilute the radioactive effluent, enough space to allow for plant and housing expansion, accessiblity by rail and road, and a twelve-hour travelling proximity to Montreal, Toronto, and Ottawa. Canada, Parliament, *House of Commons 1949 Special Committee on the Operations of the Atomic Energy Control Board*, No. 5, p. 88.

17. *Debates*, 1st Session, 21st Parliament, 1949; *CANDU?: A Review of Performance, Costs and Safety*, Glendon Energy Series, No. 1 (Streetsville, Ontario: Glendon Publications, 1981), p. 1; Eggleston, *Canada's Nuclear Story*, p. 150.

18. Stephen Hilgartner, Richard C. Bell, Rory O'Connor, *Nukespeak: The Selling of Nuclear Technology in America* (New York: Penguin Books, Ltd., 1983), p. XIV.

19. The Baruch Plan was a modified version of the Ackeson-Lilienthal Report submitted to President Truman on March 21, 1945. The Acheson-Lilienthal Report "recommended establishment under the United Nations an international 'Atomic Development Authority' which would, after the worldwide survey of raw materials, assume control of all highly concentrated uranium and thorium deposits. The authority would make its resources available for peaceful purposes only. Under the plan, the United States reserved for itself the decision as to when or whether to stop manufacturing atomic bombs of its own." President Truman and Secretary of State Byrnes requested financier Bernard M. Baruch to present the American proposal to the United Nations. Baruch would accept on the condition that he should be allowed to make changes to the Acheson-Lilienthal Report. Baruch's addition stipulated that, once accepted, "veto should be prohibited when the Security Council was considering atomic energy matters." On December 30, 1946, the United Nations Atomic Energy Commission adopted the Baruch Plan by a vote of 10-0, with the Soviet Union and Poland abstaining. After this, the dispute was transferred to the Security Council where the Soviet Union vetoed the American proposal. John Lewis Gaddis, *The United States and the Origins of the Cold War: 1941-1947* (New York: Columbia University Press, 1972), pp. 332-334.

In reserving for the Americans an opportunity to continue producing nuclear weapons, the Baruch Plan was not an effective attempt to controlling atomic technology. It did play a crucial role, however, in legitimizing American bomb production. By projecting a sincere desire to control atomic weaponry, it served to reinforce the ossification of a popular conception of a bi-polar world, with the Americans aiming for peace and the USSR as the only impediment. It was indicative of American intentions that while the Baruch Plan for International Control was being discussed, the "Baker" atomic bomb test at the Bikini Atoll on July 25, 1946, inaugerated "Operation Crossroads," one of a series of testing programs. Crossroads was finally terminated in 1958 after 23 nuclear bombs were exploded in the mid-Pacific Ocean. But considerable damage had already occurred. The Bikini Atoll was a prime example. It was "a ring of 26 small islands around a central lagoon, part of the Marshall Islands, a U.S. Trust Territory 2500 miles southwest of Hawaii. (The islands were taken from Japan in 1944.) Several of the islands were blasted away. Th lagoon is now filled with the largest single source of plutonium pollution in the world." In 1968 the U.S. government decided to authorize rehabitation of the island. Some of the original inhabitants returned in 1972 to replant coconut palms and rebuild the island. These people left the island in August 1978 after a series of investigations revealed that the island was still unsafe for human occupation. It was the excessively high radiation levels that caused the newly planted palms to bear orange coconuts in 1975. Anna Gyorgy and Friends, *No Nukes: Everyone's Guide to Nuclear Power* (Montreal: Black Rose Books, 1979), p. 6.

Clifford Elliot has reflected on the importance of the Bikini tests. He refers to Robert Scheer's interview with Thomas K. Jones, one of President Reagan's top advisors. In Sheer's *With Enough Shovels: Reagan, Bush and Nuclear War*, (New York: Bantam Books, Ltd., 1983), "Jones is quoted as saying that the United States could recover from allout nuclear war in just two to four years. He advocates everyone digging a hole in the ground and covering it with two doors and three feet of earth. 'If there are enough shovels to go 'round, everybody's going to make it' (Jones) says." Elliot cites the Bikini tests as proof of the ridiculous underestimation of the effects of atomic blasts. Clifford Elliot, "Threats to Peace, Survival", *The Observer*, Vol. 46, No. 8, February 1983, p. 28.

20. *Debates*, 2nd Session, 20th Parliament, 1946, pp. 1620, 2370, 2106, 2122, 2402-3, 2482-3, 2105.
21. Gordon Sims, "The Evolution of AECL" (M.A. Thesis, Carleton University, 1979), p. 38; *Debates*, 1st Session, 21st Parliament, 1949, p. 1273.
22. Sims, "The Evolution of AECL", p. 38.
23. Margaret Gowing, *Independence and Deterrence: Britain and Atomic Energy 1945-1952*, Vol. I: *Policy Making* (London: The Macmillan Press, Ltd., 1974), pp. 324-327. For more information on the British nuclear weapon and power program see, for example, Margaret Gowing, *Britain and Atomic Energy, 1939-45* (London: Macmillan, 1964); Margaret Gowing, *Independence and Deterrence, Vol. 1 Policy Making* (London: Macmillan, 1974); Margaret Gowing, *Independence and Deterrence, Vol. 2 Policy Execution* (London: Macmillan, 1974); and Sheila Durie and Rob Edwards, *Fuelling the Nuclear Arms Race: The Links between Nuclear Power and Nuclear Weapons* (London: Pluto Press, 1982).
24. Sims, "The Evolution of AECL", p. 39; *Debates*, 1st Session, 26th Parliament, 1963, p. 2198. In 1963, the remaining debt of $25,239,005 was "written off as a charge against general revenue." The NRU reactor was built "by the government of Canada under atomic energy commission to produce plutonium to be sold to the United States under a long-term contract. The price under the contract was to be renegotiated as of June 30, 1962. [Funds were to pay off the reactor over time but with the decreased price in June 1962,] the commission was left in a position where it had this reactor in its books at some $25 million and there was no possibility of writing it off."
25. *Debates*, 1st Session, 20th Parliament, 1949, pp. 346, 1271-1286; Canada, Parliament, *House of Commons 1949 Special Committee on the Operations of the Atomic Energy Control Board*, No. 4, p. 73; No. 5, p. 100; and *Debates*, 6th Session, 21st Parliament, 1952,

p. 960. Howe's concern over the increasing cost of the project probably encouraged his motion of October 31, 1949. This allowed for the creation of the Special Committee on the Operations of the AECB. Not surprisingly, Howe's motion was late in the session and this left only six weeks for the committee to study the issues. Also, the committee was not offered many witnesses. For example, Dr. C.J. Mackenzie, President of the AECB, appeared for the first five brief meetings; while Mr. J.L. Gray, Chief of Administration at Chalk River, and T.W. Morison, General Superintendent of Administration Services at Chalk River, appeared for the last three brief meetings. The objectivity of this committee was further curtailed by its inability to call freely for persons or papers and its own awe for the Chalk River Project. For example, Mr. Green, a committee member, asked, "Dr. Mckenzie, is there anything that you can suggest whereby we could help the project at Chalk River?"

In his reply, Dr. Mackenzie stated, "I think it is a question that you should, perhaps, discuss in your closed sessions." The new reactor must have been a point of discussion in the closed sessions, for the committee's final report recommended "that the government undertake the expansion of the present facilities by the construction of an additional reactor and such research equipment as may be required."

Howe later tried to make the committee responsible for the decision to build the reactor. "Honourable members will recall that following the report of the special parliamentary committee on atomic energy which was tabled on December 8, 1949, the government gave serious study to the recommendation that a second pile, or reactor, be added to the Chalk River establishment. The 1951-52 estimates made provisions enabling the national research council to proceed with the necessary plans and construction of the new pile."

26. Fred Knelman, *Nuclear Energy: The Unforgiving Technology* (Edmonton: Hurtig Publishers, 1976), pp. 68-69; *Debates*, 6th Session, 21st Parliament, 1952, p. 966; and *Debates*, 23rd Parliament, 1957-58, p. 1216. Knelman, expanding upon comments by Amory Lovins, in the latter's "World Energy Strategies" (Cambridge, Mass.: Friends of the Earth, Inc., Ballinger Publishing Co., 1975), p. 63, states: "There exists a global nuclear establishment, as well as national nuclear establishments. These establishments include individuals and institutions—private and public, national and international, regulatory and productive—that have a uniform perception of nuclear technology, or a global nuclear world view. This world view consists of a common belief in technological omnipotence. It accounts for the intimate relationship between utility bodies and nuclear bodies. It is guilty of tunnel vision, in that technological faith rests on fission technology and its perfectibility. The ideology is complex, technicist, elitist, manipulative, fearful of exposure and therefore sensitive, protective, and defensive in posture and policy. It rests on a well-structured set of myths translated into highly homogeneous arguments, postures and beliefs. This homogeneity is global, so that within the relatively closed networks of communication among members of the establishment there are highly predictable behavioral modes, value judgements, and polemical postures." One fundamental component of the nuclear establishment which requires additional emphasis and investigation is the profit motive. One small, but important, example was the C.D. Howe Co., Ltd. It was sub-contracted to provide engineering services for the design and supervision of construction of the NRU reactor. Of the $6,919,688 AECL paid to 34 companies providing engineering services during the fiscal years 1955-1956 and 1956-1957, $2,292,504, or 33.13%, was paid to

the C.D. Howe Co., Ltd. For a corporate breakdown of the establishment, see Appendix VI.

27. James A. Casterton, "The International Dimensions of the Nuclear Industry" (M.A. Thesis: Carleton University, 1980), p. 3.

28. *Debates*, 6th Session, 21st Parliament, 1952, pp. 966-968, 972, 3635.

29. Knelman, *Nuclear Energy*, p. 53. While Knelman was referring to a different specific example, the term is still applicable.

30. Ibid., pp. 40-67; J.L. Gray, "CANDU Milestones," Canadian Nuclear Association, *Proceedings of the 15th Annual Conference: Vol. 2, Development in Canada and Abroad*

(Toronto: June 15-18, 1975), p. 94.; *Debates* 7th Session, 21st Parliament, 1953, pp. 743, 2010-11. Knelman offers the most explicit account of the Chalk River accident. On December 12, 1952, at approximately 3:15 p.m. an assistant operator mistakenly opened four valves that could impair the moving of the reactor's control rods. If the rods were exposed without coolant, the end result could be a core melt down. Thus the first stage of the accident was caused by human error but this was soon compounded by a series of mechanical errors. This combination of human and mechanical error "is a classic example of the common hazards of nuclear energy...Four minutes after button number one had been accidentally pushed, a dull explosion was heard and the four-ton lid of the reactor vessel rose in the air. Water gushed out of the top reactor, spilling over the building floor. Radiation alarms went off and at certain points lethal doses of radiation were sensed. Messages indicated that radiation readings in the surrounding atmosphere were far above normal. An emergency procedures was instituted, sealing the reactor building. But this did not confine the contamination; the radiation-hazards director ordered an evacuation of the entire installation buildings, and grounds, for everyone but essential emergency crew." Knelman argues that "if one more control rod had jammed, we might well have lost Deep River," the village near Chalk River where the nuclear establishment lived. The explosion, though the worst accident at Chalk River, was not the first. Howe admitted, in 1953, when authorizing a committee to examine the operations of the AECB, that the Chalk River "operation has been interrupted eight times by minor explosions." The eighth "minor" explosion occurred on December 12, 1952, and necessitated re-building the reactor.

31. *Debates*, 7th Session, 21st Parliament, *1952-53, p. 2010; 1952-1953 Special Committee*, No. 2, p. 25. One lengthy comment made before committee by Dr. Mackenzie, President of AECB and AECL, deserves quotation, as it clearly reflects the degree to which individuals attempted to convince the public of the wonders of atomic energy when they did not know what would be the end result. "My own feeling is—and it is purely a personal matter—that atomic energy will develop something in a way that internal combustion power developed and that it will open up new areas. The internal combustion engine in its infancy was thought of as a substitute for coal, but it never was. It opened up the whole field of automobiles, and aircraft, and changed the whole complexion of the world. I cannot document this opinion, but I think there is a general feeling that when we get into a new form of energy, it is likely to be used in areas where there are special requirements or special advantages. It is the sort of thing I feel that we must just take on faith. I think that is a sounder way to take it than to try to document it when you do not know the actual answer."

Considering that Canadian taxpayers were paying well over $6 million annually between 1942 and March 1951, Dr. Mackenzie was advocating a rather expensive "faith."

32. See W.B. Lewis, "An Atomic Power Proposal," AECL:186, August 27, 1951.

33. J. Luntz, editor of *Nucleonics*, stated, "Ostensibly, one of the purposes of the program is for the United States to establish itself in the minds of the people of the world as the leader in the development of the peaceful atom." Quoted in Gyorgy, *No Nukes*, p. 9; The preponderance of influence exercised by the Western industrial countries is revealed in the following example. "Of 50,000 kilograms of uranium-235 earmarked for sale in 1956, only 5,000 kilos were pledged to underdeveloped nations; most went to developed Western powers (UK and Western Europe) and Japan." Robert and Leona Train Rienow, *Our New Life with the Atom* (New York: Thomas Y. Crowell Co., 1959), p. 135. Quoted in Gyorgy, *No Nukes*, p. 27; *The New York Times*, October 7, 1955, p. 4.

34. *Debates*, 2nd Session, 22nd Parliament, 1955, p. 2329; *Debates*, 7th Session, 21st Parliament, 1952-53, p. 4884.

35. *Debates*, 1st Session, 22nd Parliament, 1953-54, p. 5397; Gordon Sims, "The Evolution of AECL," p. 48; Debates, 1st Session, 22nd Parliament, 1953-54, pp. 5400-5401, 5404, 5414.

36. *Debates*, 2nd Session, 22nd Parliament, 1955, pp. 2329- 2330. While Howe offered a number of reasons for selecting Ontario Hydro, the third seems the most important. Howe stated that the "decision to accept the proposal of Ontario Hydro is based on several factors. First, as the reactor is to be used for demonstration purposes it is essential that it be operated in a power system which is sufficiently large to cope with interrupted operation or operation at a low load factor. Second, it is considered desirable that the first power reactor should be located within easy access of Chalk River, since Chalk River will be responsible for nuclear performance. Third, the financial arrangements provide that both parties will accept full responsibility for the cost of their respective portions of the project, together with any loss that may be incurred as the result of failure in operation or interrupted operation."

37. Ibid.; *Debates*, 4th Session, 24th Parliament, 1960-61, p. 2113; Casterton, "International Dimensions of the Nuclear Industry," p. 45. When discussing utility involvement, Howe mentioned two companies that had "indicated some interest." Yet, when discussing industry involvement, he stated, "...after a careful assessment of these two factors—design, engineering and manufacturing resources, and the amount of the financial contribution—Atomic Energy of Canada Limited has recommended that the contract be awarded to the Canadian General Electric Company Limited."

(Indicative of CGE's corporate strength, it contributed some $2 million toward NPD's construction.) Howe did not name any other companies. Also, James Casterton, without citing a reference, states that "Canadian General Electric was chosen after competitive bids had been called for. Seven manufacturing firms bid on the project." While it may be a case of hiding corporate involvement, it appears more likely that there were not alternative companies capable of undertaking the design and construction of nuclear reactors. Furthermore, the fact remains that no other company has ever undertaken the design and construction of a reactor in Canada, as is evident in 1958, when the Canadian state undertook the design and construction of reactors to comply with Ontario Hydro's demand that CGE not be left in a monopoly supply position; the paucity of adequate industrial capability is the only probable reason for this move.

Furthermore, in the nuclear industry, bidding on a contract is not proof of the capability of providing the necessary services; witness Jerome Spevack and Deuterium of Canada Limited.

38. For a clear and concise review of the various types of reactors, see Knelman, *Nuclear Power*, pp. 42-86. The NPD was originally designed with a large pressure vessel containing the fuel and the moderator. In April 1957, however, construction on NPD was suspended for the changeover to a new design. In the new design, the reactor core "would consist of a horizontally-oriented cylindrical tank (calandria) which contains the heavy water moderator. This tank is penetrated by a number of horizontal tubes containing the natural uranium fuel and pressurized high temperature heavy water coolant. The coolant is pumped through the tubes, removing the heat produced by fissioning of the uranium fuel, and then through the boilers where the heat is given up to produce steam which, in turn, is fed to the turbine. The pressure tube concept was adopted and is now one of the major distinguishing characteristics of the CANDU" reactor. (Casterton, "The International Dimensions of the Nuclear Industry," pp. 5-6). This change facilitated on-line refueling and thus made the CANDU an extremely proliferation-prone reactor.

The design independence has facilitated CANDU-nationalism but the Canadian nuclear industry has not even succeeded in creating a completely Canadian reactor. As Knelman states, "Canadian content in our reactor program is still less than 80 percent, about the same as India's indigenous content. Many critical components, including the large turbines, must be imported. Even when components are supplied by Canadian firms, design and engineering of this equipment is foreign. The optimism of the parents of CANDU has never diminished, but is made up of more of fantasy than reality."

39. *Debates*, 3rd Session, 22nd Parliament, 1956, p. 2841; Peyton Lyon, Tareg Y. Ismael, eds., *Canada and the Third World* (Toronto: Macmillan Co. of Canada, Ltd., 1976), p. 17. Cited in Robert Carty, Virginia Smith, *Perpetuating Poverty: The Political Economy of Canadian Foreign Aid* (Toronto: Between the Lines, Pub., 1982), p. 182; and Carty and Smith, *Perpetuating Poverty*, p. 45.

40. *Debates*, 3rd Session, 22nd Parliament, 1956, pp. 1697, 1699, 1700, 1702, 1710. For a further discussion on Canadian involvement in nuclear and non-nuclear weapons tests for the Americans see, among others, Stephen Salaff, "A Fire to Suffocate," *Canadian Forum*, Vol. 60. September 1980, pp. 14-16, and Peter von Stackelberg, "Weapons of War," *Goodwin's*, premier issue, Spring 1983, pp. 15-20.

41. *Debates*, 1st Session, 24th Parliament, 1958, p. 4524 (It was the April 1957 study which also recommended the use of horizontal pressure tubes and thus resulted in the redesigning of the NPD); J.L. Gray, "A Statement of the Nuclear Power Development Program," AECL:561 (Ottawa: February 1958), pp. 1-2, quoted in Casterton, "International Dimensions of the Nuclear Industry," pp. 6-7, 19. The February 1958 statement surrounded the announcement of the NPPD with a degree of obfuscatory rhetoric. It announced AECL's five new objectives: "1. to reduce the future dependence on a foreign source of energy; 2. to reduce the adverse effect of such imports on the balance of trade; 3. to minimize the increased load on Canada's transportation systems; 4. to reduce Canada's energy costs through the utilization of Canadian uranium; and 5. to stimulate the Canadian manufacturing sector by creating domestic and foreign markets for plant components and fabricated fuel." Years later, Gray would explain the massive change in AECL as follows: "The monopoly position of a designer-supplier of large power

stations was not acceptable to the customer [Ontario Hydro] from a competitive price point of view."

42. *Debates*, 2nd Session, 24th Parliament, 1959, pp. 4861-62, (The plant was not started up until November 15, 1966; two years behind schedule); Knelman, *Nuclear Energy*, p. 56. Ontario Hydro's option, however, was never exercised. As Knelman states, "Although Douglas Point went into the Ontario power grid in 1967, it is still owned by AECL, having never operated efficiently to date. Its cumulative availability—the percentage of total time it has operated since 1967—is only 45 percent compared with 60 percent for NPD. Part of this low availability had to do with heavy water supply, but since this is an integral part of the CANDU package, it does not qualify as an excuse for low performance." But heavy water shortages were was not the only problem. Technical problems also existed. For this reason, in April 1984 Atomic Energy of Canada announced that Douglas Point would be closed down. Donald Lawson, President of reactor operations for AECL, stated that $100 million would be required to repair the money-losing station. While dismantling the 17-year-old plant was estimated to also cost $100 million, this was what AECL had decided to do. With four new reactors planned in the 1980s, the plant was no longer needed. One should note, however, that dismantling the reactor will enable AECL to find out what is involved in the process. A reactor has never been dismantled before in Canada. This information will become valuable, as other CANDUs will grow old and burn out. "Nuclear Plant to Be Shut Down," *Winnipeg Free Press*, April 27, 1984, p. 5.

43. *Debates*, *2nd Session, 22nd Parliament, 1955, p. 2329; Debates*, 2nd Session, 24th Parliament, 1959, pp. 6110, 6105-6; and *Debates*, 3rd Session, 24th Parliament, 1960, p. 3918. In August 1959, the Americans sent a letter to Ottawa saying that the contracts would not be renewed. This was not disclosed in the House of Commons until November 6, 1959. At that time, members were informed of Eldorado's arrangements with the USAEC and the UKAEA to allow a stretch-out of deliveries to December 31, 1966.

44. *Debates*, 23rd Parliament, 1957-58, pp. 1415-16; *Debates*, 2nd Session, 24th Parliament, 1959, p. 6117. "I [Pearson speaking in the House] know of course..that the great bulk of this product [Canadian uranium] is now going into military use, and perhaps I was in a somewhat congruous positon when I was Secretary of State for External Affairs [September 10, 1948-November 15, 1948 under King and November 15, 1948-June 21, 1957 under St. Laurent] inasmuch as in that capacity it was my duty and desire, as the representative of the government at international meetings, to do everything I could... to make the use of uranium for destructive purposes unnecessary and impossible, but that at the same time, as the honourable member for Algoma East [the riding that includes Elliot Lake, the site of Ontario's largest uranium mine and Eldorado's refinery], I was doing everything I could to encourage and develop the use of that product."

45. *Debates*, 3rd Session, 24th Parliament, 1960, pp. 1495, 1426. It was not until January 19, 1960, that AECL announced that the second nuclear research centre would be located at the Whiteshell, 60 miles northeast of Winnipeg on the Winnipeg River near Lac du Bonnett. Incidentally, choosing Pinawa for its firm bedrock qualities, in the long-term, was rather fortuitous from the industry's perspective. The pre-Cambrian rock formations have facilitated the establishment of an experimental "waste disposal site" at Pinawa. Thus Pinawa could be turned into a radioactive garbage dump.

46. *Debates*, 1st Session, 26th Parliament, 1963, pp. 1228, 5588-89, 5314, 5588-89, 5315, 5376; for a more detailed account of the economic and technological disaster at the Glace Bay heavy water plant, see Philip Mathais, "A Foot in the Door of the Future: Nova Scotia's Heavy Water Plant," *Forced Growth* (Toronto: James Lorimer & Co., Pub., 1971), pp. 103-123. While four companies placed bids for the contract, not all fulfilled the Government's conditions.

The $41.5 million is broken down as follows: 200 tons of heavy water at $20.50 per pound for five years equal $41 million; and the coal subsidization equals $482,300 (106,000 tons per annum at $0.91 per ton for five years).

47. *Debates*, 1st Session, 26th Parliament, 1963, p. 5917; Canada, Treaty Series, 1963, No. 10, Atomic Energy, *Rajathan Atomic Power Station: Agreement between Canada and India*, December 16, 1963, pp. 4, 2; *Debates*, 2nd Session, 26th Parliament, p. 705, 7051-53; Casterton, "International Dimensions of the Nuclear Industry," pp. 8-9, 45. The Douglas Point reactor, which was to serve as the operating model of the next stage of reactors, was not started up until November 15, 1966, and did not provide electricity until January 7, 1967. Pickering was announced on August 20, 1964. Pickering I and II were rated at 515 MWe each. Federal equity (excluding capitalized costs) contributed equaled $116.5 million, or 35.7% of the total capital costs. (*Background Papers*, p. 309). Federal financing for RAPP I and II totalled at least $140 million. This was payable over fifteen years with about six years' grace at 6%. Robert Morrison, Edward Wonder, *Canada's Nuclear Export Policy* (Ottawa: Carleton University Press, October 1978), p. 17-18.

48. Morrison and Wonder, *Canada's Nuclear Export Policy*, p. 17. Morrison and Wonder state that of "the $63 million cost of the Pakistan Plant, $51 million was financed by Canada, half as external aid at 3/4% interest over 40 years, with 10 years' grace, the other half at 6% over 15 years with 5 years' grace."

49. Canada, AECL, *Annual Report: 1963-64*, p. 23; *Debates*, 2nd Session 26th Parliament, 1964-65, pp. 9762-3. The 1,335 tons of heavy water were broken down as follows: 1,150 tons for Douglas Point (to replace that borrowed from the USA) and the proposed Pickering stations; 35 tons for the Chalk River and Whiteshell Research Reactors; and 150 tons for the proposed Pakistan reactor. Furthermore, a surplus was demanded, as there were "several other potential requirements that could total some hundreds of tons in the same period."

50. Ibid., p. 11620; *Debates*, 1st Session, 27th Parliament, 1966-67, pp. 2145, 7079, 314, 3023.

51. *Debates*, 2nd Session, 26th Parliament, 1964-65, pp. 9763, 9765, 3919; *Debates*, 3rd Session, 26th Parliament, 1965, pp. 1173; *Debates*, 1st Session, 27th Parliament, 1966-67, p. 1148; *The Globe and Mail*, July 11, 1979, p. 9, and Casterton, "International Dimensions of the Nuclear Industry," p. 10.

52. Canada, Treaty Series: 1966, No. 27, *Atomic Energy Rajasthan Atomic Power Station: Agreement between Canada and India*, December 16, 1966, p. 2; Treaty Series: 1963, No. 10, p. 2; and *Debates*, 2nd Session 26th Parliament, 1964-65, p. 9655.

53. *Debates*, 1st Session, 27th Parliament, 1966-67, p. 14918; Jorge Sabato, "Atomic Energy in Argentina: A Case History," *World Development*, Vol. 8, August, 1973, p. 2, cited in Sims, "The Evolution of AECL," p. 125; Sims, "The Evolution of

AECL," p. 126; and *Debates*, 2nd Session, 27th Parliament, 1967-68, pp. 7940, 1141.

CHAPTER II: EXPORTING CANADIAN NUCLEAR REACTORS TO THE THIRD WORLD

1. An examination of the class dynamics is obviously a deviation from the analytical tools used by the members of the Canadian nuclear establishment. In R.W. Morrison and G. Sims, "Nuclear Power in Developing Countries: A Search for Indicators" (Ottawa: Department of Energy, Mines, and Resources, August 1980), standard analytical tools are used, "mainly aggregated statistical measurements of different aspects of the country's economic or energy situation" (p. 1). The authors conclude that "the most useful indicators seem to be the size and growth rate of electrical demand, and the scale and intensity of energy use in the economy as a whole" (p. 55). However, one cannot understand completely the reasons for an increased rate of electrical demand, for example, without a prior awareness of the international class relations. Without a class analysis, the reasons for changes in the various indicators are often undiscernible or ignored. Yet Morrison and Sims admit that their "paper ignores many obviously crucial factors, such as domestic and international politics, security or prestige considerations, and the role of individuals and institutions. It avoids the broad economic and financial situations of the countries as well as the details of cost competition between nuclear power projects and their alternatives. The terms and conditions of actual reactor contracts, which may involve considerations well beyond the purchaser's nuclear power program, are also left out of the analysis.... And it does not discuss the competition between centrally generated and locally generated electricity for the countryside' nor that between electricity and other sources of energy for the rural areas" (pp. 1-2). In short, they abstract from totality selected econometric indices in order to reveal a difficult, but promising, future for the nuclear establishment.

2. F.W. Orlando, "The Taiwan Research Reactor Project," a paper presented at the 10th Annual International Conference of the Canadian Nuclear Association (Toronto: CNA, paper no. 70-CNA-662, May 24-27, 1970), pp. 1,2; *The New York Times*, October 18, 1970, p.8; *Canadian Business*, February, 1978, p. 20; Canada, House of Parliament, House of Commons, *Debates*, 3rd Session, 28th Parliament, 1970-1972, p. 4179.

3. Donald C. Hodges, *Argentina, 1943-1976: The National Revolution and Resistance* (Albuquerque: University of New Mexico Press, 1976) offers an excellent analysis of the Peronist periods. Hodges recognizes correctly the functionalism of Peron's integration of fascist and socialist strategies; *The New York Times*, June 2, 1950, p. 7; *Atomic Scientist's Journal*, March 1956, Vol. 5, No. 4, p. 222; *The New York Times*, December 5, 1952, p. 1; Ernesto Laclau, "Argentina: Imperialist Strategy and the May Crisis." *New Left Review*, July-August 1970, No. 62, p. 6.

4. *Canada Commerce*, May 1972, pp. 20-21; *The New York Times*, June 2, 1962, p. 3; *New Scientist*, April 11, 1968, Vol. 38, No. 592, p. 65; *The New York Times*, February 23, 1968, p. 49; *New Scientist*, July 30, 1970, Vol. 47, No. 712, p. 239; Ibid., March 29, 1973, Vol. 57, No. 839, p. 726.

5. As stated in *The Financial Post*, March 24, 1973, p. 4: "Earlier sales to India and Pakistan are not considered commercial sales successes because they were part

of Ottawa's overseas-bid program. A $35-million reactor sold to Taiwan ... was for experimental rather than power generation purposes."

6. Canada, Department of Energy, Mines, and Resources, *Nuclear Industry Review: Problems and Prospects 1981 - 2000* (Ottawa: EMR, 1982) p. 266; Canada, AECL, Annual Report: 1973-74, p. 9; The Financial Post, March 10, 1973, p. 19.

7. Joe Hanlon "Repression Hits Physicists in the Argentine," *New Scientist*, July 7, 1977, Vol. 75, No. 1059, p. 5. For more information on the second Peronist period, see Hodges, *Argentina 1943-1976*; and James Petras, *Critical Perspectives on Imperialism and Social Class in the Third World* (New York: Monthly Review Press, 1978).

8. AECL, *Annual Report: 1973-74*, p. 9; James A. Casterton, "The International Dimensions of the Canadian Nuclear Industry" (M.A. Thesis: Carleton University, 1980), pp. 63-64. AECL and Casterton do not stipulate the amount of subsidization which would allow one to calculate the total cost of the reactor. AECL and the CNEA also signed a technology transfer in January 1974, EMR, *Nuclear Policy Review Background Papers* (Ottawa EMR No. ER81-ZE, 1980) p. 341.

9. Casterton, "International Dimensions," p. 82; Robert Morrison, Edward Wonder, "Canada's Nuclear Export Policy" (Ottawa: Carleton University, October, 1978), p. 69. An additional $25-million EDC loan was issued in 1978. Repayment was to begin when the reactor began service, therefore, May 1983. *Background Papers*, p. 313.

10. Canada, House of Commons, *Minutes of Proceeding and Evidence of the Standing Committee on Public Accounts*, Respecting: The Report of the Auditor General to the House of Commons for the fiscal year ending March 31, 1976, 2nd Session, 30th Parliament, 1976-77, Issue No. 9, January 25, 1977, p. 9:19; *Debates*, 2nd Session, 30th Parliament. 1976-77, p. 7705: Alastair Gillespie, Minister of Energy, Mines, and Resources, was quite specific in his explanation of AECL's marketing strategy: "The objective has been to seek the broadest possible markets, thereby staking out a preferred position for future sales to maintain a continuing workload for large, highly technical design and engineering staffs." *Debates*, 2nd Session, 30th Parliament, 1976-77, p. 7417.

11. Casterton, "International Dimensions," p. 82; *Debates*, 2nd Session, 30th Parliament, 1976-77, p. 3283; *Debates*, 1st Session, 30th Parliament, 1974-76, p. 12134; Joe Hanlon, "Repression Hits Physicists in the Argentine," *New Scientist*, July 7, 1977, Vol. 75, No. 1059, p. 5; AECL, *Annual Report*: 1972-73, p. F12. On March 31, 1973, the loss stood at $130 million. The eventual total is not public knowledge but AECL officials soon will be able to calculate the total cost, since the reactor was completed in May 1983. *The Financial Post*, September 13, 1980, p. 14. It would be interesting to know Italimpianti's profit/loss on the Argentine contract; however, such information is not public.

12. *Debates*, 2nd Session, 30th Parliament, pp. 3287, 1828, 1856, 6249. It was possible that naming Ber Gelband and Savino was part of the military's attempts to discredit the Peronist government. The Canadian Broadcasting Corporation's "The Fifth Estate" speculated that the $2.5 million was used to bribe high-ranking Argentinean military officials who were favouring light-water reactors. CBC, "The Fifth Estate," a two-part program entitled "The CANDU Affair," originally broadcast on November 8 and 15, 1977. Cited in Casterton, "International Dimensions," p. 138.

13. *Debates*, 2nd Session, 30th Parliament, 1976-77, pp. 1329, 1363, 2247, 5789.

14. The same type and make of boilers were installed at Point Lepreau, Gentilly, Bruce B. and Pickering B. It was at the latter plant where it was discovered that once the boilers were installed, hundreds of cracks developed. This alerted officials

to the problem. In 1979, the cost of replacement for Cordoba was estimated at $15 million. AECL was hoping that it could negotiate a deal similar to the Ontario Hydro-Babcox and Wilson settlement whereby the latter paid approximately 75% of the costs. Thus, in 1979, AECL's estimated cost of repair would be approximately $3.75 million plus the additional cost of delaying the project by more than a year. *The Globe and Mail*, May 25, 1979, p. 5; *The Financial Post*, September 22, 1979, p. 5; The *Financial Post*, October 6, 1979, p. 13.

15. *Debates*, 2nd Session, 30th Parliament, p. 4589; The AECL *Annual Report*: 1976-77, p. F12 reveals how entrenched was the use of sales agents. The report lists 43 agents and representatives. In the one-year period, AECL paid a total of $17,353,732 for remuneration and expenses. However, the report fails to list South Korea, Shaul Eisenberg, or the $18.5 million paid to Eisenberg. The United Development Company is listed as the Israeli agent. The list of AECL agents in 1976-77 is as follows: "C.G.R. do Brasil, Brazil; General Electric Co., U.S.A.; C.G.R. MeV, France; C.G.R. Generay, Italy; Marubeni Corporation, Japan; Equipo Para Hospitales S.A., Mexico; G.E.C. Electrical Products (Pty) Limited, South Africa; General Electric Espanola, Spain; G.E.C. Medical Equipment Limited, England; Kamol Sukosol Company Limited, Thailand; C.G.R. Benelux, Belgium; International General Electric Company (India) Private Limited, India; Equipamentos Cientificos do Brasil Limited, Brazil; Labkar Company Limited, Iran; General Electric de Colombia S.A., Colombia; Spring Port Taiwan Limited, Taiwan; A.B. Atomenergi, Sweden; E. Comm Australia Pty. Limited, Australia; Geveke Electronica, Germany; Gammaster, Netherlands; Hamco Commercial S.C.R.L., Peru; Tamathe S.R.L., Argentina; Koch & Sterzel C.G.R., Germany; The China Engineers Limited, Hong Kong; C.H.F. Mueller A.G., Germany; Dr. Serafettin Ve Ortaklari Ticaret Limited, Turkey; High Energy and Nuclear Equipment S.A., Switzerland; Societa Lombarda di Televisione S.P.A., Italy; China National Chemicals Import & Export Corporation, People's Republic of China; Roberto L. Lannes, Uruguay; Kostas Karayannis, Greece; General Machinery Company Ltd., Chile; Amtraco Corporation, Indonesia; The General Electric Company of Singapore Private Limited, Singapore; Arab Trading and Engineering Office, Syria; Costa Rica Dental and Medical Supply Co., Costa Rica; Electrische Nijverheids-Instalaties, Belgium; International Machinery Co. (Bolivia) S.A., Bolivia; Atomed Equipamento Nuclear Ltda., Brazil; Distributora Nacional C.A., Venezuela; Servicios Electronicos Int., Puerto Rico; United Development Incorporated, Israel; and Gebhart Y Asociados, Mexico"; AECL, *Annual Report: 1978-79*, p. 44; *Debates*, 1st Session, 31st Parliament, 1979, pp. 623, 2339.

16. Ernesto Laclau, *New Left Review*, p. 16; Edward Epstein, "Politicization and Income Redistribution in Argentina: The Case of the Peronist Worker," *Economic Development and Cultural Change*, July 1975, Vol. 23, No. 4, pp. 615-631 reveals how the military regimes have effectively repressed the real wages of Argentine workers. Even during the last half of Peron's first period one notices a significant roll-back. In 1965, the wages had escalated and were undoubtedly a factor in the cause of the 1965 coup.
Real Wages among Argentine Industrial Workers: 1943-1970

Year	Index of Real Wages Per Hours
1943	100
1944	111
1945	106
1946	112
1947	140
1948	173
1949	181
1950	173
1955	140
1960	120
1965	142
1970	116

17. For a discussion on the constraints of foreign-induced Third World development see, for example, Cheryl Payer, *The Debt Trap: The International Monetary Fund and the Third World* (New York: Monthly Review Press, 1974). The 1983 Argentine elections should not be construed as a change in the country's economic policy. While such an outcome is possible if the Radical Party is able to mobilize Argentine workers to change the system, it appears that the military's rationale was to allow a civilian government to try to get the country out of the worst economic crisis in the post-1945 period. For the government to succeed, the economy would require radical restructuring, which would result in imperial support for a military coup. Should the government fail, the effect would be to discredit the civilian government and facilitate the military's formal return to power.

18. Petras, *Critical Perspectives*, p. 90. Petras argues that the notion of a petty bourgeoisie "vacillating" between the imperial bourgeoisies and the domestic proletariat is insufficient to explain the ability of a section of society to maintain its existence and imprint itself on the society. Thus Petras identifies the state sector employees, civil and/or military, as an "intermediary stratum" for it has "defined a new capitalist development project tying the expansion of capitalist market relations to the expansion of the state" (p. 86). But he qualifies this by arguing that "the emergence of a state capitalist formation cannot be considered a 'historical' stage in the development of the productive forces, but rather a transitional regime, a phase between one type of exploitation and another" (p. 100).

19. *Korea Bulletin*, May 1976, Vol. 3, No. 5, (San Francisco) p. 3 cited in Yougja Yang and Gavin McCormack, "The United States in Korea," Gavan McCormack and Mark Sheldon (eds.), *Korea: North and South, the Deepening Crisis* (New York: Monthly Review Press, 1978) p. 163.

20. It was during the Korean War that the world speculated whether nuclear technology would be introduced to Korea. However, in 1950 it was not a reactor sale that was being considered; rather, it was whether US President Truman, the man who had authorized the atomic bombings of Hiroshima and Nagasaki, would use atomic bombs in the Korean conflict. *The New York Times*, December 14, 1950, p. 3; Republic of Korea, Ministry of Science and Technology, *Atomic Energy Activities in Korea*: 1977 (Seoul: 1978), p. 7; The Triga Mark-II research reactor went critical on March 30, 1962, *The New York Times*, March 31, 1962, p. 2.

21. *The New York Times*, February 9, 1975, p. 16; *The New York Times*, August 19, 1977, p. D3.

22. Gavan McCormack, "The South Korean Economy: GNP Versus the People", Gavin McCormack, Mark Sheldon, *Korea: North and South, the Deepening Crisis* (New York: Monthly Review Press, 1978), pp. 107, 92. McCormack states that

the 14% (712,00) of the labour force is unionized. However, these unions "have been carefully cultivated by management and government as instruments of social and economic control" (p. 107).

23. Ibid., p. 96; Republic of Korea, *Atomic Energy Activi- ties*, p. 7; *The New York Times*, February 9, 1975, p. 16.

24. Kim Chang Soo, "Marginalization, Development and the Korean Workers' Movement," *Ampo*, Vol. 9, No. 3, July- November 1977, p. 26 cited in Gavin McCormack, "The South Korean Economy," p. 96.

25. *International Canada*, December 1973, Vol. 4, No. 12, p. 323. It is interesting to note that while the South Korean CANDU was originally named Wolsung 1, the South Korean Electric Company changed it to KORI-3. This parallels the name of the American-supplied reactors. *Nuclear News*, August 1981, p. 91.

26. Exactly when AECL contracted Eisenberg is disputable. In Gordon Sims, "The Evolution of AECL" (M.A. Thesis: Carleton Univeristy, 1979) p. 142, it is stated that Eisenberg was engaged in 1972. However, he also argues that Eisenberg and Gray were scheduled to meet with South Korean officials in regard to the original power reactors. This would imply Eisenberg's involvement at least as early as 1968-69. (The construction on KORI-I began on December 31, 1971). Sims noted that the South Koreans cancelled the meeting and that Gray suspected American pressure, on behalf of Westinghouse, as the reason. Now, either Eisenberg was already under contract at this point or was verbally assured of a commission at the conclusion of a reactor contract. It seems highly unlikely that he would be participating without one or the other.

27. *Debates*, 2nd Session, 30th Parliament, 1976-77, pp. 1636, 1843-44, 1855-56, 2433, 1855-56, 1916. House of Commons, *Public Accounts Committee*, No. 21, March 17, 1978, pp. 21:13-14; *Debates*, 2nd Session, 30th Parliament, 1976-77, pp. 1632, 3601, 3659; *Debates*, 3rd Session, 30th Parliament, 1977- 78, p. 926.

28. *International Canada*, May 1975, Vol. 6, No. 5, p. 130; *International Canada*, June 1975, Vol. 6, No. 6, p. 186; *Canada Commerce*, July-August 1975, Vol. 139, No. 7, p. 64; *The New York Times*, May 29, 1975, p. 55; *The Globe and Mail*, January 30, 1976, p. B3; Casterton, "The International Dimensions of the Canadian Nuclear Industry," pp. 69, 83; *International Canada*, May 1979, Vol. 10, No. 4, p. 127; *Modern Power and Engineering*, October 1978, Vol. 72, No. 10, p. 9; *The Globe and Mail*, September 28, 1978, p. B4; *The Globe and Mail*, May 3, 1979, p. B5; *The Globe and Mail*, July 3, 1974, p. B1; Sims, "The Evolution of AECL," p. 142; *The New York Times*, February 1, 1976, p. 111; *The New York Times*, July 4, 1979, pt. IV, p. 2; *The New York Times*, February 21, 1980, p. D9; *The New York Times*, February 21, 1980, p D9.

29. Committee on Nuclear Issues in the Community, *Nuclear Issues: In the Canadian Energy Context*, National Conference Proceedings, Vancouver, March 7-9, 1979 (Ottawa: Royal Society of Canada for CONIC, 1979); *Debates*, 3rd Session, 30th Parliament, 1977-78, pp. 4826, 5310; *Debates*, 4th Session, 30th Parliament, 1978-79, p. 2643.

30. *Debates*, 2nd Session, 30th Parliament, 1976-77, pp. 2059, 3287; House of Commons, *Public Accounts Committee*, No. 21, March 17, 1978, pp. 21:10, 21:10-21:11, 21:14, 21:16, 21:15, 21:17; *Debates*, 2nd Session, 30th Parliament, 1976-77, pp. 7418, 3290; Sims "The Evolution of AECL," p. 52; see AECL, *Annual Report: 1978-79*, p. 6 for a brief discussion of the reorganization.

31. Sylvia Ann Hewlett, Richard S. Weinert, eds., *Brazil and Mexico: Patterns in Late Development* (Philadelphia: Institute for the Study of Human Issues, 1982), p. 26. Hewlett and Weinert offer a good analysis of Mexican economic development.

See also Donald Hodges, Ross Gandy, *Mexico 1910 - 1976: Reform or Revolution?* (London: Zed Press, 1979); *The Financial Post*, October 14, 1969, p. 13; *The New York Times*, August 25, 1973, p. 34; ENR, May 14, 1981; *The Winnipeg Free Press*, May 17, 1982, p. 38.

32. *International Canada*, May 1979, Vol. 10, No. 5, p. 132; January 1976, Vol. 7, No. 1, p. 1; January 1979, Vol. 10, No. 1, pp. 6-7; *Executive*; August 1980, Vol. 22, p. 24; *Oilweek*, January 22, 1979, Vol. 29, No. 50, p. 4, ENR, May 14, 1981, p. 30, *Energy Analects*, August 14, 1981, Vol. 10, No. 31, p. 1, *The Winnipeg Free Press*, June 11, 1982, p. 12.

33. Robert Jungk, *The Nuclear State* (London: John Calder Publishers, Ltd., 1979).

34. The full cost of nuclear technology should also include an examination of reactor safety and the storage and/or dumping of radioactive garbage in sparsely populated areas (the Canadian government's euphemism is nuclear waste disposal). However, both these subjects are beyond the scope of this work. For more information on Canada's disposal program see Walter Robbins, *Getting the Shaft: The Radioactive Waste Controversy in Manitoba* (Winnipeg: Queenston House, 1984). Robbins' book is interesting, informative, and inspires one to action.

CHAPTER III: CANADIAN CONTRIBUTIONS
TO GLOBAL NUCLEAR PROLIFERATION

1. The nuclear weapons number game has resulted in a large section of academia continuously engaged in trying to count the missiles. While initially of importance, the range of overkill in which the world now finds itself has served to decrease the relevance of the numbers game. However, it serves a very important function of confusing and masking the reality of the situation from the general public which concludes that "experts" are required and thus strengthens the perpetuation of the arms race. Nevertheless, a good assessment is contained in Gwyn Prins, ed., *Defended to Death: A Study of the Nuclear Arms Race*, Cambridge University Disarmament Seminar (Harmondsworth: Penguin Books, 1983) pp. 296-321.

2. India argues that it is not a nuclear weapon state, as it only exploded a "nuclear device." I fail to see the difference. For a further discussion on "peaceful nuclear explosions," see Appendix IV, The Non-Proliferation Treaty.

3. Fred H. Knelman, *Nuclear Energy: The Unforgiving Technology* (Edmonton: Hurtig Publishers, 1976) p. 145; Theodore B. Taylor, Mason Willrich, *Nuclear Theft: Risk and Safeguards* (Cambridge, Mass: Ballinger Publishing Co., 1974); Theodore B. Taylor, "Diversion by Non-Governmental Organizations," Mason Willrich, ed., *International Safeguards and Nuclear Industry* (Baltimore: The Johns Hopkins University Press, 1973) pp. 176-198.

4. Albert Wohlstetter, Thomas A. Brown, Gregory Jones, David McGarvey, Henry Rowen, Vincent Taylor and Roberta Wohlstetter [hereafter referred to as Wohlstetter *et al.*], "The Military Potential of Civilian Nuclear Energy: Moving Towards Life in a Nuclear Armed Crowd," *Minerva*, Vol. 15, Nos. 3-4, Autumn-Winter 1977, pp. 387-538.

5. Canada, Treaty Series, 1945, No. 13, *Declaration on Atomic Energy*, at Washington, November 15, 1945, (Ottawa: Queen's Printer, 1945) p. 3; Wohlstetter, *et al.*, "The Military Potential of Civilian Nuclear Energy," p. 450; Walter LaFeber, *America, Russia, and the Cold War: 1945-1976* (New York: John Wiley and Sons, Inc., 1976), pp. 128-172.

6. Wilfred Eggleston, *Canada's Nuclear Story* (Toronto: Clarke, Irwin & Co., Ltd., 1965), pp. 148-49; Canada, *Debates of the House of Commons*, 1st Session, 23rd Parliament, 1957-58, pp. 3335, 989, 1538-9, 2178.
7. Edward Teller, a Hungarian immigrant to the USA, was part of Robert Oppenheimer's Manhattan Project team and has since remained a vehement supporter of the development of virtually anything nuclear. Teller is known best for his work with Stanislow Ulam that resulted in the development of the Hydrogen bomb. When Oppenheimer voiced his opposition to the H-bomb program he "was subsequently hounded by the 'Red-baiting' witch-hunters of the House of Un-American Activities Committee, and accused of Communistic leanings and implicit treachery." [Gwyn Prins, ed., *Defended to Death*, p. 73] Unopposed, Teller's work continued and led to a series of test explosions: first, the "George" shot of the "Greenhouse" series on Eniwetok Atoll in the Pacific on May 8, 1951; and second, the "Mike" shot, which yielded 10 Megatons (Mt) of TNT equivalent, roughly, to 800 Hiroshimas. However, the third test is commonly referred to as the first "successful" H-bomb detonation. On March 1, 1954, at Bikini Atoll, the "Bravo" shot, the first of the "Castle" series, resulted in a blast twice as large as expected in the calculations—14.8 Mt, or over a thousand Hiroshimas. [Ibid.]

The "Bravo" shot resulted in massive radiation contamination over three of the Marshall Islands and the Japanese trawler, the FUKURYU MARU—the Lucky Dragon. The impact on Western consciousness of the horrible fate of the crew of the Lucky Dragon and the continued bomb testing program was instrumental in the mass mobilizations opposed to atmospheric testing. The British Campaign for Nuclear Disarmament is possibly the best remembered group that began in this period.

The mass public demonstrations resulted in a series of diplomatic moves at the international level which could have resulted in a general and complete disarmament, had the Americans not been so adamantly opposed to any attempt to limit their nuclear offensive. The Cambridge Univesity Disarmament Seminar refers to the 1955 Geneva Summit meeting as "the last chance for general and complete disarmament (GCD)" [Ibid., p. 76].

While the Americans effectively thwarted the last attempt for an international GCD, the Administration still had to contend with the domestic popular mobilizations in the USA and indirectly in Europe and Japan. It was at this point that Edward Teller came, once again, to serve the purposes of covering up the American nuclear escalation. It must be recognized, however, that Teller's work at trying to establish "clean bombs" and "peaceful nuclear explosions," in the acceptable jargon of American nuclear strategy, was not entirely a result of ardent partriotism but also a good degree of self-seeking promotion. In July 1952, Teller and Dr. Ernest Lawrence founded what became known as the Lawrence Livermore Laboratory in Livermore, California, east of San Francisco. Had a GCD been signed, Teller's budget would undoubtedly have been cut. Nevertheless, he was able to maintain and expand his program and obfuscate American weapons testing with his erroneous notions of "clean bombs" and "peaceful nuclear explosions." As William Epstein states in *The Last Chance: Nuclear Proliferation and Arms Control*, (New York: The Free Press, 1976) p. 172: "many members of the American arms control community believe that both the notion of clean bombs and that of underground peaceful nuclear explosion were invented by these scientists because of their fears that nuclear tests might be halted and permanently ended."

Edward Teller—or E.T., as Helen Caldicott has called him —has continued his advocacy of PNEs. In the 1960s he advocated the use of 300 bombs, averaging 600 Kt each, to dig a new Panama Canal. (*Northern News* Vol. 6, No. 5, June 1983, p. 14.) His creation of the concept of PNEs has served to diminish the horror of what he is talking about. Furthermore, the notion of PNEs as a useful obfuscatory concept has spread to other nuclear programs. Canada, for example, has considered using PNEs to blast into the Alberta tar sands. India declared that it exploded a nuclear "device" for the purpose of a PNE. And the NPT has enshrined the uses of PNEs with the minor qualifier that they must be under international supervision.

Teller is still active in promoting nuclear weapons development and serves the interests of the US Pentagon by publishing articles which try to diminish the American threat to global survival and the results of a nuclear war; witness his November 1982 *Reader's Digest* article "Six Dangerous Myths about Nuclear War." While the article's erroneous assumptions have been thoroughly critiqued by Frank Von Hippel's "The Myths of Edward Teller" in the March 1983 *Bulletin of the Atomic Scientists*, it is regrettable that a large number of *Digest* readers will never read Von Hippel's critique. To the uninformed person, Teller's article contains the implicit soother where "we're good—they're bad." However, a quote by Teller and A.L. Latter reveals an obvious imbalance: "It would be desirable if sites could be found which are so remote from populous areas that the tests could be concluded without regard to the direction of the winds. Unfortunately, the bombs are too big and the planet is too small." [E. Teller and A.L. Latter, *Our Nuclear Future*, 1958, p. 94, cited in Gwyn Prins, ed., *Defended to Death*, p. 75].

8. Robert W. Morrison, Edward F. Wonder, *Canada's Nuclear Export Policy* (Ottawa: Carleton University Press, 1978), p. 62. Robert Carty, Virgina Smith *Perpetuating Poverty: The Political Economy of Canadian Foreign Aid*, Perspective on Underdevelopment Series (Toronto: Between the Lines, 1981) p. 46; *External Affairs*, May 1956, Vol. 8, p. 113; *Debates*, 1st Session, 30th Parliament, 1974-76, p. 6856. In a June 1983 telephone conversation with Robert M. Smith, Director of Safeguards Development at AECL's Whiteshell Nuclear Research Establishment, the author was informed of a relatively correct method of calculating CANDU plutonium production. The formula is as follows: first, take the MW(e) size of the reactor and multiply by three to receive the approximate MW(th) figure; multiply this figure by 365 for the per annum period at 100% capacity; multiply this figure by .8 for the grams plutonium produced per MW working day; and finally, multiply by the estimated rate of per annum capacity. Thus the 40-MW CIRUS operated at 75% capacity calculates as follows: $(40 \times 365 \times .8 \times .75) \div 1000 = 8.76$ kg plutonium-239 per annum at 75% capacity. To calculate the number of bombs producible from a given quantity of plutonium-239, the author has used the conservative IAEA estimate that 8 Kg of Pu-239 are required for a nuclear explosive device. The Canadian nuclear establishment, however, contends that a nuclear bomb could be produced from 15 lbs. (6.81 Kg) of Pu-239. *Debates*, 1st Session, 30th Parliament, p. 8142. For the purposes of this thesis, the higher range estimate and Smith's formula will be used. CIRUS was started up in July 1960.

9. *External Affairs*, March 1964, Vol. 16, p. 115; Stockholm International Peace Research Institute, The Nuclear Age (Stockholm: Almqvist & Wiksell International, 1974), p. 129; and Walter Stewart, "How We Learned to Stop Worrying and

Sell the Bomb," *Macleans*, November 1974. Cited in Morrison and Wonder, *Canada's Nuclear Export Policy*, p. 18.

10. *Nuclear News*, August 1981, pp. 89-90; Interview with an AECL Spokesperson, June 1983.

11. *Debates*, 3rd Session, 28th Parliament, 1970-72, p. 4184. The TRR originally was to be under bilateral safeguards with Canada, but when diplomatic negotiations were being served, Taiwan placed the TRR under the IAEA system via a unilateral submission effective October 13, 1969. SIPRI, *The Nuclear Age*, p. 130.

12. *The New Scientist*, May 23, 1974, Vol. 62, No. 902; SIPRI, *The Nuclear Age*, pp. 113, 81. The estimated one bomb per week calculation was based on 1980 stockpiles.

13. *Debates*, 1st Session, 30th Parliament, 1974-76, p. 6858; *Debates*, 2nd Session, 26th Parliament, 1964-65, p. 9655; *Debates*, 3rd Session, 28th Parliament, 1970-72, p. 2587; *Executive*, September 1974, Vol. 16, p. 41.

14. Sharp's statement was quoted in SIPRI, *SIPRI Yearbook 1975*, (Stockholm: Almqvist & Wiksell International, 1975), p. 517; *Debates*, 1st Session, 30th Parliament, 1974-76, pp. 7971, 1108, 1751.

15. *Debates*, 1st Session, 30th Parliament, 1974-76, p. 2428; for more information on Edward Teller and PNEs, see footnote No. 7 above; for an example of the Indian advocacy of PNEs, see N. Seshagiri, *The Bomb: Fallout of India's Nuclear Explosion*, (Delhi: Vikas Publishing House PVT., Ltd., 1975); *The New York Times*, May 30, 1979, p. 8; for a brief collection of the post detonation declarations, see SIPRI, *SIPRI Yearbook 1975*, pp. 517-520; and *Debates*, 1st Session, 30th Parliament, 1974-1976, p. 2429. India did not use Canadian uranium in CIRUS.

16. Canadian private companies were not allowed to contract out to complete RAPP II; *Debates*, 1st Session, 30th Parliament, 1974-76, p. 2429; Canada, *Atomic Energy: Exchange of Notes between Canada and the Republic of Argentina*, Buenos Aires, September 10 and 12, 1974 (Ottawa: Queen's Printer, 1974, No. 33) p.4; *International Canada*, July/August 1974, Vol. 5, Nos. 7 and 8, p. 139; *The New York Times*, February 3, 1978, p. 11; SIPRI, *Nuclear Energy and Nuclear Weapon Proliferation*, South Korea had signed the NPT on July 1, 1968, but did not ratify the treaty until April 23, 1975; Robert Morrison and Edward Wonder, *Canada's Nuclear Export Policy*, pp. 72-73; telephone conversation with James Casterton, AECB, March 9, 1984; telephone conversation with Terrance Lonergan, Department of External Affairs, March 15, 1984; Debates, 1st Session, 30th Parliament, 1974-76, p. 5675.

17. *Debates*, 1st Session, 30th Parliament, 1974-76, pp. 7077, cited on p. 7080, 7520, 7858, 7971, 7972, 9237, 8077.

18. *The New York Times*, February 3, 1978, p. 11; *Debates*, 1st Session, 30th Parliament, 1974-76, p. 9012; for the plutonium calculation, see above footnote no. 8; *Debates*, 1st Session, 30th Parliament, 1974-76, p. 6993, Fred Knelman, *Nuclear Energy: The Unforgiving Technology*, (Edmonton: Hurtig Publishers, 1976), p. 23. The South Korea reprocessing plant issue was resolved by the Korean decision to forgo purchasing the plant. This, in turn, made the South Korean contract signing with Canada somewhat more palatable. Though the Canadians had discussed the issue with the South Koreans on a number of occasions, one can assume that it was US intervention that was probably critical. As Myron B. Kratzer, US Acting Assistant Secretary of State for Oceans, Environment and Scientific Affairs, told the US Senate Government Operations Committee, after acknowledging the American discussion, "The South Korean Government reached the decision that the cancellation of its plans was in its own best interest." [quoted in *The New York Times*, January 30, 1976, pp. 1, 4]. What was not clear was whether the Canadian government would have withheld the CANDU reactor had South

Korea insisted on purchasing the reprocessing plant. Parliament was simply informed, four days after the nuclear cooperation agreement was signed, that the South Koreans had cancelled the anticipated purchase of the French reprocessing plant. On December 22, 1976, it was admitted that the South Korean commitment had been received before the agreements were signed. Yet the US State Department only announced the South Korean decision on January 29, 1976—three days after Canada signed the nuclear cooperation agreement with South Korea. Thus it appears that other than the Government's December 1976 statements, little proof is available to reveal a South Korean decision prior to the January 26, 1976, signing with Canada. One could conclude that the South Korean decision to not purchase a French reprocessing plant possibly was not a prerequisite to the Canadian cooperation agreement. The South Korean decision, while encouraged by the Canadian state, may have been used for political purposes to try to bolster the appearance of the Government as a sincere advocate of non-proliferation. See *Debates*, 1st Session, 30th Parliament, 1974-76, p. 10493; *Debates*, 2nd Session, 30th Parliament, 1976-77, p. 2259; *The New York Times*, January 30, 1976, p. 1.

19. *Debates*, 1st Session, 30th Parliament, 1974-76, p. 8827; It is interesting to note that upon subsequent repetitions of the same question MacEachen, when answering, conveniently omitted the cost and environmental reasons. It is possible he recognized that these were not politically useful. Allan MacEachen, however, was not the only Liberal member who played down the impact of reactor exports on Third World societies; he was supported by his Parliamentary Secretary, Monique Begin. Douglas Roche tried to remind Begin that General E.L.M. Burns, the long-time head of the Canadian disarmament team, opposed sales to autocratic and unstable governments. Roche repeated Burns's recognition that if the South Koreans wanted to produce nuclear bombs, no international inspection agreement was going to stop them. Begin was not interested in examining the nature of South Korean society, particularly when she asked, "Who are we to pass judgement on political systems under which other people choose to live?" See *Debates*, 1st Session, 30th Parliament, pp. 10493, 11999, 8830, 8514.

20. Canada, *Atomic Energy Agreement between Canada and Argentina*, Treaty Series: 1976, No. 12 (Ottawa: Queen's Printer, 1976), p. 8. It is interesting to note that the May 1983 start-up of Embalse did not receive the publicity of other reactor exports; Canada, *Atomic Energy Agreement between Canada and the Republic of Korea*, Treaty Series: 1976, No. 11 (Ottawa: Queen's Printer, 1976), p. 10; *Debates*, 1st Session, 30th Parliament, 1974-76, pp. 10489, 10495.

21. See, for example, Allan Wyatt, *The Nuclear Challenge: Understanding the Debate* (Toronto: The Book Press Limited, 1978, particularly Chapters 9-11, pp. 129-161; Edward P. Thompson, "An Army of Redresses." *The Making of the English Working Class*, (Harmondsworth: Penguin Books, Ltd., 1980) pp. 515-639.

22. *Debates*, 1st Session, 30th Parliament, 1974-76, pp. 6997, 10491, 10493. One should note that MacEachen did not feel content with simply listing three reasons opposing a moratorium. Apparently he felt compelled to add a threat that a moratorium might have a negative effect in this situation. However, he failed to explain exactly how the negative effect could occur; *Debates*, 1st Session, 30th Parliament, 1974-76, p. 12072, 12057, 12087-88. One could argue that it is impossible to "effectively" safeguard a nuclear power plant export. Thus the moratorium should in fact be a shut-down of the federal export program. One would anticipate that were a moratorium declared, this point would be democratically debated in inter- and extra-parliamentary forums.

23. The federal government's statement was quoted in SIPRI, *SIPRI Yearbook 1975*, p. 517, my emphasis; *Debates*, 1st Session, 30th Parliament, 1974-76, pp. 11616, 12060, 12066, 13615-16.
24. For the plutonium calculation, see above footnote no. 8; *The Globe and Mail*, June 19, 1980, p. 3; *Debates*, 1st Session, 30th Parliament, 1974-76, p. 11239. For a journalistic approach to the Pakistani-Libyan pact and the Pakistani bomb program, see: Philip Tibenham, Chris Olgiati, Steve Weissman and Herbert Edwards, "Libya Played Banker for Daring Espionage." *The Globe and Mail*, June 19, 1980, pp. 1, 3; Tibenham *et al.*, "To What Extent Did the French Know Karachi's Intentions?" *The Globe and Mail*, June 20, 1980, p. 13; Tibenham *et al.*, "Network to Get Key Pieces Is Alive and Based in Paris," *The Globe and Mail*, June 21, 1980, pp. 1, 4; and Steve Weissman, Herbert Krosney, *The Islamic Bomb: The Nuclear Threat to Israel and the Middle East*, (New York: Times Books, Inc., 1981).
25. *Debates*, 1st Session, 30th Parliament, 1974-76, p. 2255. Shortly after the December 22, 1976, safeguard announcement, the Government attempted to increase the safeguards on recipients of Canadian uranium. Thenceforth, the December 1974 safeguards requirement were obligatory. On January 1, 1977, the Government suspended uranium contracts worth approximately $300 million to the EEC, Japan, Switzerland, and restricted shipments to the USA. The Government did allow the existing contracts to be delivered during the renegotiation process. This "period of grace" pending renegotiation was extended from one to two years. But it did not take long to settle the issue. The suspension was lifted for the USA in mid-November 1977; the EEC, in December 1977; and Japan, on January 26, 1978. The Swiss negotiations continued for an extended period, as the Swiss government argued that it did not have the legislative authority to enforce the Canadian desired degree of control over technology transfers. For more information, see Canada, Department of External Affairs, "Canada's Nuclear Safeguard Policy" (Ottawa: Department of External Affairs, 1978), pp. 4-9.
26. *Debates*, 2nd Session, 30th Parliament, 1976-77, p. 2256.

CHAPTER IV: URANIUM SALES

1. June Taylor, Michael D. Yokell, *Yellowcake: The International Uranium Cartel*, (New York: Pergamon Press, 1979), p. 22; Eldorado Nuclear Ltd., *Annual Report: 1970*, pp. 19-20; Canada, House of Commons, *1952-53 Special Commit- tee on the Operations of the Government in the Field of Atomic Energy*, No. 3, pp. 47-48; Brian Easlea, *Fathering the Unthinkable: Masculinity, Scientists, and the Nuclear Arms Race* (London: Pluto Press, 1983), p. 67; Wilfred Eggleston, *Canada's Nuclear Story*, (Toronto: Clarke Irwin and Co., Ltd., 1965), p. 44; Robert Bothwell, "Radium and Uranium: Evolution of a Company and a Policy," *Canadian Historical Review*, Vol. LXIV, No. 2, June 1983, p. 135; Eggleston, *Canada's Nuclear Story*, pp. 44-45; Bothwell "Radium and Uranium," pp. 38-45; "Reviews," *Maclean's* Vol. 78, February 6, 1965, p. 50; Canada, House of Commons, *1952-53 Special Committee*, No. 3, pp. 54, 58.
2. Canada, Atomic Energy Control Board, *Annual Report 1947- 48*, pp. 12-13; *Debates*, 1st Session, 21st Parliament, 1949, p. 2356; *Debates*, 4th Session, 20th Parliament, 1948, p. 2356; *CIM Bulletin*, May 1976, Vol. 69, No. 769, p. 69; Canada, House of Commons, *Debates*, 23rd Parliament, 1957-58, p. 4147; *Debates*, 3rd Session, 24th Parliament, 1960, pp. 1377, 3918; *The Financial Post*, March 7, 1959, p. 48; W.D.G. Hunter, "Canada's Uranium Industry: A Crisis of Survival," *Business*

Quarterly, Vol. 26, No. 4, Winter 1961, p. 227; *Debates*, 2nd Session, 24th Parliament, 1959, pp. 2663, 6119; and Ruth Marossi, "Canada's Uranium Crisis," *The Bulletin of the Atomic Scientists*, Vol. 17, No. 7, pp. 281-82.

3. *The Financial Post*, April 25, 1959, p. 15; *Debates*, 2nd Session, 24th Parliament, 1959, pp. 6105-61; *Debates*, 23rd Parliament, 1957-58, p. 4147, *Debates*, 3rd Session, 24th Parliament, 1960, p. 3918; *Debates*, 2nd Session 24th Parliament, 1959, pp. 2661, 2663, 571; *The Financial Post*, April 18, 1959, p. 15; *Debates*, 2nd Session, 24th Parliament, pp. 571, 6117, 6106; *The Financial Post*, January 31, 1979, p. 3, *Debates*, 4th Session, 24th Parliament, p. 5688.

4. For a discussion of the 1963 missile debate, see John Warnock, "The Debate over Nuclear Weapons," *Partner to Behemoth: The Military Policy of a Satellite Canada* (Toronto: New Press, 1070), pp. 183-201: *Debates*, 25th Parliament, 1962-63, p. 3097; John Warnock, *Partner to Behemoth*, pp. 194, 196, 201. Pearson was true to his campaign statements, for the missiles did arrive in Canada. They were "secretly delivered" to La Macaza, Quebec, on New Year's Eve, December 31, 1966. Warnock adds that "this must have brought chuckles of delight in Washington, for it was the anniversary of the assault on Quebec City by the U.S. revolutionary forces, under General Richard Montgomery in 1776."

5. Taylor, Yokell, *Yellowcake*, p. 32; *Debates*, 1st Session, 26th Parliament, 1963, p. 1636; Pearson's announcement was made to "the chair[person] of the committee which was charged with the investigation of the economic status of Elliot Lake and the chair[person] of the industrial committee of the Bancroft and district chamber of commerce." *Debates*, 1st Session, 26th Parliament, 1963, pp. 1636, 1908; *Debates*, 2nd Session, 26th Parliament, 1964-65, p. 2861; *Debates*, 1st Session, 26th Parliament, pp. 1636, 1908, 1228.

6. *Debates*, 3rd Session, 26th Parliament, 1965, pp. 1948, 1949, 1602, 1980. Gordon Edwards, "Fission Chips: Canada and the H-Bomb," *Transitions*, Journal of the Canadian Coalition for Nuclear Responsibility, Spring 1983, p. 19.

7. *Debates*, 3rd Session, 26th Parliament, 1965, pp. 957-8; *The Financial Post*, April 3, 1966, p.21; *Debates*, 1st Session, 27th Parliament, 1966-67, pp. 991-2, 1324; *Debates*, 2nd Session, 26th Parliament, 1964-65, pp. 11718, 11884.

8. *The Financial Post*, October 22, 1966, p. 5; *Debates*, 1st Session, 27 Parliament, 1966-67, p. 8813; *The Financial Post*, December 24, 1966, p.5; *Canadian Nuclear Technology*, Vol. 5, No. 6, Nov.-Dec. 1966, p. 35; *The Financial Post*, March 23, 1968, p. M11; *The Financial Post*, September 13, 1969, p.35.

9. *The Financial Post*, December 1, 1973, p. 1; *The Financial Post*, September 13, 1969, p. 35; *The Financial Post*, March 23, 1968, p. M11; *The Financial Post*, January 29, 1966, pp. 1, 5, 23; *The Financial Post*, May 25, 1968, pp. 23-24; Eldorado Nuclear Limited, *Annual Report: 1968*, pp. 4-5. In 1968, initial production was scheduled for the second quarter of 1970. It was to include custom refining of UF_6 and sale of Eldorado-produced uranium in the form of UF_6.

10. *The Financial Post*, August 1, 1970, p. 24; *The Financial Post*, March 27, 1971, p. M9; *The Financial Post*, March 22, 1969, p. M15; *The Financial Post*, March 23, 1968 p. M11; *Debates*, 2nd Session, 28th Parliament, 1969-70, pp. 42523, 5250-51; *The Financial Post*, January 2, 1971, p. 13; *The Financial Post*, August 1, 1970, p. 24; *Debates*, 2nd Session, 28th Parliament, p. 5252. Aside from the cartel, the federal government considered supporting construction of a uranium enrichment facility. The proposed plant would have consumed 25% of the power generated annually by the James Bay Hydro Electric Power Project and all of Canada's 1974 known uranium reserves within twenty-two years. The enrichment facility, however, primarily was a provincial project of Quebec's Premier Bourassa. The

estimated $3 billion price tag to be shared among the Ottawa, Quebec, and French governments was an important factor that diminished federal support. Debates, 1st Session, 30th Parliament, 1974-76. p. 2877. For further discussion of the failed plans, see Fred Knelman, "Uranium—The Embarrassment of Enrichment," Nuclear Energy: The Unforgiving Technology, pp. 180- 200.

11. June H. Taylor, Michael D. Yokell, *Yellowcake; The International Uranium Cartel* (New York: Pergamon Press, 1979), pp. 57, 66; On the issue of Canadian instigation of the cartel, the authors are more specific: "Some United States cartel investigators believe it was RTZ [the British controlled international mining conglomerate, Rio Tinto Zinc] which conceived of a uranium cartel, and through officers in its Canadian subsidiary, Rio Algom, got the Canadian government to take a lead in initiating calls for other governments to participate.... The RTZ uranium group includes Palabora Mining Corporation in South Africa, Rossing Uranium in Namibia, Conzinc Riotinito of Australia, Mary Kathleen Uranium, Rio Algom of Canada, and its United States subsidiary which has a mill in Utah, the only foreign-owned mill in the United States." p. 73. It is interesting to note that MacNabb was also vice-president of Uranium Canada Ltd., a marketing board responsible primarily for overseeing the Canadian uranium stockpile. "The President of Uranium Canada Ltd., Jack Austin, was also MacNabb's superior as Deputy Minister for Energy, Mines, and Resources. Taylor and Yokell, *Yellowcake*, p. 70.

12. Taylor and Yokell, *Yellowcake*, pp. 68, 81, 82, 84, 102, 122, 123, 61-62.

13. *Debates*, 2nd Session, 30th Parliament, 1976-77 pp. 7999, 8074; Taylor and Yokell, *Yellowcake*, p. 62; *Debates*, 2nd Session, 30th Parliament, 1976-77 pp. 7991; *The Financial Post*, January 2, 1971, p.13; *Debates*, 3rd Session, 30th Parliament, 1977-78, pp. 215-16, 219, 224. An interesting sidenote to the cartel was provided in mid-December 1983. It revealed continued state protection for those involved. Eldorado Nuclear and Uranium Canada (two Crown corporations) and Denison Mines, Rio Algom, Gulf Minerals, and Uranez Canada (private corporations) were taken to court in 1981 by the federal justice department on price-fixing charges. It was not surprising that the private companies were not charged; the Trudeau government had already promised that to Gulf, at least. But the ruling for Eldorado Nuclear and Uranium Canada was most interesting. As Paul McKay states in "Supreme Court Let U-Cartel off Hook," *The Nuclear Free Press*, No. 20, Winter 1984, p. 3, "Based on century old legal precedents established in England and colonial England, the Supreme Court of Canada ruled...that two federal crown corporations...are immune from prosecution under existing federal legislation." This meant, in effect, that "the government could interpret the ruling as a 'carte-blanche to engage in illegal activities and...encourage other (corporate) citizens to do likewise.'"

14. *Debates*, 3rd Session, 30th Parliament, 1977-78, pp. 1228-29, 5561-62; *The Globe and Mail*, November 9, 1977, p. B2. Eldorado Nuclear Limited, *Annual Reports*, 1969- 1978.

15. Taylor and Yokell, *Yellowcake*, p. 98. Another motive for limiting the cartel was the fear that too high a price for uranium could further limit reactor sales and, therefore, also uranium. *The Globe and Mail*, November 9, 1977, p. B2; Taylor and Yokell, pp. 98, 99; *New Scientist*, June 26, 1975, Vol. 66, No. 955, pp. 710-11; *The Financial Post*, July 5, 1975, p. 3; *The Globe and Mail*, June 18, 1976, p. B.10.

16. *One Sky Report*, May 1982, p. 22, Mark Hertsgaard, "Le president Reagan bouleverse les bases de la politique nucleaire," *Le Monde Diplomatique*, juin 1982, pp. 4, 5. Hertsgaard discusses Reagan's plan to use the power industry's spent fuel bundles

to compensate for the military's plutonium shortage so that the latter could complete Reagan's military build-up; In December 1981, Eldorado announced its decision to close its operations in Uranium City, Saskatchewan. Canadian mining interests have devised new ways to counter the opposition to mine closures. The Rabbit Lake, Cluff Lake, and after 1983, Key Lake Mines operate without establishing a permanent town. Instead, miners are simply flown in. *Star-Phoenix*, December 19, 1982, cited in *One Sky Report*, May 1982, p. 2.

17. *Uranium and Electricity*, Eldorado Nuclear, Ltd. (Ottawa: 1982) p. 15, cited in Carole Giangrande. *The Nuclear North: The People, the Regions, and the Arms Race* (Toronto: House of Anansi Press Ltd., 1983) pp. 87, 212. Giangrande offers an excellent account, based on documented evidence and many personal interviews, of the impact of nuclear technology, particularly uranium mining, on the common Canadian citizen. Her work clarifies the manner in which opposition to nuclear related industries varies from region to region. She argues that if the Canadian anti-nuclear/peace movement is to effect changes, its impact is dependent upon recognizing and coordinating the regional concerns rather than remaining primarily a southern urban response; see Ingride Alesich, "Atomic Cafe: The Saskatchewan Version," *Briarpatch*, Jan/- Feb., 1984, Vol. 13, No. 1, pp. 8-10, for more information on the Key Lake spills. One of the main causal factors was corporate cheapness; packed sand was used to build the reservoir containment walls rather than something that didn't dissolve when wet. For a breakdown of corporate involvement in Saskatchewan uranium exploitation, see Walter Davis, *The Yellowcake Road: Corporate Uranium and Saskatchewan* (Saskatoon: Saskatoon Citizens for a Non-Nuclear Society, 1981).

CHAPTER V: REVIVING THE SALE OF REACTORS: THE LATE 1980s AND BEYOND

1. Atomic Energy of Canada Limited, *Annual Report 1977-78*, p. F6; Canada, Department of Energy, Mines, and Resources, *Nuclear Policy Review Background Papers* (Ottawa: EMR, Report No. ER81-2E, 1980), pp. 275, 351.

2. *Nuclear News*, August 1981, pp. 85-104, Wohlstetter, *et al.*, "The Military Potential of Civilian Nuclear Energy," *Minerva* Vol. 15, Nos. 3-4, Autumn-Winter 1977, p. 401. While the actual number of nuclear power reactors would have declined somewhat due to cancellations, it serves a good working figure. It is important to recognize that the actual number of reactors in the world appears problematic even for the nuclear industries to determine. Witness the discussion in *AECL Ascent*, Spring 1983, p. 6. *Ascent* notes the discrepancy between the number of on-line reactors estimated by the IAEA and *Nuclear News* as 294 power reactors with a total of 173,108 MWe capacity in 25 countries versus 276 power reactors totalling 167,103 MWe in 24 countries, respectively. This is a difference of 18 reactors, 6005 MWe, and one country. While Paul Vlajcic of *Nuclear News* admits the discrepancy may be due to their agency's policy of not counting power reactors under 30 MWe and their difficulty in obtaining information on the USSR, the discrepancy still appears rather large. This is compounded when one recognizes that the IAEA and *Nuclear News* also dispute the number of US power reactor cancellations in 1982 with the figures 16 and 18 plants, respectively. However, this would not be the first time that the IAEA has been suspiciously over-inflating the promises and obfuscating the drawbacks of the nuclear industries.

3. See for example Amory B. Lovins, L. Hunter Lovins, Leonard Ross, "Nuclear Power and Nuclear Bombs," *Foreign Affairs*, Vol. 58, Summer 1980; Mark Hertsgaard, "Le president Reagan bouleverse les bases de la politique nucleaire," *Le Monde Diplomatique*, juin 1982, pp. 4, 5. For material pertaining to the American nuclear escalation of the late 1970s and early 1980s, see: Gwyn Prins, ed., *Defended to Death: A Study of the Nuclear Arms Race*; Raymond Williams, "The Politics of Nuclear Disarmament," *New Left Review*, No. 124, Nov.-Dec, 1980, p. 39; Robert Aldridge, *The Counterforce Syndrome: A Guide to U.S. Nuclear Weapons and Strategic Doctrine*; Emma Rothschild, "The American Arms Boom," E.P. Thompson and Dan Smith, eds., *Protest and Survive* (New York: Monthly Review Press, 1981) pp. 108-121; George Kistiakowsky, "The Arms Race and Nuclear War: An Interview," E.P. Thompson and Dan Smith, *Protest and Survive*, pp. 122-136.

4. Wohlstetter, *et al.*, "The Military Potential of Civilian Nuclear Energy," A SIPRI Monograph (Cambridge, Mass: The MIT Press, 1975), p. 81.

5. Amory B. Lovins, L. Hunter Lovins, Leonard Ross, "Nuclear Power and Nuclear Bombs," p. 1142. For discussions of some of the technical, social, and political aspects of enrichment technology, see: Frank Barnaby, "'he Nuclear Fuel Cycle," *The Nuclear Age*, pp. 46-62; J. Beckman, "Gas Centrifuges for Cheaper Isotope Separation," C. F. Barnaby, *Preventing The Spread of Nuclear Weapons*, pp. 90-99; J. H. Coates, B. Barre, "Practical Suggestions for the Improvement of Proliferation Resistance with the Enriched Uranium Fuel Cycle," SIPRI, Nuclear Energy & Nuclear Weapon Proliferation, pp. 40-59; P. Baskma, "Jet Nozzle and Vortex Tube Enrichment," SIPRI, *Nuclear Energy & Nuclear Weapon Proliferation*, pp. 61-71; K.L. Kompa, "Laser Separation of Isotopes," SIPRI, *Nuclear Energy & Nuclear Weapon Proliferation*, pp. 73-90.

6. Amory B. Lovins, L. Hunter Lovins, *Energy/War: Breaking The Nuclear Link—A Prescription for Nonproliferation* (New York: Harper Colophone Books, 1981), p. 21. The Lovinses state that while the Oak Ridge design has been criticized, its broad feasibility was confirmed by a US government study, Nonproliferation Alternatives System Assessment Program (NASAP) [The nine-volume NASAP report was published by the US Department of Energy in June 1980 as document DOE/NE-0001/1-9.] NASAP concluded "that a plant separating tens of bombs' worth per year could be built in 1-2 years for tens of millions of dollars, a smaller one for less." For a discussion of some of the technical, social, and political aspects of reprocessing, see: Union of Concerned Scientists, "Nuclear Fuel Reprocessing: Radiological Impact of West Valley Plant," David R. Brower, Jim H. Harding, *The Nuclear Fuel Cycle*, pp. 149-207; Frank Barnaby, "The Nuclear Fuel Cycle," *The Nuclear Age*, pp. 44-62; Gene I. Rochlin, Plutonium, *Power, and Politics: International Arrangements for the Disposition of Spent Nuclear Fuel* (Berkeley: University of California Press, 1979) pp. 67-130; K. Hannerz, F. Segerberg "Proliferation Risks Associated with Different Back-End Fuel Cycles for Light Water Reactors," SIPRI, *Nuclear Energy & Nuclear Weapon Proliferation* (London: Taylor & Francis, Ltd., 1979) pp. 91-103; Dr. Abrahamson, "Reprocessing and Waste Management," SIPRI, *Nuclear Energy & Nuclear Weapon Proliferation*, pp. 105-111; B.T. Feld, "Can Plutonium Be Made Weapon-Proof?" SIPRI, *Nuclear Engergy & Nuclear Weapon Proliferation*, pp. 113- 119.

7. Gordon Edwards, "Canada's Nuclear Industry and the Myth of the Peaceful Atom," Ernie Regehr and Simon Rosenblum, *Canada and the Nuclear Arms Race*, with a foreword by Margaret Laurence. (Toronto: James Lorimer & Company, Publishers, 1983). pp. 147, 148. Edwards states: "The nuclear review was carried out by an interdepartmental committee of government officials, with assistance

and advice from AECL, Eldorado Nuclear Limited, the Atomic Energy Control Board, and the Canadian Nuclear Association—all organizations which are dedicated to the promotion of nuclear technology. However, there was no opportunity for groups critical of nuclear power to make their views known effectively. Despite a written mandate from sixty-five organizations across Canada, which was communicated personally to Marc Lalonde, then minister of energy, the Canadian Coalition for Nuclear Responsibility was prevented from even making a presentation to the minister or to the review committee."

It is interesting to note that the leaked "Internal Review" bears many similarities to the *Nuclear Industry Review* and the *Nuclear Policy Review Background Papers*. The leaked document is less rhetorical and obfuscatory and clearly reveals policy options. See Canada, Department of Energy, Mines, and Resources, Nuclear Policy Review Background Papers (Ottawa: Minister of Supply and Services, Report No. ER81-2E, 1981); *Nuclear Industry Review: Problems and Prospects, 1981-2000* (Ottawa: Minister of Supply and Services, 1982); and Canada, Inter-Agency Review, *Policy Review of the Nuclear Power Industry in Canada*, Reiner Hollback, EMR, Draft report leaked to the Ottawa Press, June, 1981 (Montreal: Canadian Coalition for Nuclear Responsibility, 1981).

8. Canada, Inter-Agency Review, *Policy Review of the Nuclear Power Industry In Canada*, Reiner Hollbach, EMR (Montreal: CCNR, 1981) pp. 88-89 [hereafter referred to as Internal Review].

9. Ibid., pp. 90-91; see Paul McKay *Electric Empire: The Inside Story of Ontario Hydro* (Toronto: Between The Lines, 1983); for more on the Canadian radioactive refuse program, see R.S. Dixon, E.L.J. Rosinger, eds., *Third Annual Report of The Canadian Nuclear Fuel Waste Management Program* (Pinawa: AECL-6821, December, 1981) p. 87; *Ascent*, Vol. 3, No. 2, 1982, p. 27. T.E. Rummery, E. L.J. Rosinger "The Canadian Nuclear Fuel Waste Management Program," paper presented at the International Conference on Radioactive Waste Management sponsored by the Canadian Nuclear Society, Winnipeg, Manitoba, September 13-16, 1982; G.R. Simmons, A. Brown, C.C. Davidson, G.L. Rigby, "The Canadian Underground Research Laboratory," IAEA, International Conference on Radioactive Waste Management, Seattle, WA, USA, May 16-20, 1983, IAEA-CN-43/167; AECL, "Nuclear Fuel Waste Management," January, 1981. Despite volumes of industry material, the waste disposal issue has at times become a public relations nightmare as successive communities mobilize to try to run AECL out of town. For the struggle in Massey, Ontario (20 miles south of the East Bull Lake test-drilling site), see Mikell Billski, "Nuclear Sacrifice: A Northern Legacy," Part 1: "Massey VS. AECL: A Northern Town Takes On Southern Nuclear Interests." *The Nuclear Free Press*, Fall 1982, pp. 4-5.

10. CBC, "The Journal," August 3, 1983. The immediate Ontario Hydro response to the Pickering accident was to advertise the studies it was conducting and the cost of replacing the unproduced electricity. While the implicit assumptions are that everything is under control and "nuclear power is cheap," in actual fact it revealed the ridiculousness of depending on one dangerous and unpredictable energy source. See also, "What Happened at Pickering," *The Nuclear Free Press*, Fall 1983, Issue 19, pp. 1, 8.

11. Internal Review, pp. 92-96; Thomas Claridge, "Ontario Hydro May Abandon Heavy Water Plant," *The Globe and Mail*, June 27, 1983, pp. 1, 2. In a March 1984 telephone conversation, an AECL official stated that support for Lepreau II was high but that a number of contentious points impeded its construction. First, Lepreau II primarily was for the export market, and firm US contracts

had yet to materialize. Second, the percentage of federal funding still was unsettled. And third, there were demands for a no-strike labour contract.

12. Canada, Department of EMR, *Nuclear Industry Review: Problems and Prospects 1981-2000* (Ottawa, 1982), pp. 45- 48. A similar notion of power exports to the US existed in 1972. The plan involved a US reactor company's building a $2 billion 12,000-MWe plant in Nova Scotia and exporting the power to the US. *Debates*, 4th Session, 28th Parliament, 1972, pp. 3023-4; Gordon Edwards, *Canada's Nuclear Dilemma...And How to Avoid It!* (Montreal: Canadian Coalition for Nuclear Responsibility, 1981), pp. 3-5. In 1979 the industry estimated that the three types of decommissioning would be priced as follows: first, dismantling and removal, a straight $30 million; second, encasement would cost $17.5 million plus $60,000 per annum for 65 years; and third, mothballing would cost $6 million plus $80,000 per annum *ad infinitum*. These prices are, however, unverified guesses and subject to error and inflation. Thus the 1979 estimate of $30 million for dismantling and removal had, by January 1983, escalated to $40 million. The only power plant to have been dismantled fully was the 30-MW demonstration reactor at Elk River, Minnesota. The job cost $6.5 million and suggests that a 1,200-MWe plant would require $260 million. This price range is similar to the $100 million for a 600-MW CANDU estimated by Gordon Edwards of the Canadian Coalition for Nuclear Responsibility (For more information, see: G. N. Unsworth, "Decommissioning CANDU Nuclear Power Stations" (Mississauga: AECL-6332, April, 1979): "Ill-fated Quebec Nuclear Power Plant Headed for an Expensive End," *Winnipeg, Free Press*, January 6, 1983, p. 30; Rasa Gustaltis, "What Do You Do with a Used Nuclear Plant?" *Canadian Dimension*, July- August 1979, Vol. 14, No. 1, p. 40; *Canadian Business*, January 1978, p. 17-18). For the formula used to calculate the CANDU plutonium production, see Chapter 3, footnote No. 8 above; Internal Review, p. 103; Interview with an AECL official, March 1984.

13. Internal Review, pp. 107-116; Steve Weissman, Herbert Krosney, The Islamic Bomb (New York: Times Books, 1981), p. 91.

14. Internal Review, pp. 118, 119, 121; Gordon Edwards, "Canada's Nuclear Industry and the Myth of the Peaceful Atom," pp. 148, 154.

15. Western nuclear reactor suppliers have been trying to sell to Romania since the early 1960s. For ideological reasons, there have been occasional public statements arguing against nuclear transfers to Warsaw Pact nations. But with a relatively fixed Western export market, nuclear suppliers easily overcame any political concerns in their attempt to find a purchaser.

Speculation of a Canadian sale to Romania began in 1967. Jerome Spivak, President of Deuterium Canada, Ltd., twice flew to Bucharest in 1967 in an attempt to sell a heavy water plant should the Romanians choose a CANDU. In January 1968, a Romanian delegation toured Canadian nuclear reactors and research establishments and requested a Canadian General Electric tender on a 300-350 MWe reactor. The Canadian Exports Credits Insurance Corporation was an interested potential financier. The Canadians were hopeful. The Romanian visit was succeeded by speculation that they would purchase uranium refining and fuel fabrication plants to process their indigenous uranium supplies. This would complement the anticipated 300-MWe CANDU and heavy water plant.

The visit by the Romanian delegation, however, probably was only a preliminary review, as the contract bidding soon was opened to other international suppliers. By August 1968, Canada, France, West Germany, and Sweden were competing for the contract. The Americans eventually placed a bid, apparently for two reasons. The first and most obvious was that they hoped to receive a reactor contract. The second was due to a concern of an imminent Soviet invasion of Czechoslovakia. With the hope of increasing its influence in neighbouring Romania, the US overcame its earlier concern of Congressional opposition to an Eastern bloc nuclear sale. But the American efforts, like those of the other nuclear suppliers, were in vain; the Romanians did not contract a reactor at this time due to a lack of capital. *New Scientist* June 11, 1964, Vol. 22, No. 395, p. 655; *The Financial Post*, January 6, 1968, p. 31; *The Financial Post*, March 2, 1968, pp. 1, 5; *The Globe and Mail*, November 5, 1977, p. B14. American negotiations with Romanian officials began in July 1968 and resulted in the November 1968 signing of a nuclear cooperation agreement. *The New York Times*, July 9, 1968, pp. 1, 11; November 22, 1968, p. 19. It is possible that the Romanians initiated contact with the US. If such were the case, the agreement would have been mutually beneficial: increased US influence in Romania and increased Romanian contacts with the West. Both could have served to strengthen Romania's maneuverability with the Soviet Union.

16. *Debates*, 1st Session, 30th Parliament, 1974-76, p. 2429, AECL, *Annual Report*: 1976-77, p. T8; *International Canada*, October 1977, Vol. 8, No. 10, p. 227; *The Globe and Mail*, November 22, 1978, p. B1; *The Globe and Mail*, November 19, 1977, p. B2, *The Globe and Mail*, July 29, 1978, p. B3.

17. *The Globe and Mail*, November 22, 1978, p. B1. The December 1978 cost of uranium (U_3O_8) was $130 per kg. The Canadian export policy required the most refined form possible; therefore, it is usually exported as uranium hexaflouride (UF_6) which adds approximately $5.50 to $6 per kg. However, two steps are required for converting U_3O_8 into CANDU fuel; first, conversion to ceramic grade uranium dioxide (UO_2) which adds approximately $6 per kg.; and second, UO_2 fabrication into CANDU fuel adds a further increase of about $40 per kg. Therefore, in December 1978, the 6,240 fuel bundles (each with 20 kg of fuel) required for an initial fuel charge would cost $21,964,800. *Debates*, 4th Session, 30th Parliament, 1978-79, p. 2090, Interview with an AECL Official; *The Globe and Mail*, December 16, 1978, p. B12; *The Globe and Mail*, December 21, 1978, p. B13; *The Globe and Mail*, July 29, 1978, p. B3. Even if Canadian officials had succeeded in negotiating the CANDU fuel and heavy water contracts, the Canadian content still would have been less than 20% ($186,964,800 of $1 billion).

18. *Ascent*, Summer 1979, Vol. 1, p. 27; *The Financial Post*, October 11, 1980, p. 17; *The Financial Post*, October 8, 1980, p. B3; *Energy Analects*, August 7, 1982, p. 4; *The Globe and Mail*, June 25, 1982, p. 3; *The Winnipeg Free Press*, December 18, 1982, p. 61; *The Globe and Mail*, January 4, 1983, p. B2; *The Winnipeg Free Press*, September 10, 1982, p. 5; John Tobias Interview, CANADA-AM, CTV Television News, Friday, January 6, 1984; Guy Hunter, Clifford Maynes, "The Romanian Deal: Canada Renews Credit for Reactor Sales—But Romanians Would Rather Deal in Strawberries," *The Nuclear Free Press*, Issue 19, Fall 1983, p. 4; AECL, *Annual Report*: 1981-82, pp 9-10.

19. Alice Krueger "Irradiation Labelling: We May Not Be Told If Food's Been Treated" (sic), *The Winnipeg Free Press*, Sept. 17, 1983, p. 55; Joan Havemann, "Food Irradiation-Brought to You by Atomic Energy of Canada," *Briarpatch*, April, 1983, Vol. 12, No. 3, p. 18; *Debates*, 1st Session, 30th Parliament, 1974-76, p. 8827; Havemann, "Food Irradiation," *Briarpatch*, p. 19; *Debates*, 4th Session, 30th Parliament, 1978-79, pp. 1319, 2113, 2258; "Government Fears Argentine CANDU May Spawn Bombs," *The Ottawa Citizen*, April 23, 1983. A copy was

provided through the generosity of Energy Probe, pp. 1-3; Gordon Edwards, "Canada's Nuclear Industry and the Myth of the Peaceful Atom," Ernie Regehr, Simon Rosenblum, *Canada and the Nuclear Arms Race* (Toronto: James Lorimer & Co., Pub., 1983), p. 151. Refusing to load CANDU fuel bundles en route to Argentina, however, was not the first time Saint John longshore workers mobilized to block the Canadian nuclear export program. Edwards states that a similar event occurred in the summer of 1979 when they refused to load a heavy water shipment intended for Argentina. The workers "demanded the release of sixteen trade unionists who had been imprisoned without charges in Argentina. The action was organized by the No CANDU for Argentina Committee, and had the full backing of the Canadian Labour Congress, representing 2.5 million Canadian workers. A few days after the boycott, six of the trade unionists were released from Argentine prisons." (Edwards, p. 146); "Government Fears," *The Ottawa Citizen*, April 23, 1983, pp. 2-3; Burt Solomon, "Argentina: Bent on a Home-Grown Nuclear Program," *The Energy Daily*, November 9, 1082, pp. 2, 4. The anticipated capacity of Argentina's facility is disputed. Solomon states 15 kg of P-239 would be reproduced annually. However, Catesby Leigh in "Argentina 'Could' Test Bomb in 2 years," *Kingston Whig-Standard* (AECL provided the undated article, available at Pinawa Library, PIOI-O2O) cites two additional estimates. The first, by an unnamed Argentinean CNEA official, is 40 kg., or five bombs, annually. The second, provided by the US Congressional Research Service, is 87 kg., or nearly eleven bombs, annually "'at full capacity.'"

20. Albert Wolhstetter *et al.*, "The Military Potential of Civilian Nuclear Energy," *Minerva*, Vol. 15, Nos. 3-4, Autumn-Winter, 1977, p. 387.

APPENDIX I: FEDERAL GOVERNMENT EXPENDITURES SUBSIDIZING NUCLEAR ENERGY RESEARCH AND DEVELOPMENT, 1947-1979 (IN $ MILLIONS)

Year	AECL R & D Expenditures Funded by Appropriations	AECB Research Expenditures Funded by Appropriations	Capital Stock Contributions Financing NRU Reactor and CRNL Facilities	Total R & D Support
1978-79	119.120	—	—	119.120
1977-78	216.061[a]	—	—	216.061
1976-77	195.549[b]	—	—	195.549
1975-76	93.576	11.346	—	104.922
1974-75	85.921	10.375	—	96.296
1973-74	87.918	7.245	—	95.163
1972-73	78.206	7.896	—	86.102
1971-72	77.048	11.720	—	88.768
1970-71	68.942	7.100	—	76.088
1969-70	69.000	5.400	—	74.400
1968-69	68.600	3.959	—	71.195
1967-68	66.500	2.500	—	69.000
1966-67	57.983	2.000	—	59.983
1965-66	52.667	1.600	0	54.267
1964-65	45.158	1.250	0	46.408
1963-64	70.163[c]	.900	13.761	57.302[d]
1962-63	37.062	.770	—	37.832
1961-62	33.933	.650	—	34.633
1960-61	38.218	.650	—	38.828
1959-60	29.408	.400	1.098	31.156
1958-59	25.684	.400	4.714	30.798
1957-58	21.131	.300	8.863	30.394
1956-57	21.544	.300	11.001	32.845
1955-56	18.626	.300	12.554	32.886
1954-55	14.645	.300	6.967	20.506
1953-54	12.360	.300	4.009	16.669
1952-53	12.610	.300	24.794	17.704
1951-52	12.076	.200	—	12.276
1950-51	7.177	.150	—	7.327
1949-50	6.618	.150	—	6.768
1948-49	5.747	.143	—	5.890
1947-48	5.573	.150	—	5.723
	1,754.824	79.154	60.239	2,355.449

a. Includes the $87.571 million budgetary expenditure covering the write-off of the Gentilly I debt.
b. Includes the $85.491 million expenditure when the interest payments on Gentilly I and Douglas Point reactor were forgiven.
c. Includes the $25.239 million expenditure for the NRU reactor debt write-off.
d. Includes the $20 million investment in Chalk River that was transferred to AECL for $1.00.

SOURCE: Department of Energy, Mines, and Resources, Canada, *Nuclear Policy Review Background Papers* (Ottawa, EMR, Report No. ER81-2E, 1980), p. 307.

APPENDIX II: MAJOR CANADIAN EXPORT EFFORTS TO FIRST WORLD COUNTRIES

United Kingdom

Cooperation between Canada and Britain has been maintained since the Second World War. However, Canadian opportunities to penetrate the British reactor market, while continually publicized, have never materialized. But there were two periods in the British nuclear program when the importation of foreign technology was seriously considered—first in 1961-1963 and again in 1971-1974.

While Britain succeeded in completing and starting the world's first commercial reactor at Calder Hall in October 1956, by the early 1960s the ensuing technological and financial difficulties of the British nuclear program prompted the United Kingdom Atomic Energy Authority (UKAEA) to consider importing a foreign reactor technology.

As a result, AECL engaged the UKAEA in negotiations throughout 1963. By late October, the two parties had concluded a UK-Canada Nuclear Power Agreement. But instead of a reactor sale, AECL sold the CANDU technical information to the British for $750,000.

The second period of anticipation for AECL was even less fruitful. By the early 1970s, the Canadian program was anxiously looking for exports. Some officials stated that Britain was considering 18 CANDU reactors. But the British decision to pursue the Steam Generated Heavy Water Reactor (SGHWR) quelled AECL's reactor export plans. AECL, trying to reap some profit or an opening into the British market, worked to negotiate another technology exchange and supply of heavy water for the British reactors. Two years after the 1975 agreement, the UKAEA shelved active work on the SGHWR project and committed itself to two more AGRs. While the Three Mile Island disaster tended to raise questions about the safety of American light water reactors (LWR) and thus encourage CANDU exporters, the prospects of a sale have been negligible. Even the Canadian Department of Energy, Mines, and Resources concluded, in 1980, that should Britain order any new reactors (they have not for 13 years), they will be light water reactors.[1]

United States

While AECL had glimmers of for hope in possible sales to the UK, similar possibilities never occurred with the USA. Instead, the connections between the two countries have included uranium, heavy water (Canada purchased it from an American-owned plant in British Columbia), plutonium, and information flows. It appears that the CANDU technology has not been sold to the Americans, although it may have been provided free of charge. It is not surprising that AECL was incapable of penetrating the American market, which was well supplied with its own corporations involved in reactor production. In fact, American light water reactors (LWR) have dominated the global reactor market. As of June 1977, LWRs accounted for 90.4 percent of the Western world's reactors that were operating or under construction. The remaining 9.6 percent included the British and French gas-graphite design, the British SGHWR, and the CANDU.

Thus Canadian officials found the American market impossible to break into with reactor sales or technology exports. Since the early 1980s, however, the Canadian nuclear industry considered the possibility of building CANDUs on the Canadian side of the Canada-USA border in order to supply power to northeastern American states and to give Canadian reactor contractors some business. This plan appeared as a drastic attempt to resuscitate the Canadian nuclear program.[2]

France

Atomic Energy of Canada Limited's close contact with the Commissariat a l'Energie Atomique (CEA) did not increase the chance of a reactor sale. The French based their system on LWRs and were inclined to move toward the fast breeder reactors—not the CANDU. Two notable agreements between France and Canada, however, were concluded in 1968. The first, signed in October 1968 by AECL and CEA officials, was a technology transfer. Due to the secrecy surrounding the agreement's contents, the new Trudeau government was criticized in the House of Commons. Members of Parliament questioned why Canada was selling its technology for a rumoured $1 million when the Government was spending $68 million on research in 1968 and had spent $1 billion on nuclear research in the last 20 years. It was obvious that technology transfers were insufficient to support the industry, but the Canadian government appeared willing to take what was available.

The second AECL-CEA agreement was somewhat more lucrative, as it relieved the Canadian coporation of some of its nuclear waste for a profit. Concluded in 1968, it allowed for the sale of irradiated fuel bundles from the NPD and Douglas Point reactors. The 120 to 160 kgs of plutonium contained in these rods—enough for 15 to 20 nuclear bombs—were shipped to a reprocessing plant at Mol, Belgium. The transport of the radioactive material continued from August 1969 to May 1972, with an estimated value to AECL of $1.5 million.[3]

Japan

Canadian hopes were raised in September 1971 when AECL and the Power Reactor and Nuclear Fuel Development Corporation (PNC) of Japan concluded a five-year agreement allowing for a technology transfer. Japan was interested in the CANDU-BLW, a pressure tube reactor moderated with heavy water and cooled with boiling light water. The performance of the CANDU-BLW at Gentilly, however, would explain decreased Japanese interest.

A second chance arose in 1976 when the Electric Power Development Company (EPDC) expressed interest in introducing the CANDU in Japan. The EPDC and other developmentoriented companies investigate new generating technology. EPDC and AECL soon signed a $1.7-million contract for a more comprehensive study. AECL stated that they "hoped to produce a conceptual plant design which whould enable EPDC to obtain the permission of the Japanese regulatory authority to commit a CANDU project in Japan in about 1981."

Two factors precluded additional AECL involvement in the Japanese market. The first relates to the nature of the Japanese nuclear establishment. While EPDC examined the various reactor types, it was the nine major regional utilities that selected the specific reactor. The utilities "are strongly associated with one of three Japanese suppliers (which)...in turn license their systems from either Westinghouse or General Electric." Thus it was American control of the Japanese market which precluded the introduction of the CANDU reactor. A second factor dashed AECL's hopes of the Japanese reactor sale. Canadian officials had hoped that Japan would introduce the CANDU as an intermediate step between the light water reactor and the fast breeder. In August 1979, however, the Japanese Atomic Energy Commission announced its support for the advanced thermal reactor.[4]

Australia

Canada's nuclear association with Australia was formalized in an August 4, 1959, international agreement on atomic cooperation. But it was not until the late 1960s that Australia seriously considered purchasing a nuclear power reactor. There was a flurry of international activity when the Australian Atomic Energy Commission (AAEC) requested that proposals be received by June 15, 1970, for the proposed 500-MWe nuclear power reactor at Jervis Bay, 140 miles south of Sydney. The estimated $70-million contract received bids from nine firms. AECL succeeded in making it to the final selection round with three other bidders: Nuclear Power Group Ltd. (UK), Kraftwerk Union (FDR), and Westinghouse Electric International Corp. (USA). But Canada's hopes ended when the Australians cancelled their plans, citing an unwillingness to undertake the expense. While Canada and the rest of the nuclear suppliers kept struggling for an opening into the Australian market, the AAEC appeared content with two research reactors and development of Australia's uranium resources for export.[5]

Greece

After Canadian General Electric decided, in 1968, to withdraw from the design and production of nuclear reactors, Greece was one of the first countries to which AECL directed its marketing efforts. The Canadian corporation wanted to receive the Greek contract, estimated at $75 million. But AECL's preliminary bid, issued in 1969, was rejected when the Greek officials chose a British steam-generating heavy water reactor.

Canadian officials stated they were upset and surprised by the realities of the international market. They felt their chances were good in that Greece and Canada had negotiated the initial financing and that the Canadian offer was backed by the Canadian Exports Credits Insurance Corporation. But the Canadian bid did not match the British offer. The UK contracted to purchase 40,000 tons of Greek tobacco worth $65 million over a twelve-year period. In return, the Greeks would buy a 450-MWe reactor. There was also some speculation that a UK-Greece arms deal was negotiated at the same time as the reactor contract. *The Financial Post* stated that since it was known in Ottawa that the American bid was rejected due to America's refusal to sell arms to the Greek government, it was assumed that Britain had agreed to the arms sale.[6]

Italy

The Canadian nuclear industry has been trying to enter the Italian market since the late 1960s. The first contract, signed in 1970, allowed for a technology transfer of CANDU heavy water and boiling light water reactor technology. The five-year agreement was signed with the Comitato Nazionale per l'Energia Nucleare (CNEN), the Italian research and development commission, and the Ente Nazionale per l'Energia Elettrica (ENEL), the national electric agency. The amount paid for the technology transfer by the CNEN and the ENEL was kept secret. One could speculate that it was a gift intended to increase the possibility of a reactor contract.

Frustrated with only a technology transfer, the Canadian nuclear industry tried two marketing strategies. The first, bidding for a direct sale, was attempted between 1970-1974. To supplement this approach, AECL worked with Italimpianti in bidding on the Argentine reactor in the hope that this alliance would allow AECL to enter two markets. The AECL-Italimpianti partnership did not result in an Italian contract, as ENEL awarded the four reactor contracts to an Italian licensee of US technology.

Unable to make a direct sale, AECL adapted its strategy to accommodate the ENEL's preference for higher Italian content. Thus, in December 1976, AECL entered into a licensing agreement with Progettazione Meccaniche Nucleari (PMN). The agreement, which received Canadian Cabinet approval in late 1977, applied to the Italian domestic market and allowed PMN to export CANDU reactors. For the Italian market, AECL would provide assistance to PMN in the preparation of a reactor proposal to ENEL. Should the PMN bid be accepted, AECL would be hired as the nuclear consulting engineers, provide the design of the nuclear steam supply system, and supply the heavy water. PMN would be responsible for the design and contracting of the remainder of the nuclear plant. The AECL license was granted to PMN on the payment of a fee—the amount of which was a closely guarded secret—and the commitment to purchase at least $60 million worth of Canadian-supplied goods and services.

The second part of the agreement, PMN's right to export CANDU reactors, hinged on the prior receipt of a domestic Italian contract. Under the terms of the agreement, PMN could not export the CANDU "until five years after the first CANDU unit is committed in Italy or two years after a second unit is committed in Italy (whichever comes first)." A second stipulation required that, prior to the settlement of an export contract, PMN must have purchased at least $35 million worth of equipment and services supplied by private Canadian nuclear industries. A third stipulation stated that PMN could export only on a non-exclusive basis. Thus PMN could not market CANDU reactors in a country that already was designated as the exclusive territory for another company. At the time of the agreement, this excluded PMN from marketing in Canada.

The third stipulation also required that PMN not sell to countries that did not agree to comply with the 1974 Canadian safeguards policy (discussed in Chapter 3). The Canadian government supported the Italian licensing and argued that they had firm control of the destination of Canadian nuclear technology: unless the third party agreed to comply with Canadian safeguards, the sale would be forbidden. But the Government's assurance was false on at least two counts. First, verbal and written compliance with existing safeguards did not ensure against a contravention of the agreement—witness the Indian explosion. Second, there did not appear to be a Canadian veto backed up with some form of effective sanctions for preventing an Italian decision to sell to a third party not approved by Canada.

Yet despite Government assurances and all AECL's attempts at receiving either a direct reactor sale or a partial contract through a license, the Canadian nuclear industry was unsuccessful. Two reasons explained the failures and the slight possibility of future sales. The first reason related to the structure of the international and Italian nuclear estalishments. The international hegemony of American nuclear suppliers was reflected in the predominance of US licensees in the Italian domestic market. A brief examination of its complex structure revealed the small role played by the Canadian licensee.

PMN was part of a state industrial group controlled by IRI Finmeccanica. The Finmeccanica group was comprised of AMN-Impianti Termicie Nucleari of Genoa, an engineering company that specialized in the design and supply of boiling light water (BLW) reactors; Ansaldo Societa Elettromeccanica of Genoa, responsible for the group's manufacturing activities in the thermo-electromechanical field; Breda Termomeccanica of Milan, which supplied BLW heavy components such as pressure vessels and steam generators for the Italian market and export to the USA; Italimpianti of Genoa, an engineering company with which AECL established a partnership for the marketing of the Argentine Cordoba reactor and the construction of the non-nuclear half of the plant; and finally Progettazione Meccaniche Nucleari (PMN). Thus PMN was only one part of a large conglomerate supplying a variety of reactor types. Furthermore, the Finmeccanica group competed with other industrial groups: first, the Elettronucleare Italiana Consortium, which was made up of Breda Termomeccania, Fiat, Franco Tosi, and Ercole Marelli; and second, the Societa per Imprese Nucleari, which was comprised of FBM Construzioni Meccaniche (Milan), SNIA Viscosa (Milan), Tecnomasio Italiano Brown Boveri (Milan), Babcox and Wilcox (New York), and Stone & Webster Engineering (Boston). The preponderance of the American light water reactor producing corporations and Italian licensees thus was a major factor that precluded AECL's receipt of the four reactor contracts awarded in the early 1970s.

The small foothold of the Canadian licensee was aggravated by the second reason for the absence of a Canadian sale—the status of the Western and Italian economies. The tightening of the Western, and specifically the Italian, financial market in the late 1970s explained why PMN failed to receive the reactor contracts in Sardinia even though the bids were unopposed. As of August 1982, Italy was one of the most heavily indebted European nations, with $46.5 billion owed to Western banks. It was exceedingly difficult for Italy to generate capital on the international market due to the liquidation of its largest private banking group, the Banco Ambrosiano of Milan. Furthermore, the ENEL had an extremely difficult time borrowing money. The state electric company tried to raise $40 million on the West German bond market. But with the international banking community's insistence on a higher than normal interest rate for ENEL, the Bank of Italy advised ENEL not to complete the deal. Unless there was a considerable improvement in the Italian economic situation, the country would remain unable to embark upon its program of eight reactors. If the market improved, however, Italy would finance the first four reactors that it had already awarded to an American licensee. This would then leave AECL in a market dominated by American LWRs should Italy decide upon further reactors. PMN's receipt of a reactor contract, therefore, appeared very unlikely.[7]

Footnotes

1. Canada, House of Commons, *Debates*, 1st Session, 26th Parliament, 1963, p. 3856. *Debates*, 2nd Session, 29th Parliament, 1974, pp. 8, 86; *Debates*, 1st Session, 30th Parliament, 1974-76, p. 2450; Canada, Department of Energy, Mines, and Resources, *Nuclear Policy Review* Background Papers, Report No. ER81-2E, 1980, p. 267.
2. Irvin C. Bupp, Jean-Claude Derian, *The Failed Promise of Nuclear Power: The Story of Light Water* (New York: Basic Books, Inc., Pub., 1981), p. 9. Bupp and Derian offer an excellent introduction to the export of American LWRs; Canada, Department of Energy, Mines, and Resources, *Nuclear Industry Review: Problems and Prospects 1981-2000*, Ottawa 1982, pp. 45-48. A similar notion existed in 1972. The plan involved a U.S. reactor company building a $2 billion 12,000-MWe plant

in Nova Scotia and exporting the power to the U.S.A. *Debates*, 4th Session, 25th Parliament, pp. 3023-4.

3. *Debates*, 1st Session, 28th Parliament, 1968-69, pp. 1214, 2140-1; AECL, *Annual Report: 1968-69*, p. 30; *Debates*, 4th Session, 28th Parliament, 1972, p. 8142.

4. AECL, *Annual Report: 1971-72*, p. 38; AECL, *Annual Report: 1977-78*, p. 15; EMR, *Nuclear Policy Review*, p. 267.

5. *The Financial Post*, August 8, 1959, p. 13; *The Financial Post*, July 30, 1960, p. 1, *Debates*, 3rd Session, 28th Parliament, 1970-72, p. 3917; *India Quarterly*, Vol. 25, No. 4 October-December 1969, pp. 374-384; *The Financial Post*, June 20, 1970, p. 38; *The Financial Post*, September 12, 1970, p. 8; *Bulletin of Atomic Scientists*, April 1979, Vol. 35, No. 4, pp. 40-44.

6. *The Financial Post*, May 10, 1969, p. 1; *Debates*, 1st Session, 28th Parliament, 1968-69, p. 8520; *Debates*, 2nd Session, 28th Parliament, 1969-70, p. 1141.

7. *The Globe and Mail*, November 30, 1976, p. 32; CHEN-FIEN-ENEL 20th Nuclear Congress of Rome, *The Nuclear Power Industry in Italy*, March 20-21, 1975, Rome, pp. 3-9; *Energy Analects*, November 3, 1978, p. 3; *The Globe and Mail*, August 10, 1982, p. 37; *The Globe and Mail*, August 14, 1982, p. 34. For more information on the Italian program and Canadian marketing attempts, see: *International Canada*, October 1978, Vol. 9, No. 10, p. 220 and July - August 1975, Vol. 6, Nos. 7 and 8, p. 213; *Foreign Trade*, June 21, 1969, Vol. 131, Nos. 4 and 5, pp. 25-26; *Atom*, June 1979, No. 272, p. 157.

APPENDIX III: "ATOMS FOR PEACE" AND THE INTERNATIONAL ATOMIC ENERGY AGENCY

While Eisenhower's "Atoms for Peace" program immediately launched the global expansion of the American nuclear industry, it was many years before the nominal non-proliferation aspects—mainly the creation of an international authority for regulating the expansion—were implemented. Eisenhower made his bold speech to the United Nations General Assembly in December 1953, but it was not until October 20, 1956, that the Statute of the International Atomic Energy Agency was ready for signing, 1959 that draft regulations were discussed, 1961 that the Agency's first safeguards document, "The Agency's Safeguard System (1961)," was created, 1964 that the safeguards included power reactors over 100 MW(th), and September 1965 that a working safeguards system was established. This policy of promotion before control has typified American strategy since the creation of the Baruch Plan in 1946. [1]

Promotion, as compared to the regulation of atomic energy, was more in the American interest and thus was easily and quickly achieved. The first major move was the passage of the 1954 United States Atomic Energy Act (USAEA). This cancelled the secrecy that had existed since the 1946 McMahon Act. It had served the important function of precluding the dissemination of technical nuclear information until the United States had secured its leadership in the power reactor field. While the McMahon Act was unable to thwart rival nuclear programs completely, particularly in Britain and Canada, its replacement with the Atomic Energy Act of 1954 was greeted with great enthusiasm by American "industrial allies and rivals of the 'First World.'"[2] The reasons for the support were obvious. The 1954 act opened the flow of American information, offered legitimacy to all domestic nuclear programs, and promised future export markets. To aid American and foreign nuclear programs, the USAEA authorized massive development of the "peaceful" program, bilateral agreements for peaceful purposes, private ownership of major nuclear facilities and special fissionable material (under license, though this requirement was revoked in 1964), and international activities of private enterprise if they operated under bilateral state agreements and the recipients promised to develop only "peaceful" nuclear industries. [3] The act thus inaugurated the horizontal proliferation of nuclear research and power programs and the overhang proliferation of nuclear weapon capability.

It can be argued that the "Atoms for Peace" program, while implying an American interest in an international control (but encouraging nuclear exports in the interim period until the IAEA was created), also served an important military function. It hid from prominent view a very aggressive American escalation of the arms race in the mid-1950s. In a review of American nuclear arms policy that demystifies the jargon of the military strategists, Robert Aldridge argues that the Americans were trying to achieve "counterforce" capability long before the Soviet Union. In *The Counterforce Syndrome*, Aldridge states that counterforce has, by definition, offensive connotations.

> It means that nuclear missiles are aimed at strategic military targets in the Soviet Union such as command and communication centres. Since these targets are 'hard'—deeply entrenched and coated with thick concrete—a high explosive force is desirable and precision is mandatory. These are the targets of a disabling nuclear strike.

Aldridge contends that the pursuit of counterforce capability is only explainable as a desire to launch a first strike attack against the Soviet Union. Of utmost importance, however, is Aldridge's statement that "counterforce has been the Pentagon's clandestine military doctrine since at least the 1950s."[4]

While one might argue that the Americans' quantitative and qualitative escalation of the arms race was simply coincidental with the delay in the creation of an effective IAEA, two occurrences disprove the contention. The first was the American opposition to a negotiated general and complete disarmament (GCD). The Soviets, in September 1954, had accepted a British and French proposal that had combined the Western preference for control measures with the Soviet desire for prohibiting the manufacture of nuclear weapons. A Cambridge University disarmament seminar has described this point as the second and last time since 1945 that a GCD was possible. The chance of this occurring, however, was frustrated "primarily as a result of the hardening of the American position at Geneva" in August 1955. The American proposal involved only control measures and did not include the prohibition of nuclear bomb production.

A second factor implicating a military purpose to "Atoms for Peace" relates to the role of C.D. Jackson. He was a key figure in propagating the slogans "atoms for peace" and "a bigger-bang-for-the-buck." The latter was used to justify to the American taxpayer the Pentagon's primary dependence upon nuclear weapons. Albert Wohlstetter, who had served as a consultant to the US Department of Defense, the State Department, the Arms Control and Disarmament Agency, and was a Rand Corporation staff member from 1953 to 1962, has described C.D. Jackson as Eisenhower's "advisor on psychological warfare."[5]

Eisenhower's speech was thus part of a very complex process. The "Atoms for Peace" program rhetorically appealed to a concern for international control in order to launch the American nuclear power program which, independently, was of great political and corporate importance but it also obfuscated the US military escalation. When, in 1954-55, the international situation appeared to be forcing a restriction on American arms escalation, "Atoms for Peace" was there to divert domestic attention to the "benevolent civilian atom." The nuclear power industry was fundamental in hiding the military applications and provided an expanded market for the reactor-producing private corporations—Westinghouse and General Electric, the two most notable. This function has been maintained to the present day. Not until the power program had become an entrenched industry on a global scale was it possible to slowly increase the international control mechanisms.

Until then, the 1956 IAEA Statute clearly had established the Agency's priorities. Not surprising was the prevalence of the American preference of promotion over control. Article I announced the Agency's intention "to accelerate and enlarge the contribution of atomic energy to peace, health and prosperity throughout the world." It was Article II, however, that required the Agency to "ensure, so far as it is able, that assistance provided by or at its request or under its supervision or control is not used in such a way as to further any military purpose." The clause "so far as it is able" was limited in three ways. First, the establishment of the safeguards system was delayed nearly twelve years, until September 1965; second, the largest portion of the IAEA budget was consistently allocated to promotional activities such as information, reports, technical assistance, and the encouragement of nuclear power, particularly in underdeveloped countries; and third, the safeguards system included a series of built-in structural limitations. The impact of the first two points was clear. Delaying the safeguard system allowed some reactors, such as CIRUS, to be exempted from international control. And the IAEA regulators were placed in a constant and losing competition with IAEA promoters. But the impact of the third factor was less obvious. Thus the following discussion focusses on the IAEA's structural limitations to reveal the Agency's inadequacy as a mechanism for halting the proliferation of nuclear weapons.[6]

To block the acquisition of atomic bombs, the Statute of the International Atomic Agency foresaw the need for four functions: information gathering, design approval, deposition, and the imposition of sanctions. By reviewing these functions and the manner in which they were, or were not, implemented, one can better understand the Agency's faults. It is important to remember that while the following discusses the Agency's nuclear weapon non-proliferation work, the majority of the IAEA's annual budget was spent on the promotion of nuclear power technology.

I. Information Gathering

The Agency's main non-proliferation function involved gathering information on the increasing number of nuclear facilities. There were, however, two important restric-tions. The Agency's safeguards were not required for every facility nor was the Agency responsible for safeguarding unreported materials. Paul Szasz calls this the IAEA's "most severe limitation." Szasz states that a country could have an unregistered source of nuclear material, such as a uranium mine, which could be used in a clandestine production facility. Unfortunately, he diminishes the relevance of this point by stating that special inspection rights may be demanded which, while not impossible, are unlikely due to the built-in disincentives in the IAEA system. This dependence upon voluntary compliance was prevalent throughout most of the IAEA's safeguards. [7]

Material accountancy

The Agency's information gathering function was based on three principles: material accountancy, containment, and inspections. Material accountancy has been the most heavily relied upon method. The Agency works to achieve this task and maintain a relatively small budget by depending upon the national organizations to record the inflow and outflow of material in the various parts, or material balance areas, of the power reactor or nuclear facility. The national organization was required to maintain the records and from these compile the reports which were to be submitted to the IAEA for review. The types and frequency of reports submitted vary from the regular reports, which may be submitted on a basis varying from monthly to annual, to the special reports which must be submitted without delay if the Agency harbours any serious suspicions of diversion or finds an inconsistency in the regular reports submitted.

Containment

The containment principle has changed dramatically from when the IAEA was first conceived. Containment was to have involved the actual IAEA ownership and control of nuclear materials and supplies. This appears to have been a result of the American desire for a monopolistic agency exercising wide powers of control as envisaged in the Baruch Plan. The Soviets opposed this on the basis of their previous experiences with other international organizations, such as the United Nations Security Council, where the Americans quickly achieved domination. The containment concept, as originally planned, has periodically arisen with the notion of international or regional reactor or fuel parks that would be spaced around the globe for regional use but under IAEA control. Aside from the apparent ecological and economic problems, particularly of transporting the material or power to the required areas, the international fuel or power centres have been opposed primarily due to private and competitive reasons. While the Europeans have moved in this direction and cooperated on a number of major projects, the Americans have remained hesitant. One could anticipate, however, that should the worldwide nuclear industries maintain their low economic viability while public opposition increases, the Americans may favor the original containment concept to decrease costs and legitimize the activity.

For these reasons, the containment principle has yet to be implemented as originally planned. Instead, the containment issue changed from ownership or control of the materials, which would imply physical security—a responsibility the Agency has objected to for financial reasons—to a form of aiding the task of material accountancy. The Agency's inspectors record a certain type and amount of nuclear material prior to its enclosure in a large container which was affixed with an Agency seal. The process required the presence of an inspector if the seal was to be broken. Thus containment obviously has decreased in importance as a method of preventing nuclear proliferation.

Inspections

The Agency gathered information through four types of inspections: ad hoc, routine, special, and additional. Ad hoc inspections were carried out primarily at the onset of the safeguards to determine the accuracy of the reports initially submitted. This form of ad hoc inspection required at least one week's notice and included only those locations where the reports and the inspection indicated the presence of nuclear material. A second type of ad hoc inspection may occur in the exporting and receiving countries engaged in a nuclear transfer. Only twenty-four hours' notice was required, and the area of inspection was limited to that specified in the notification of transfer previously sent to the IAEA.

Routine inspections were used to verify the accuracy of a state's reports from its records, to verify record accuracy, and to obtain information on suspected possible causes of material unaccounted for (MUF). The Agency established formulae which specified the maximum number of inspectors involved in, and the frequency and duration of, inspections for specific types of nuclear material or facilities. These inspections had three warning time periods. The first required a twenty-four hour notice for plutonium or uranium enriched to at least 5 percent. The second required at least a one-week warning for all other nuclear material. The third type was a surprise inspection. During this form, the inspector had access to all the required records. The surprise inspections, however, limited the inspector's freedom of access to crucial points identified in the Agency's Subsidiary Agreement. As well, surprise inspections allowed that the "state should be informed of the projected general pattern of announced and unannounced inspections."

The third type was special inspections. These inspections were used to verify the information contained in the special reports submitted to the Agency after an unusual incident or accident. But even these inspections were compromised by the necessity of prior state consultation whereby the time and scope of access were determined.

The fourth and final type was additional inspections. This type of inspection was considered extraordinary in that it was based on the Agency's conclusion that the information provided by the state was incomplete and incapacitated the Agency's approval of no diverson. However, once again, these inspections were limited, as state consultation was required to conduct the inspection and approve any additional locations for inspection.

It is apparent that the IAEA inspections were not overly stringent. Possibly the most serious inspection was the surprise inspection. Yet even this required that the inspection be limited to specific previously agreed-upon areas, and the country was to be informed of the general pattern of surprise routine inspections. Insufficient as the structural organization of inspection types may appear, the process was aggravated when one considers the inspectors.

The Agency assigned inspectors that would be acceptable to the state under inspection, to decrease the hostility to inspection. However, due to the limited number of inspectors—there were only forty-five in 1971—and the large number of reactors in a variety of countries with many different languages, there was bound to develop a fraternity of sorts between the inspectors and the national technicians and scientists. While one could argue that such professional intimacy precluded diversion or at least enabled the inspector to detect an uneasiness among the staff and thus suspect diversion, one can argue the opposite and say that the inspectors would be open to bribery. While this is not intended as a slur on IAEA inspectors, one must recognize that such an event is not impossible. There have been allegations of bribery within the Canadian nuclear program, and one cannot conclude that the situation would differ radically at the international level.[8]

It was the inspection aspect of the Agency's information gathering function that received the most publicity. From the IAEA's viewpoint, it was the threat of inspection that supposedly served to ensure that each state was correct and truthful in its recording responsibilities and in the reports it submitted. For the nuclear suppliers, the employment of inspectors was advertised to the domestic populations as a guarantee that the nuclear exports were safe from diversion to nuclear weapon production. But it is important to realize five points. First, inspections were very restricted. Second, they were not very thorough or frequent if the Agency had no suspicions. Third, inspections were secondary to material accountancy. Fourth, material accountancy was compromised, as it was only one of the original IAEA non-proliferation functions. And fifth, non-proliferation strategies received a smaller portion of the Agency's budget than the promotional aspects. Thus the threat of detection was not as serious as the Agency would have one believe.

II. Design Approval

Aside from the information gathering function, the IAEA was also entrusted with the task of design approval. This function was intended to ensure that a nuclear facility was used only for peaceful purposes. However, the IAEA soon abandoned this function due to its uselessness. One can review, for example, a 200-MWe CANDU reactor and approve it for peaceful purposes. But the Agency recognized that it was less the specific technology than the use to which it was put that was the determining factor of whether it would be confined to peaceful purposes. The design approval function was thus reduced to design review. This facilitated the Agency's monitoring and material accountancy. In this way, the Agency required the minimum amount of information and thus served to increase the maintenance of design secrets. In fact, concern over commercial secrets may have been an important reason for the diminution of the design approval function.

III. Deposition

Deposition was the third function originally foreseen for the IAEA. This would have required the IAEA to protect all fissionable material placed in its custody in geographically scattered depots. The main reason for the failure to implement this function was possibly the Agency's constant concern with keeping operating costs to a minimum. One cannot argue, for example, that it was national self-interest which destroyed this function for, as it was originally planned, the state was to deposit only fissionable material that was in excess of its immediate needs.

IV. Imposition of Sanctions

The Agency's fourth function was the imposition of sanctions. While arguably the most important IAEA function, it is apparent that the built-in bureaucratic tendencies of aiming for cost effectiveness and promotion over regulation served to diminish the potential usefulness of this function. To understand how this function would be implemented, one must examine briefly the system as a whole.

The IAEA safeguards were intended to permit the timely detection of diversions. This system was based on the hope that the threat of detection would serve to inhibit potential divertors. There are serious concerns, however, that the Agency's emphasis on promotion impeded its limited regulatory function. Even the USA has seen the necessity to divide the USAEC into the regulatory NRC and the promo-tional Department of Energy (DOE). Nevertheless, the IAEA continued to subordinate its regulatory function to the needs of the promotion of nuclear power. In a sense, this outcome was understandable in that the USA was the Agency's largest financial contributor. Also, from the Agency's perspective, it was functional for the perpetuation and expansion of its existence to increase the use of nuclear power. Unfortunately, this reversed emphasis often served to limit the regulatory staff's ability to fulfill its function of timely detection; IAEA reporting was often six months behind schedule. To alleviate this situation, the Agency implemented a higher threshold to decrease the number of false alarms which, in turn, decreased annual expenses.

Impediments also existed if diversion was suspected. The normal route was to negotiate a special routine or additional inspection with the state suspected of diversions. Thus one must add to the six-month accounting lag at best a week for establishing the inspection criteria and implementation. Assuming therefore that the suspicion was confirmed on the first inspection and did not require subsequent negotiations and inspection to verify the diversion, a report is compiled and submitted to the IAEA board of governors. The board, which incidentally was comprised of representatives from almost all the world's significant uranium producers, was not in permanent session. Instead, the board was convened for two major sessions a year and two minor sessions before and after the IAEA's annual General Conference. While the member states have the technical authority to convene the board on seventy-two hours' notice, it appears that this right was not exercised excessively.

After investigation, the board could submit its report to the United Nations General Assembly and inform the UN of the possible sanctions to be imposed. These could range from a request to return any nuclear material made available to the recipient country to a call for a nuclear embargo. It is apparent that the former sanction would require the unlikely compliance of the diverting country while the latter would be effective only if the country were dependent upon foreign assistance. The Agency appeared to console itself with the technical possibility that the General Assembly could call for a UN military intervention—a most unlikely event.[9]

Summary

It is apparent that the IAEA Safeguards System was encumbered with a number of serious limitations. The two most important were: the priority of promotion over regulation which served to limit the Agency's ability to fulfill its limited non-proliferation obligations effectively; second, assuming that diversion was detected—by timely means or not—there existed a series of bureacratic impediments which decreased the probability of applying the Agency's limited sanctions. It was for these reasons that, while the Agency found many suspicious indications of diversion, it has never taken any action. Or when the Agency detected diversion of quantities too small for a bomb, it chose not to even inform the supplying countries—thus ignoring the long-term cumulative effects of diversion. It was with these matters in mind that Amory and L. Hunter Lovins succinctly asked:

> If an alert, incorruptible, omnipresent inspector instantly detected a big, blatant diversion and succeeded in getting the news instantly from his field post to the Inspector-General, thence to the Director-General and the Board of Governors, thence to the Security Council (subject to veto)—would the exhaustive re-examinations on which they would all doubtlessly insist even have been officially notified in all the UN languages before a bomb went off?[10]

Footnotes

1. Bernhard G. Bechheofer, "Historical Evolution of Internationl Safeguards," Mason Willrich, ed., *International Safeguards and Nuclear Industry*, pp. 21-44; Gwyn Prins, ed., *Defended To Death*, p. 71.
2. The phrase is used by Noam Chomsky, *Towards a New Cold War: Essays on the Current Crisis and How We Got There* (New York: Pantheon Books, 1982) p. 15. It clearly delineates the general unity in opposing Communism but does not ignore the inter-capitalist rivalries.
3. Bernard Bechhoefer, "Historical Evolution of International Safguards." p. 25.
4. Robert C. Aldridge, *The Counterforce Syndrome: A Guide to U.S. Nuclear Weapons and Strategic Doctrine* (Washington: Institute for Policy Studies, 1981), pp. 4,7.

5. Gwyn Prins, ed., *Defended to Death*, P. 78; Wohlstetter, *et al.*, "The Military Potential of Civilian Nuclear Energy," p. 451; Albert Wohlstetter, Victor Gilinsky, Robert Gillette, Roberta Wohlstetter; *Nuclear Policies: Fuel without the Bomb* (Cambridge, Mass.: Ballinger Publishers, 1978). p. 106.

6. C.F. Barnaby, *Preventing the Spread of Nuclear Weapons*, Pugwash Monograph I (London: Souvenir Press, 1969), p. 313; Benjamin Sanders, *Safeguards against Nuclear Proliferation*, A SIPRI Monograph (Stockholm: Almqvist & Wiksell International, 1975), p. 4; and Wohlstetter, *et al.*, "The Military Potential of Civilian Nuclear Energy," p. 438. It appears that the creation of the IAEA also served to internationalize the cost of regulating what have been predominantly American nuclear exports. It seems that financing the IAEA safeguards is based roughly on domestic capacity. Paul C. Szasz ("International Atomic Energy Safeguards," Mason Willrich, ed., *International Safeguards and Nuclear Industry*, P. 128) states that in 1972 the US paid approximately 31.5%. But data revealed by the Stockholm International Peace Research Institute (SIPRI) shows that in 1974, the US domestic market alone comprised 35.3% of the world's installed nuclear capacity (see Frank Barnaby, SIPRI Director, *The Nuclear Age*, p. 44). Furthermore, on June 30, 1981, 86.17% of the world's 535 power reactors (30 MWe and over) that were operable, under construction, or on order were in the Western bloc, the exceptions being the anticipated Canadian sale to Romania and Westinghouse sale to Yugoslavia (*Nuclear News*, August 1981, pp. 85-104). And, of the Western total, in June 1977, American-derived light water technology accounted for 90.4% of the Western world's reactors that were operating or under construction. (Irwin C. Bupp and Jean-Claude Derian, *The Failed Promise of Nuclear Power: The Story of Light Water*, New York: Basic Books, Inc., Pub., 1981, p. 9). Thus one can conclude that the US does not directly finance the safeguarding of the reactors it has exported, and it has profited from the internationalization of nuclear safeguards.

7. Paul C. Szasz, "International Atomic Energy Safeguards," Mason Williams, ed., *International Safeguards and Nuclear Industry*, p. 95. Szasz has produced an excellent descriptive article on the international safeguards system. However, it appears that Szasz's article is lacking the criticism necessary to view the system as it actually exists.

8. Ibid., pp. 87-88, 97-101, 103, 105, 126, 107-107. Szasz recognizes the debates over IAEA inspectors but considers only the advantages. He states that "over the years, an inspector is likely to become well acquainted with a substantial number of members of the relevant scientific community in a state to which he is assigned, and he may be able to suspect significant clandestine activity merely by observing the movements of his acquaintances. Moreover, no state can rely on all its scientists and technicians being uniformly discreet, content and loyal solely to national objectives; if an inspector's ear is available it may hear tales." While Szasz is correct on this point, he fails to recognize that the Agency cannot rely on all its scientists, technicians and inspectors being uniformly discreet, content and loyal solely to international objectives.

9. Ibid., pp. 99, 88; Lawrence Scheinman, "The Nuclear Safeguards Problems," D. F. Ford, T. C. Hollocher, H. W. Kendall, J. J. MacKenzie, L. Scheinman, and A. S. Schurgin, *The Nuclear Fuel Cycle: A Survey of Public Health, Environmental and National Security Effects of Nuclear Power* (Cambridge, Mass: Friends of the Earth for the Union of Concerned Scientists, 1974), p. 58; Victor Gilinsky, "Diversion by National Governments," Mason Willrich, ed., *International Safeguards*

and Nuclear Industry, pp. 173-174; Paul C. Szasz, "International Atomic Energy Safeguards," pp. 108, 116, 121.

10. Amory B. Lovins, J. Hunter Lovins, Leonard Ross, "Nuclear Power and Nuclear Bombs," *Foreign Affairs*, Vol. 58, Summer 1980, pp. 1145-1146; Amory B. Lovins, L. Hunter Lovins, *Energy/War Breaking the Nuclear Link* (New York: Harper Colophon Books, 1981), p. 32.

APPENDIX IV: THE LIMITATIONS OF THE TREATY FOR THE NON-PROLIFERATION OF NUCLEAR WEAPONS (NPT)

During the 1960s, the world's nuclear suppliers slowly realized that the IAEA had to be supplemented with a more stringent set of controls to limit the horizontal proliferation of nuclear weapons. Among others, three reasons were most obvious: the IAEA safeguards system had many loopholes; within this system, compliance was voluntary and specific to each facility rather than applicable to a country's total nuclear program; and, by 1965, the "nuclear club" had increased to five members. The nuclear suppliers—which were predominantly from Western countries—recognized it to be in their interests to increase the scope of the international safeguards system. This would protect their perceived state interests and legitimize further the export of technology, material, and supplies. The result was the Treaty for the Non-Proliferation of Nuclear Weapons (NPT), which was opened for signature on July 1, 1968, and, after the required number of signatories, entered into force on March 5, 1970.

The NPT was an eleven-article treaty to which 106 countries were ratified parties as of March 1979. In many ways it was a considerable improvement over the original IAEA. But as discussed below, the Treaty's six major articles ensured its ineffectiveness as a means of stopping any of the four forms of nuclear weapon proliferation. As a Cambridge University disarmament seminar concluded, the NPT was "self-defeating in its own drafting."[1]

Articles I and II were inextricably linked. They compelled the nuclear weapon states (NWS) and non-nuclear weapon states (NNWS), respectively, not to transfer/receive "nuclear weapons or other nuclear explosive devices directly or indirectly." The NWS were not to encourage or induce NNWS to manufacture or acquire nuclear weapons or other nuclear explosive devices. Conversely, NNWS were not to seek or receive such assistance. Explicit in the first two articles was the creation of a two class world system in an attempt to perpetuate the status quo. The world was divided into one group comprised of the five nuclear powers—USA, USSR, UK, France and China—and a second group which included all the remaining countries. While some might argue that this was a positive beginning to halting nuclear proliferation, the following articles revealed the mistaken assumptions upon which the two articles were predicated.

Article III, a blatant attempt to ensure that the first two articles were fulfilled, was a case in point. Under the Article, each non-nuclear weapon state party to the Treaty undertakes to accept safe-guards, as set forth in an agreement...with the International Atomic Energy Agency['s]...safeguard system, for the exclusive purpose of verification of the fulfillment of its obligations assumed under this Treaty with a view to preventing diversion...to nuclear weapons or other nuclear explosive devices....The safeguards required by this Article shall be applied on all source or special fissionable material in all peaceful nuclear activities within the territory of such State, under its jurisdiction, or carried out under its control anywhere.

The Article was premised on the assumption that non-nuclear weapon countries were the only location of weapons proliferation. Thus it was simply aimed at preventing horizontal proliferation and ignored, for example, the issue of vertical proliferation within the nuclear weapon states.

The second part of Article III was addressed to the nuclear suppliers and required that they not provide

(a) source or special fissionable material [this does not include uranium ore], or (b) equipment or material especially designed or prepared for the processing, use of production of special fissionable material, to any non-nuclear weapon State for peaceful purposes, unless the source or special fissionable material shall be subject to the safeguards required by this Article.

This clause was the converse of the first. However, the phrase "safeguards required by this Article" refers to "each non-nuclear weapon State party to the Treaty." Thus, while Article III restricted the importation and exportation of material and supplies to Treaty members, it was conspicuously silent on the exportation, or the limitations thereof, to states that were not party to the Treaty. The nuclear suppliers thus remained free to pursue their commercial and political objectives in continuing nuclear exports while the non-nuclear weapon states party to the Treaty were scrutinized more than those states not party to the Treaty. Thus the NPT had a built-in disincentive for signing the Treaty.

The first clause of Article IV entrenched the standard IAEA practice whereby

Nothing in this Treaty shall be interpreted as affecting the inalienable right of all the Parties to the Treaty to develop research, production and use of nuclear energy for peaceful purposes without discrimination and in conformity with Articles I and II of this Treaty.

Thus promotion of nuclear power was of greater importance than the prevention of nuclear weapons proliferation. This part of Article IV has since been used to legitimize nuclear exports. Against growing domestic opposition to nuclear exports, Article IV is loudly proclaimed as an international obligation com-pelling the supply of nuclear technology.

202

The second clause of Article IV entrenched the promotion over prevention intent and attempted to decrease the discrimination against non-nuclear weapon states party to the Treaty. Those

> in a position to do so shall...co-operate in contributing alone or together with other States or international organizations to the further development of the applications of nuclear energy for peaceful purposes, especially in the territories of non-nuclear weapon States party to the Treaty, with due consideration for the needs of the developing areas of the world.

To some, this clause may have invoked notions of human beings gathering together willingly and harmoniously in an attempt to solve the energy problems of developing countries and thus creating a more egalitarian world where everyone marches happily into an illuminated future. Unfortunately, such a scenario fails to account for the reality in which nuclear transfers occur. The Treaty failed to expropriate international transfers; thus the existing system remained whereby an oligarchy of national nuclear establishments sold their technology in a quasi-competitive market. Thus the second clause of Article IV did not result in any preferential treatment for NPT signatories which possibly could have been an incentive for additional Treaty members. Instead, the clause—by not stating otherwise—resulted in an equivalent commercial market system for non-nuclear weapon states regardless of whether or not they were party to the Treaty. In this sense, the only real function of this clause was to legitimize further the exports from the nuclear suppliers.

Article V of the NPT possibly was the most compromising. It stated that

> Each Party to the Treaty undertakes to take appropriate measures to ensure that, in accordance with this Treaty, under appropriate international procedures, potential benefits from any peaceful applications of nuclear explosions will be made available to non-nuclear weapon States party to the Treaty on a non-discriminatory basis and that the charges to such Parties for the explosive devices used will be as low as possible and exclude any charges for research and development.

The term "peaceful nuclear explosion" (PNE) was a mutilation of the English language for which we have Edward Teller, an American, to thank. Stated bluntly, a nuclear explosion results in massive destruction and radiation poisoning. Affixing the adjective "peaceful" has not changed the reality of the situation but was effective in evoking an incorrect assumption that were a nuclear explosion peaceful, it would in some way result in less destruction and radiation. Teller and other Americans used the concept of PNEs effectively to thwart the late 1950s opposition to nuclear testing. PNEs were advertised as useful for blowing up mountains and clearing harbours. In fact, Teller and associates at the Lawrence Livermore Laboratory in California attempted to develop a "clean" bomb, one without, or with at least considerably less, radiation. Their failure did not inhibit the entrenchment of PNE acceptability among American officials, other nuclear weapon states and, eventually, Article V of the NPT.

Article VI was a weak and ineffective attempt at redressing the imbalances created by the Treaty's division of the world into two groups and implied that vertical proliferation was of importance—though secondary. Under the Article,

> Each of the Parties to the Treaty undertakes to pursue negotiations in good faith on effective measures relating to cessation of the nuclear arms race at an early date and to nuclear disarmament, and on a treaty on general and complete disarmament under strict and effective international control.

Five points regarding the Article's content require comment. First, note that the Article used "pursue" and not "pursue and conclude." Evidently, such precise terminology would have been unacceptable to the major nuclear weapon powers.[2]

Second, the phrase "in good faith," while possibly included to compensate for the Treaty's failure to compel the nuclear weapon states to conclude a general disarmament treaty, was far from adequate. Considering the gravity of the voracious escalation of the arms race, it was a travesty that the Treaty for the Non-Proliferation of Nuclear Weapons was so feeble as to suggest only something as elusive as "good faith."

Third, the word "effective," while not delineating a concrete suggestion, was of value, as it recognized that a number of "disarmament" agreements have been concluded that did not fulfill the true meaning of the word. As a Cambridge University disarmament seminar concluded, agreements in the post-1963 period have been of two types:

> first, there have been agreements not to do things which it was unlikely that anybody would wish to do....[and second,] agreements not to do what cannot be done at the time that the agreement is made.

As an example of the first type, they cited the Sea-bed Treaty, in force since 1972, which compelled the signatories not to place nuclear weapons on the ocean floor. They repeated the Chinese criticism at the time of the Treaty's signing: the issue in demilitarizing the sea was not the sea-bed, it was the missile-carrying submarine. An example of the second type was the Outer Space Treaty, in force since 1967. The signatories pledged not to militarize space, yet are quickly violating the Treaty "under a thin 'civilian' disguise." A third category was implicit in the Cambridge group's work that "DIS-armament" treaties should fulfill the literal definition of the term and not simply limit or regulate an otherwise unlimited arms race. There were two prime examples: the 1963 Partial Test Ban Treaty (PTBT) allowed under-ground explosions and enabled a situation where 60 percent of the nuclear explosions since 1945 have occurred after the signing of the PTBT; and the SALT agreements committed neither the USA nor the USSR "to surrender any weapon that it really wished to keep."

But there were additional problems with the NPT's recognition that the world required "effective measures relating to the cessation of the nuclear arms race." The Treaty failed to specify when its members were to begin pursuing in good faith the effective yet unspecified negotiations relating to nuclear disarmament. And finally, the Article included no reference to the imposition of sanctions should the disarmament negotiations fail to occur.[3]

Remembering that the NPT was drafted by primarily the nuclear weapon states makes its obvious loopholes more understandable. To prevent the potential disruption of the anarchy which prevailed in the international nuclear market, it was in the interests of the nuclear suppliers that the Treaty include the previously discussed internal contradictions and discriminatory assumptions between the nuclear weapon states and the non-nuclear weapon states, and between the NPT and non-NPT signatories within the non-nuclear group of nations. The non-mandatory nature of the NPT thus enabled those nations which perceived it to be in their national interest to not sign and ratify the NPT, to continue engaging in international nuclear transfers and use the Treaty's discriminatory assumptions to legitimize their non-compliance.

Footnotes

1. Briefly, the remaining five articles are as follows: Article VII states that the Treaty is not to impede the negotiation of nuclear free zones. Article VIII discusses the amending procedures and the need for a Review Conference in five years and subsequent conferences if the majority of the members approve. Article IX discusses the depository governments, when ratification occurs for contemporary and subsequent members, and includes the Treaty's definition of a nuclear weapon state as "one which has manufactured and exploded a nuclear weapon or other nuclear explosive device prior to 1 January, 1967." Article X lists a state's withdrawal rights after three months' notice and states that the Treaty is valid for twenty-five years after entry into force (therefore, until March 5, 1995). An NPT Conference would be held to determine—with majority approval —whether to continue indefinitely or for a fixed period or periods. Article XI lists the languages of the Treaty and states that all are authentic. For the complete text of the Treaty, see IAEA, *Internationl Treaties Relating to Nuclear Control and Disarmament*, IAEA Legal Series No. 9 (Vienna: International Atomic Energy Agency, 1975) pp. 35-40; SIPRI, *Nuclear Energy and Nuclear Weapon Proliferation* (London: Taylor and Francis Ltd., 1979), p. 366; and Gwyn Prins, ed., *Defended To Death: A Study of the Nuclear Arms Race*, A Cambridge University Disarmament Seminar. (Harmondsworth: Penguin Books, 1983), p. 125.
2. IAEA, *International Treaties*, pp. 36-38.
3. Gwyn Prins, ed., *Defended to Death*, p. 125. For a brief discussion of American violations, see Robert Aldridge, *The Counterforce Syndrome*, pp. 14-20; Gwyn Prins, ed., *Defended to Death*, pp. 124, 127; IAEA *International Treaties*, p. 38; and, for a list delineating the status of most national nuclear programs, see Frank Barnaby, *The Nuclear Age*, pp. 63-75.

APPENDIX V: THE LONDON CLUB

The increasing disillusionment among segments of the nuclear supplying countries over the limited effectiveness of the Non-Proliferation Treaty (NPT) resulted in an attempt to increase the coordination within the oligarchy of nuclear suppliers. The immediate causes for concern were the May 18, 1974, Indian nuclear explosion, the West German decision to sell a complete fuel cycle to Brazil, and the French interest in marketing reprocessing plants to Pakistan and South Korea. Thus a series of meetings began in London in 1975 and continued for more than two years. The location and secrecy of the meetings, as well as the exclusive membership requirement, resulted in the name "The London Club."

The suppliers' club originally was comprised of the USA, Canada, the UK, France, the Federal Republic of Germany, Japan, and the USSR. Slowly, it increased its membership. By June 1976, the meetings included Sweden, Belgium, the Netherlands, Italy, the German Democratic Republic, and attendence was expected for Czechoslovakia and Poland, but representatives did not attend until later. By January 1978, there were fifteen members, including Switzerland, Czechoslovakia, and Poland.

It is important to note the preponderance of Western capitalist nations represented in the London Club. The ratio of six to one and eleven to four in the original and final membership groups, respectively, was not surprising, as the West had been most responsible for the proliferation of nuclear power. Eisenhower's "Atoms for Peace" program was a great success from a narrowly defined marketing perspective.

A second important point on the Club's composition requires attention. While the London Club meetings were known for their eventual production of a set of nuclear export guidelines, it was the original seven members that concluded the agreement and then opened up the membership for less important suppliers of nuclear technology and uranium. The latter group enabled the East European representation to increase. The reasons for this strategy were obvious: first, the exclusion of the additional suppliers ensured that there would not be undue pressure for an "effective" set of guidelines; and second, by later including the membership, it served to give the appearance that the agreement was effective. It was implicit that the aid of additional suppliers would ensure the termination of horizontal weapon proliferation. In turn, this implication legitimized continued nuclear exports. As did the IAEA and the NPT, the London Club perpetuated the priority of sales before safety.

The guidelines' weaknesses were revealed in the clause "The following fundamental principles for safeguards should apply to nuclear transfers to any non-nuclear weapon state for peaceful purposes." There was no obligation whatsoever for the nuclear suppliers to comply with the London Club's guidelines. Furthermore, the guidelines actually did not involve any significant cost to the nuclear suppliers. Instead, they transferred the costs to the importing country and the already overburdened IAEA. Thus the guidelines were functional for the leading nuclear suppliers. They involved no additional cost and legitimized export sales. As well, they placed the blame for proliferation on the importing country. Nor were the guidelines backed up by enforceable rules. By examining the ten categories of guidelines, one can understand the uselessness of the agreement as a means of preventing nuclear weapon production.[1]

The first category related to the prohibition of nuclear explosives.

> Suppliers should authorize transfers of items identified in the trigger list only upon formal governmental assurances from recipients explicitly excluding uses which would result in any nuclear explosive device.

Aside from the use of "should" which resulted in no commitment to comply with the guideline, this clause was seen, by some, as a positive recognition that a peaceful nuclear explosion was in fact a bomb. Thus India had proven the obvious. But while this was an important step in repairing the misleading approach traceable to the work of Edward Teller, a governmental assurance was far from sufficient to prevent its violation.

Physical protection was the second category. Once again the nuclear suppliers did not bear additional responsibility for continued exports. For, while the guidelines advise that trigger list material "should be placed under effective physical protection," this "is the responsibility of the (recipient)...country." Furthermore, the guideline did not even suggest a universal standard of physical protection. Instead, "the levels of physical protection on which these measures have to be based should be the subject of an agreement between supplier and recipient."

The issue of safeguards was the focus of the third guideline. The original seven nuclear suppliers revealed their distaste for the NPT's insistence on full-scope safeguards when they suggested that "suppliers should transfer trigger-list items only when covered by IAEA safeguards." This reversal was aggravated, however, when it was agreed that "exceptions should be made only after consultation with the parties to the understanding." Thus the nuclear suppliers were requesting the perpetuation of the pre-1968 NPT status quo. Yet in 1968 it had been the status quo that agreed to the creation of the NPT. One could conclude that the decrease in reactor sales during the first half of the 1970s precipitated this regressive move.

The next three categories of guidelines referred to exportation of trigger-list or sensitive materials and facilities. While it was important that many of these items were mentioned, the effect of doing so was fruitless due to the absence of "effective" safeguards. The London Club's two major suggestions were briefly as follows: first, suppliers should require an IAEA safeguards agreement on all triggerlist exports; and second, the suppliers "should exercise restraint in the transfer of sensitive facilities, technology and weapons-usable material." Note that there was no mention of forbidding such exports. But, of course, such a suggestion would thwart the freedom of suppliers' exports. Third, that suppliers should urge multinational regional fuel cycle centres. The guideline, while mentioning the IAEA, did not limit such activities to one organization and thus served to potentially undermine an already weak agency. Fourth, that "suppliers should be informed if a recipient country embarks upon the production of greater than 20% enriched uranium." Once again, while important, there was no obligation for them to comply.

The seventh category referred to the controls on supplied or derived weapons grade material. It stated that

> suppliers recognized the importance...of including in agreements on supply of nuclear materials or of facilities which produce weapons-usable material, provisions calling for mutual agreement between the supplier and the recipient on arrangements for reprocessing, storage, alteration, use, transfer or retransfer of any weapons-usable material involved. Suppliers should endeavor to include such provisions whenever appropriate and practicable.

While the guideline initially may have conveyed a concern that the potentially harmful use of the supplies and material required a part in the decision-making process of the material's fate, one can also discover an implicit concern that was not so noble. It appeared possible that this guideline, if implemented, could be important to the nuclear suppliers once they expanded to a commercial basis their reprocessing and storage capabilities. Should the nuclear market expand in the manner that many nuclear suppliers foresee, it would be advantageous to have a say in the future use of the material when the same suppliers just happened to provide—for a fee—storage and reprocessing services.

The final major guideline referred to the retransfer of trigger-list items. It suggested that suppliers should supply trigger-list items only after

> the recipient of the retransfer or transfer will have provided the same assurance as those required by the supplier for the original transfer.

A second request stated that "the supplier's consent should be required" for such transfers. While an important guideline, the fact that it was not a required item for a nuclear export diminished its nominal effectiveness.

The remaining parts of the London Club's guidelines pertained primarily to promoting—but not requiring— the IAEA safeguards, the construction of equipment facilitating the application of the safeguards, and the guidelines for consultation among the suppliers. Guideline 16, however, requires additional comment. In the fifth paragraph, the nuclear suppliers stated that they "will jointly reconsider their common safeguards requirements, whenever appropriate." Whatever potential for increasing the effectiveness of the guidelines intended in this statement was thoroughly negated by paragraph 16. It stated that "unanimous consent is required for any changes in these guidelines." One need not be overly cynical to doubt the likelihood of such an occurrence. What appeared to be the intent of this very ungenerous—but ingenious— clause was that the original seven nuclear suppliers were not about to have the new invitees coalesce into a formation intending to use the "Club" as a vehicle for strengthening the existing NPT safeguard regime and prohibiting assistance until such time. It appeared, therefore, that the London Club's eight newcomers were required to play by the rules of the original seven.[2]

Footnotes

1. *The New York Times*, February 24, 1976, p. 1; *International Canada*, Vol. 7, No. 6, June 1976, p. 190; *International Canada*, Vol. 7, No. 1, January 1976, p. 17.
2. Stockholm International Peace Research Institute, *SIPRI Yearbook 1978* (Stockholm: Almqvist & Wiksell International, 1979), Appendix 2A. The London Club's nuclear export guidelines are reprinted on pp. 35-42. There are six major components discussed in the London Club's Trigger List. They are: complete nuclear reactors, pressure vessels, reactor control rods, fuel reprocessing plants, fuel fabrication plants, and isotope separation plant equipment.

APPENDIX VI: A BREAKDOWN OF THE CANADIAN NUCLEAR ESTABLISHMENT (1974)*

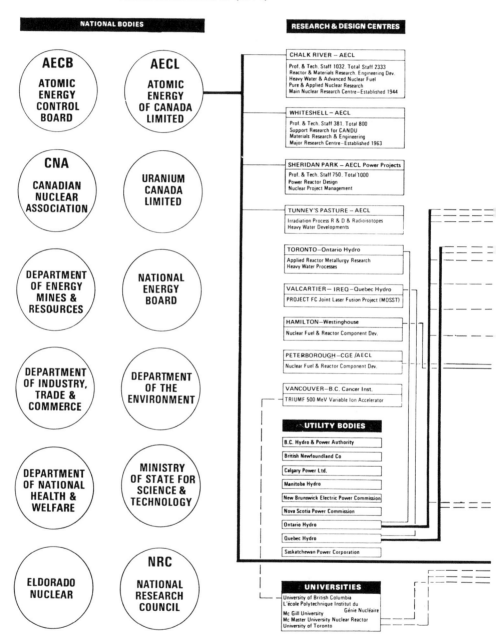

* Source: *Nuclear Engineering International*, June 1974.

REACTOR AND FUEL CYCLE DATA

URANIUM MILLING MINING OPERATIONS

COMPANY	LOCATION	NOMINAL CAPACITY TONNES/DAY	SHORT TONS/DAY
Active			
Denison Mines	Elliot Lake, Ont.	5,400	6,000(a)
Eldorado Nuclear	Eldorado, Sask.	1,600	1,800
Rio Algom Mines			
−Quirke Mill	Elliot Lake, Ont.	4,100	4,500
Inactive (b)			
Can-Fed Resources	Bancroft, Ont.	1,400	1,500
Preston Mines	Elliot Lake, Ont.	2,700	3,000
Rio Algom Mines			
−Nordic Mill	Elliot Lake, Ont.	3,400	3,700
−Panel Mill	Elliot Lake, Ont.	2,700	3,000
Stanrock Uranium Mines (d)	Elliot Lake, Ont.	2,700	3,000(c)
Under Construction			
Gulf Minerals Canada	Rabbit Lake, Sask.	1,800	2,000

(a) Present leaching capacity limited to about 4,000 tonnes (4,400 short tons) per day. Mill expansion to
6,400 tonnes (7,100 short tons) per day scheduled for 1975.
(b) Capacities listed refer to capacities at time of closure, other past producing mills have been dismantled.
(c) Partly dismantled, recovery of uranium from mine water only, 1964 to 1970.
(d) Amalgamated with Denison Mines Limited effective February 12, 1973.

POWER AND PROTOTYPE REACTORS

NAME	TYPE	NETT MWe	DATE OP
NPD−2/ROLPHTON	CANDU−PHW	22.5	6/1962
DOUGLAS POINT GS−1	CANDU−PHW	208	10/1966
PICKERING GS−A1	CANDU−PHW	512	3/1971
PICKERING GS−A2	CANDU−PHW	512	10/1971
PICKERING GS−A3	CANDU−PHW	512	1/1972
PICKERING GS−A4	CANDU−PHW	512	6/1973
GENTILLY 1	CANDU−BLW	250	1971
GENTILLY 2	CANDU−PHW	640	1979
BRUCE GS−A1	CANDU−PHW	752	1977
BRUCE GS−A2	CANDU−PHW	752	1976
BRUCE GS−A3	CANDU−PHW	752	1978
BRUCE GS−A4	CANDU−PHW	752	1979
BRUCE GS−B5	CANDU−PHW	750	1981
BRUCE GS−B6	CANDU−PHW	750	1982
BRUCE GS−B7	CANDU−PHW	750	1983
BRUCE GS−B8	CANDU−PHW	750	1983
PICKERING GS−B5	CANDU−PHW	500	1980
PICKERING GS−B6	CANDU−PHW	500	1981
PICKERING GS−B7	CANDU−PHW	500	1981
PICKERING GS−B8	CANDU−PHW	500	1982
DARLINGTON GS−A1	CANDU−PHW	750	1982
DARLINGTON GS−A2	CANDU−PHW	750	1983
DARLINGTON GS−A3	CANDU−PHW	750	1984
DARLINGTON GS−A4	CANDU−PHW	750	1984

OVERSEAS CANDU REACTORS

NAME/LOCATION	TYPE	MW(e)	DATE OP
India			
RAPP−1/Rajasthan	CANDU−PHW	202	1973
RAPP−2/Rajasthan	CANDU−PHW	202	1975
MAPP−1/Kalpakkam	CANDU−PHW	202	1976
MAPP−2/Kalpakkam	CANDU−PHW	202	1979
NAPP−1/Narora	CANDU−PHW	200	1981
NAPP−2/Narora	CANDU−PHW	200	
Pakistan			
KANUPP/Karachi	CANDU−PHW	125	1972
Argentina			
EPEC Rio Tercero 1	CANDU−PHW	600	1978
EPEC (no order yet)	CANDU−PHW	−	−
Republic of Korea			
Asan	CANDU−PHW	600	1980
(option)	CANDU−PHW	600	−

RESEARCH & TRAINING REACTORS

NAME/LOCATION	MW(th)	MAX. TH.FLUX n/cm²/s	MODERATOR	COOLANT	FIRST CRIT
ZEEP/Chalk River	0.001		D_2O	D_2O	8/1945
NRX/Chalk River	40	5.12×10^{13}	D_2O	H_2O	7/1947
NRU/Chalk River	110	2.5×10^{13}	D_2O	D_2O	11/1957
PTR/Chalk River	zero	5×10^9	H_2O	H_2O	11/1957
ZED 2/Chalk River	zero	1.0×10^9	D_2O	D_2O	9/1960
TUR/Toronto Univ.	zero		D_2O	D_2O	1958
Slowpoke 1/Toronto Univ.	0.020	1.0×10^{11}	H_2O	H_2O	1970
MNR/Hamilton, Ont.	2	2.2×10^{13}	H_2O	H_2O	2/1959
WR-1/Whiteshell	40		D_2O	Organic	11/1965
Slowpoke 2/Tunney's Past	0.020	1.0×10^{11}	H_2O	H_2O	1971
OVERSEAS CANADIAN SUPPLIED RESEARCH REACTORS					
CIRUS/Trombay, India	40	6.3×10^{13}	D_2O	H_2O	7/1960
TRR/Taiwan	40	5.3×10^{13}	D_2O	H_2O	1/1973
Republic of Korea	40	under negotiation			

(Table continues on next page)

211

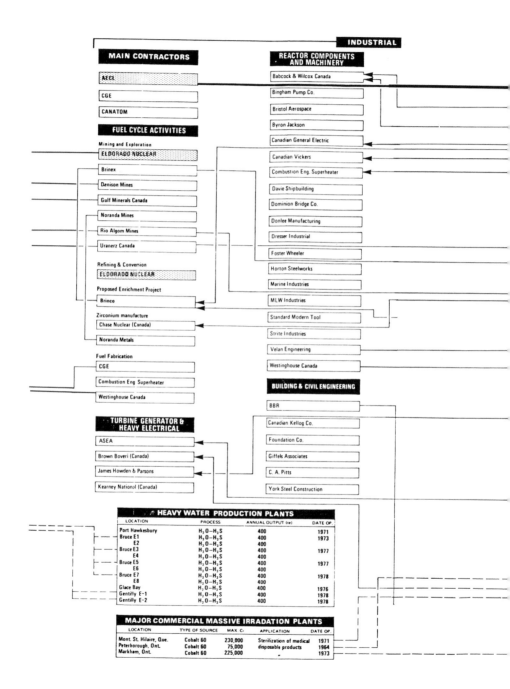

INDUSTRIAL

MAIN CONTRACTORS

- AECL
- CGE
- CANATOM

FUEL CYCLE ACTIVITIES

Mining and Exploration
- ELDORADO NUCLEAR
- Brinex
- Denison Mines
- Gulf Minerals Canada
- Noranda Mines
- Rio Algom Mines
- Uranerz Canada

Refining & Conversion
- ELDORADO NUCLEAR

Proposed Enrichment Project
- Brinco

Zirconium manufacture
- Chase Nuclear (Canada)
- Noranda Metals

Fuel Fabrication
- CGE
- Combustion Eng Superheater
- Westinghouse Canada

TURBINE GENERATOR & HEAVY ELECTRICAL

- ASEA
- Brown Boveri (Canada)
- James Howden & Parsons
- Kearney National (Canada)

REACTOR COMPONENTS AND MACHINERY

- Babcock & Wilcox Canada
- Bingham Pump Co.
- Bristol Aerospace
- Byron Jackson
- Canadian General Electric
- Canadian Vickers
- Combustion Eng. Superheater
- Davie Shipbuilding
- Dominion Bridge Co.
- Donlee Manufacturing
- Dresser Industrial
- Foster Wheeler
- Horton Steelworks
- Marine Industries
- MLW Industries
- Standard Modern Tool
- Strite Industries
- Velan Engineering
- Westinghouse Canada

BUILDING & CIVIL ENGINEERING

- BBR
- Canadian Kellog Co.
- Foundation Co.
- Giffels Associates
- C. A. Pitts
- York Steel Construction

HEAVY WATER PRODUCTION PLANTS

LOCATION	PROCESS	ANNUAL OUTPUT (te)	DATE OP.
Port Hawkesbury	$H_2O - H_2S$	400	1971
Bruce E1	$H_2O - H_2S$	400	1973
E2	$H_2O - H_2S$	400	
Bruce E3	$H_2O - H_2S$	400	1977
E4	$H_2O - H_2S$	400	
Bruce E5	$H_2O - H_2S$	400	1977
E6	$H_2O - H_2S$	400	
Bruce E7	$H_2O - H_2S$	400	1978
E8	$H_2O - H_2S$	400	
Glace Bay	$H_2O - H_2S$	400	1976
Gentilly E-1	$H_2O - H_2S$	400	1978
Gentilly E-2	$H_2O - H_2S$	400	1978

MAJOR COMMERCIAL MASSIVE IRRADATION PLANTS

LOCATION	TYPE OF SOURCE	MAX. Ci	APPLICATION	DATE OP.
Mont. St. Hilaire, Que.	Cobalt 60	230,000	Sterilization of medical	1971
Peterborough, Ont.	Cobalt 60	75,000	disposable products	1964
Markham, Ont.	Cobalt 60	225,000	"	1973

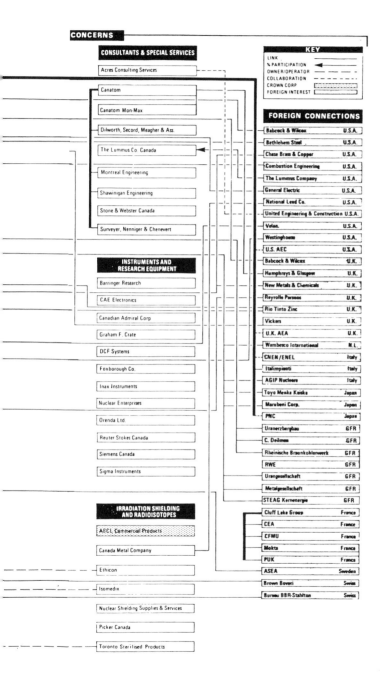

CONCERNS

CONSULTANTS & SPECIAL SERVICES

Acres Consulting Services

Canatom

Canatom Mon-Max

Dilworth, Secord, Meagher & Ass.

The Lummus Co. Canada

Montreal Engineering

Shawinigan Engineering

Stone & Webster Canada

Surveyer, Nenniger & Chenevert

INSTRUMENTS AND RESEARCH EQUIPMENT

Barringer Research

CAE Electronics

Canadian Admiral Corp

Graham F. Crate

DCF Systems

Foxborough Co.

Inax Instruments

Nuclear Enterprises

Orenda Ltd.

Reuter Stokes Canada

Siemens Canada

Sigma Instruments

IRRADIATION SHIELDING AND RADIOISOTOPES

AECL Commercial Products

Canada Metal Company

Ethicon

Isomedix

Nuclear Shielding Supplies & Services

Picker Canada

Toronto Sterilised Products

KEY

LINK
% PARTICIPATION
OWNER/OPERATOR
COLLABORATION
CROWN CORP
FOREIGN INTEREST

FOREIGN CONNECTIONS

Babcock & Wilcox	U.S.A.
Bethlehem Steel	U.S.A.
Chase Brass & Copper	U.S.A.
Combustion Engineering	U.S.A.
The Lummus Company	U.S.A.
General Electric	U.S.A.
National Lead Co.	U.S.A.
United Engineering & Construction	U.S.A.
Velan	U.S.A.
Westinghouse	U.S.A.
U.S. AEC	U.S.A.
Babcock & Wilcox	U.K.
Humphreys & Glasgow	U.K.
New Metals & Chemicals	U.K.
Reyrolle Parsons	U.K.
Rio Tinto Zinc	U.K.
Vickers	U.K.
U.K. AEA	U.K.
Wambesco International	N.L.
CNEN/ENEL	Italy
Italimpianti	Italy
AGIP Nucleare	Italy
Toyo Menka Kaisha	Japan
Marubeni Corp.	Japan
PNC	Japan
Uranerzbergbau	GFR
C. Deilman	GFR
Rheinische Braunkohlenwerk	GFR
RWE	GFR
Urangesellschaft	GFR
Metalgesellschaft	GFR
STEAG Kernenergie	GFR
Cluff Lake Group	France
CEA	France
CFMU	France
Mokta	France
PUK	France
ASEA	Sweden
Brown Boveri	Swiss
Bureau BBR-Stahlton	Swiss

213

APPENDIX VII: CORPORATIONS WITH TIES TO THE URANIUM CARTEL (Location)

1. Rio Tinto Zinc (Great Britain)
    Rio Algom (Canada)*
       Rio Algom (US)
    Palabora Mining (South Africa)
    Rössing Uranium (Namibia)
    Conzinc Riotinto of Australia (CRA) (Australia)
       Mary Kathleen Uranium (Australia) (49% owned
       by Australian government)
2. Uranex (France) — marketing only (government owns 1/3 share)
3. Imetal (France)
    Cie. de Mokta (France)
       Compagnie des Minerais d'Uranium de
       Franceville (COMUF) (Gabon) (French
       government owns shares)
    Penarroya (France)
       Compagnie Française des Minerais
       d'Uranium (CFMU) (France) (government
       owns 15%)
4. Pechiney Ugine Kuhlmann (France)
    CMFU (France) - minority interest.
5. Nuclear Fuels Corporation (South Africa) marketing only
6. Anglo-American (South Africa)**
       Charter Consolidated (Great Britain) - 33/7%
       Engelhard Minerals (United States) - less than
       10%, marketing only
       RTZ (Great Britain) - less than 8%
       Anglo-American (South Africa) - 10%
7. Gulf Oil Corporation (United States)
       Gulf Minerals Canada (Canada)
       General Atomic Company (50% owned by Gulf Oil
       Corporation, 50% by Scallop Nuclear, Inc.)
8. Getty Oil Development Company (United States)
       Getty Mining Pty., (Australia) - 35% of a
       partnership with Pancontinental Mining
9. Eldorado Nuclear (Canada) (government-owned company)
10. Noranda (Canada)
       Noranda (Australia)
       Kerr-Addison (Canada) - with Gulf Minerals Canada
11. Denison Mines (Canada)
12. Electrolytic Zinc (Australia)
13. Peko-Wallsend (Australia)

14. Pancontinental Mining (Australia) - 65% of a partnership with Getty Oil Development Company (United States)
15. Queensland Mines (Australia)
16. Uranium Canada (UCAN) (government-owned corporation)
17. Ranger Mines (Australia) (government owns 72%)
18. Western Mining Corporation (Australia)

  *   Indentation indicates subsidiary relationship.
**   Note: Anglo-American owns 35.7% of Charter Consolidated, which in turn owns 10% of Anglo-American. Charter Consolidated also holds stock in RTZ (Great Britain), less than 8%.

Source: June Taylor, Michael Yokell, *Yellowcake: The International Uranium Cartel* (New York, Pergamon Press, 1979), pp. 71-72.

SELECTED BIBLIOGRAPHY

BOOKS

Aldridge, Robert C. *The Counterforce Syndrome: A Guide to U.S. Nuclear Weapons and Strategic Doctrine.* Washington; Institute for Policy Studies, 1978.

Alperovitz, Gar. *Atomic Diplomacy: Hiroshima and Potsdam, The Use of the Atomic Bomb and the American Confrontation with Soviet Power.* New York: Vintage Books, 1965.

Bacon, Hilary, and Valentine, John. *Power Corrupts: The Arguments against Nuclear Power.* London: Pluto Press, 1981.

Barnaby, C.F., ed. *Preventing the Spread of Nuclear Weapons.* Pugwash Monograph I. London: Souvenir Press, 1969.

_____. *The Nuclear Age.* Stockholm International Peace Research Institute. Cambridge, Mass.: The MIT Press, 1975.

Barnet, Richard J., and Muller, Ronald E. *Global Reach: The Power of Multinational Corporations.* New York: Simon and Schuster, 1974.

Beal, Barry. *Energy and Industry: The Potential Energy Development Projects for Canadian Industry in the Eighties.* Toronto: James Lorimer and Co., Pub. in association with the Canadian Institute for Economic Policy, 1980.

Bertell, Rosalie. *No Immediate Danger: Prognosis for a Radioactive Earth.* London: Women's Press, 1985.

Brown-John, C. Lloyd. *Canadian Regulatory Agencies: Quis Custodiet Ipsos Custodes?* Toronto: Butterworth and Co. (Canada) Ltd., 1981.

Bupp, Irvin C., and Derian, Jean-Claude. *The Failed Promise of Nuclear Power: The Story of Light Water.* New York: Basic Books, Inc., Pub., 1978.

Caldicott, Helen. *Nuclear Madness: What You Can Do!* Brookline, Mass.: Autumn Press, Inc., 1978

Calvocoressi, Peter. *World Politics since 1945.* New York: Longman Group Ltd., 1977.

Carty, Robert, and Smith, Virginia. *Perpetuating Poverty: The Political Economy of Canadian Foreign Aid.* Toronto: Between the Lines, 1981.

Carty, R. Kenneth, and Ward, W. Peter. *Entering the Eighties: Canada in Crisis.* Toronto: Oxford University Press, 1980.

Cave Brown, Anthony, ed. *Dropshot: The American Plan for World War III against Russia in 1957.* New York: The Dial Press, 1978.

Cervenka, Zdenek and Rogers, Barbasa. *The Nuclear Axis: Secret Collaboration between West Germany and South Africa.* New York: Time Books, 1978.

Chomsky, Noam. *Towards a New Cold War: Essays on the Current Crisis and How We Got There.* New York: Pantheon Books, 1982.

Clarke, Robert, and Swift, Richard. *Ties That Bind: Canada and the Third World.* Toronto: Between the Lines, 1982.

Commoner, Barry. *The Politics of Energy.* New York: Alfred A. Knopf, Inc., 1979.

Curtis, Richard, and Hogan, Elizabeth. *Perils of the Peaceful Atom : The Myth of Safe Nuclear Power.* New York: Ballantine Books, 1979.

Davis, Walter. *The Yellowcake Road: Corporate Uranium and Saskatchewan*. Saskatoon: Saskatoon Citizens for a Non-Nuclear Society, 1981.

De Leon, Peter. *A Cross-National Comparison of Nuclear Reactor Development Strategies*. Santa Monica: Rand Corporation, Report p-5739, October 1976.

Doern, G. Bruce. *Government Intervention in the Canadian Nuclear Industry*. Montreal: The Institute for Research on Public Policy, 1980.

Doerr, Audry D. *The Machinery of Government in Canada*. Toronto: Methuen Publications, 1981.

Dow, James. *The Arrow*. Toronto: James Lorimer and Co., Pub., 1979.

Durie, Sheila, and Edwards, Rob. *Fuelling the Nuclear Arms Race: The Links between Nuclear Power and Nuclear Weapons*. London: Pluto Press, 1982.

Dwivedi, O.P., ed. *Resources and the Environment: Policy Perspectives for Canada*: Toronto: McClelland and Stewart Ltd., 1980.

Easlea, Brian. *Fathering the Unthinkable: Masculinity, Scientists, and the Nuclear Arms Race*. London: Pluto Press, 1983.

Eayrs, James. *In Defence of Canada: Peacemaking and Deterrence*. Studies in the Structure of Power Series: Decision Making in Canada, Vol. 6. Toronto: University of Toronto Press, 1980.

_____. *In Defence of Canada: Growing Up Allied*. Studies in the Structure of Power Series: Decision Making in Canada, Vol. 8. Toronto: University of Toronto Press, 1980.

Ebinger, Charles K. *International Politics of Nuclear Energy*. The Washington Papers, Vol. VI, No. 57. The Center for Strategic and International Studies, Georgetown University, Washington, D.C., Beverly Hills: Sage Publications, 1978.

Eggleston, Wilfred. *Canada's Nuclear Story*. Toronto: Clarke, Irwin & Co., Ltd., 1965.

Elliot, Mary, ed. *Ground for Concern: Australia's Uranium and Human Survival*. Harmondsworth: Penguin Books, Ltd., 1977.

Epstein, William. *The Last Chance: Nuclear Proliferation and Arms Control*. New York: The Free Press, 1976.

Faulkner, Peter. *The Silent Bomb: A Guide to the Nuclear Energy Controversy*. New York: Vintage Books, 1977.

Foote, Raymond L. *The Case of Port Hawkesbury: Rapid Industrialization and Social Unrest in a Nova Scotia Community*. Canadian Experiences Series. Toronto: PMA Books, 1979.

Ford, D.F.; Hollocker, T.C.; Kendall, H.W.; Mackenzie, J.J.; Scheinman, L; and Schurgin, A.S. *The Nuclear Fuel Cycle*. Cambridge, Mass.: Friends of the Earth for the Union of Concerned Scientists, 1974.

Gaddis, John Lewis. *The United States and the Origins of the Cold War, 1941-1947*. New York: Columbia University Press, 1972.

Gatt-Fly. *Power to Choose: Canada's Energy Options*. Toronto: Between the Lines, 1981.

Giangrande, Carole. *The Nuclear North: The People, the Regions, and the Arms Race*. Toronto: House of Anansi Press, Ltd., 1983.

Goldstick, Miles. *Uranium Mining in Canada: Some Health and Environmental Problems*. Limited printing, 3rd Working Draft. Vancouver: British Columbia Survival Alliance, December 1980.

Gowing, Margaret. *Britain and Atomic Energy: 1939-1945*. London: Macmillan & Co. Ltd., 1965.

_____. *Independence and Deterrence: Britain and Atomic Energy*. Vol. I: *Policy Making*. Vol. 2. *Policy Execution*. London: The Macmillan Press, Ltd., 1974.

Graeub, Ralph. *The Gentle Killers: Nuclear Power Stations*. London: Willmer Brothers, Ltd., 1974.

Greenwood, Ted; Feiveson, Harold A.; and Taylor, Theodore B. *Nuclear Proliferation: Motivations, Capabilities, and Strategies for Control.* New York: McGraw-Hill Book Co., 1977.

Griffiths, Franklyn, and Polanyi, John C. *The Dangers of Nuclear War: A Pugwash Symposium.* Toronto: University of Toronto Press, 1979.

Ground Zero. *Nuclear War: What's in It for You?* New York: Pocket Books, 1982.

Gyorgy, Anna, and Friends. *No Nukes: Everyone's Guide to Nuclear Power.* Montreal: Black Rose Books, 1979.

Halle, Louis J. *The Cold War as History.* New York: Harper Torchbooks, 1975.

Halliday, Fred. *Soviet Policy in the Arc of Crisis.* Washington: Institute for Policy Studies, 1981.

Hammerstrom, Gary. *The Hazards of Nuclear Energy: A Policy and Planning Approach.* Croton-on-Hudson, N.Y., Policy Studies Associates, 1977.

Harding, Bill. *Nukenomics: The Political Economy of the Nuclear Industry.* Regina, Saskatchewan: Regina Group for a Non-Nuclear Future, 1979.

_____. *Uranium Mining in Northern Saskatchewan: Correspondence with the Primer.* Regina: Regina Group for a Non-Nuclear Society, 1979.

Harvard Nuclear Study Group. *Living with Nuclear Weapons.* New York: Bantam Books, 1983.

Hewlett, Richard G.; and Henderson, Oscar E. *A History of the United States Atomic Energy Commission: The New World, 1939-46.* Pennsylvania State University Press, 1976.

Hewlett, Sylvia Ann, and Weinert, Richard S., eds. *Brazil and Mexico: Patterns in Late Development.* Philadelphia: Institute for the Study of Human Issues, 1982.

Hilgartner, Stephen; Bell, Richard C.; and O'Connor, Rory. *Nukespeak: The Selling of Nuclear Technology in America.* Harmondsworth: Penguin Books, Ltd., 1983.

Hodges, Donald, and Gandy, Ross. *Mexico 1910-1976: Reform or Revolution.* London: Zed Press, 1979.

Hooker, C.A.; MacDonald, R.; Van Hulst, R.; Victor, P. *Energy and the Quality of Life: Understanding Energy Policy.* Toronto: University of Toronto Press, 1981.

Hoyle, Fred, and Hoyle, Geoffrey. *Commonsense in Nuclear Energy.* San Francisco: W.H. Freeman and Co., 1980.

Hyde, H. Montgomery. *The Atomic Bomb Spies.* London: Hamish Hamilton, Ltd., 1980.

Jones, Rodney W. *Nuclear Proliferation: Islam, the Bomb, and South Asia.* The Washington Papers, Vol. IX, No. 82. The Center for Strategic and International Studies. Beverly Hills: Sage Publications, 1981.

Jungk, Robert. *The Nuclear State.* Translated by Eric Mosbacher. London: John Calder Pub., Ltd., 1979.

Kaplan, Fred M. *Dubious Specter: A Skeptical Look at the Soviet Nuclear Threat.* Washington: Institute for Policy Studies, 1980.

_____. *The Wizards of Armageddon.* New York: Simon and Schuster, 1983.

Knelman, Fred H. *Nuclear Energy: The Unforgiving Technology.* Edmonton: Hurtig Publishers, 1976.

LeFeber, Walter. *America, Russia, and the Cold War 1945-1975.* New York: John Wiley and Sons, Inc., 1976.

Law, Charles; and Glen, Ron. *Critical Choice: Canada and Nuclear Power: The Issues behind the Headlines.* Toronto: Corpus, 1978.

Laxer, James. *Canada's Energy Crisis.* Toronto: James Lorimer and Co., Pub., 1975.

Leiss, William, ed. *Ecology versus Politics in Canada.* Toronto: University of Toronto Press, 1979.

Lens, Sidney. *The Day before Doomsday: An Anatomy of the Nuclear Arms Race.* New York: Doubleday & Co., Inc., 1977.

Leonard and Partners, Ltd. *Economic Impact of Nuclear Energy Industry in Canada.* Ottawa: Canadian Nuclear Association, 1978.

Loewenheim, Francis L.; Langley, Harold D.; and Jonas, Manfred, eds. *Roosevelt and Churchill: Their Secret Wartime Correspondence.* Toronto: Clarke, Irwin & Co., Ltd., 1975.

Lovins, Amory B. *Soft Energy Paths: Toward a Durable Peace.* New York: Harper Colophon Books, 1979.

———. *World Energy Strategies: Facts, Issues, and Options.* New York: Harper Colophon Books, 1980.

Lovins, Amory B., and Lovins, L. Hunter. *Energy/War: Breaking the Nuclear Link.* New York: Harper Colophon Books, 1981.

Lovins, Amory B., and Price, John H. *Non-Nuclear Futures: The Care for an Ethical Energy Strategy.* New York: Harper Colophon Books, 1980.

Lyon, Peyton V., and Ismael, Tareq Y. *Canada and the Third World.* Toronto: Macmillan of Canada, 1976.

McCormack, Gavin and Sheldon, Mark. *Korea: North and South, the Deepening Crisis.* New York: Monthly Review Press, 1978.

McKay, Paul. *Electric Empire: The Inside Story of Ontario Hydro.* Toronto: Between the Lines, 1983.

McMullan, Doris; Hornby, Ian; Collins, Jim; and McAulay, John. *The Nuke Book: The Impact of Nuclear Development.* Ottawa: Pollution Probe, 1976.

Maddox, Robert James. *The New Left and the Origins of the Cold War.* Princeton: Princeton University Press, 1974.

Mandelbaum, Michael. *The Nuclear Question: The United States and Nuclear Weapons, 1946-1976.* New York: Cambridge University Press, 1979.

Marmorek, Jan. *Everything You Wanted to Know about Nuclear Power (But Were Afraid to Ask).* Toronto: The Pollution Probe Foundation, 1978.

Mathias, Philip. *Forced Growth: Five Studies of Government Involvement in the Development of Canada.* Toronto: James Lorimer and Co., Pub., 1971.

Melman, Seymour. *The Permanent War Economic: American Capitalism in Decline.* New York: Touchstone Books, 1974.

Milliband, Ralph. *The State in Capitalist Society: The Analysis of the Western System of Power.* London: Quartet Books, Ltd., 1980.

Morrison, Robert W., and Wonder, Edward F. *Canada's Nuclear Export Policy.* Ottawa: Carleton University Press, 1978.

Morrison, R. W., and Sims, G. *Nuclear Power in Developing Countries: A Search for Indicators.* Ottawa: Published under an Energy, Mines, and Resources Research Agreement, August 1980.

Mueller, Peter. *On Things Nuclear: The Canadian Debate.* Toronto: Canadian Institute for International Affairs, 1977.

Nelkin, Dorothy, and Pollak, Michael. *The Atom Besieged: Antinuclear Movements in France and Germany.* Cambridge Mass.: The MIT Press, 1982.

Nelles, H.V. *The Politics of Development: Forest, Mines, and Hydro-Electric Power in Ontaro, 1849-1941.* Toronto: Macmillan of Canada, 1974.

New Left Review, ed. *Exterminism and Cold War.* London: Verso Editions and New Left Books, 1982.

Ornstein, Michael. *Canadian Policy-Makers' Views on Nuclear Energy.* Toronto: York University Institute for Behavioural Research, 1976.

Patterson, Walter C. *Nuclear Power.* Harmondsworth: Penguin Books, Ltd., 1978.

Payer, Cheryl. *The Debt Trap: the International Monetary Fund and the Third World.* New York: Monthly Review Press, 1974.

Peat, David. *The Nuclear Book: What Happened at Harrisburg? And Can It Happen Here?* Canada: Deneau and Greenberg Pub., Ltd., 1979.

Petras, James. *Critical Perspectives on Imperialism and Social Class in the Third World.* New York: Monthly Review Press, 1978.

Pringle, Peter, and Spigelman, James. *The Nuclear Barons.* New York: Holt, Rinehart and Winston, 1981.

Prins, Gwyn, ed. *Defended to Death: A Study of the Nuclear Arms Race.* A Cambridge University Disarmament Seminar. Harmondsworth: Penguin Books, 1983.

Redick, John R. *Military Potential of Latin American Nuclear Energy Programs.* Sage Professional Papers in International Studies Series. Beverly Hills: Sage Publications, 1972.

Reece, Ray. *The Sun Betrayed: A Report on the Corporate Seizure of U.S. Solar Energy Development.* Montreal: Black Rose Books, 1979.

Regehr, Ernie. *Making a Killing: Canada's Arms Industry.* Toronto: McClelland and Stewart, Ltd., 1975.

————. *Militarism and the World Military Order: A Study Guide for Churches.* Geneva: Commission of the Churches on International Affairs of the World Council of Churches, 1980.

Regehr, Ernie, and Simon Rosenblum, eds. *Canada and the Nuclear Arms Race.* Forward by Margaret Laurence. Toronto: James Lorimer and Co., Pub., 1983.

Robbins, Walter. *Getting the Shaft: The Radioactive Waste Controversy In Manitoba.* Winnipeg: Queenston House, 1984.

Rochlin, Gene I. *Plutonium, Power, and Politics: International Arrangements for the Disposition of Spent Nuclear Fuel.* Berkeley: University of California Press, 1979.

Rosenblum, Simon. *The Non-Nuclear Way: Creative Energy Alternatives for Canada.* Regina: Regina Group for a Non-Nuclear Society, 1981.

Sampson, Anthony. *The Seven Sisters: The Great Oil Companies and the World They Shared.* New York: Bantam Books, Inc., 1980.

Sanders, Benjamin. *Safeguards against Nuclear Proliferation.* Stockholm International Peace Research Institute. Cambridge, Mass.: The MIT Press, Ltd., 1975.

Seshagiri, N. *The Bomb!: Fallout of India's Nuclear Explosion.* Delhi: Vikas Publishing House, PVT, Ltd., 1975.

Shapira, Yoram. *Mexican Foreign Policy under Echeverria.* The Washington Papers Vol. VI, No. 56. The Center for Strategic and International Studies. Beverly Hills: Sage Publications, 1978.

Sherwin, Martin J. *A World Destroyed: The Atomic Bomb and the Grand Alliance.* Toronto: Random House (Canada) Ltd., 1975.

Smith, Daniel M. *The American Diplomatic Experience.* Boston: Houghton Mifflin Co., 1972.

Solomon, Lawrence. *The Conserver Solution: A Blueprint for the Conserver Society.* A project of the Pollution Probe Foundation. Toronto: Doubleday Canada, Ltd., 1978.

Stacey, C.P. *Arms, Men, and Governments: The War Policies of Canada, 1939-1945.* Ottawa: The Queen's Printer for Canada, 1970.

Stavrianos, L.S. *Global Rift: The Third World Comes of Age.* New York: William Morrow and Co., 1981.

Stephenson, Lee, and Zachar, George R. *Accidents Will Happen: The Case against Nuclear Power.* The Environmental Action Foundation. New York: Perennial Library, 1979.

Stockholm International Peace Research Institute. *SIPRI Yearbook 1975*. Stockholm: Almqvist & Wiksell International, 1976.

———. *Nuclear Energy and Nuclear Weapon Proliferation*. London: Taylor & Francis, Ltd., 1979.

Stretton, Hugh. *Capitalism, Socialism, and the Environment*. Cambridge: Cambridge University Press, 1978.

Tanzer, Michael. *The Race for Resources: Continuing Struggles over Minerals and Fuels*. New York: Monthly Review Press, 1980.

Taylor, June H., and Yokell, Michael D. *Yellowcake: The International Uranium Cartel*. New York: Pergamon Press, 1979.

Thompson, E.P., and Smith, Dan, eds. *Protest and Survive*. New York: Monthly Review Press, 1981.

Tupper, Allan, and Doern, G. Bruce. *Public Corporations and Public Policy in Canada*. Montreal: The Institute for Research on Public Policy, 1981.

Walters, Robert E. *The Nuclear Trap: An Escape Route*. Harmondsworth: Penguin Books, Ltd., 1974.

Warnock, John W. *Partner to Behemoth: The Military Policy of a Satellite Canada*. Toronto: New Press, 1970.

Weissman, Steve, and Krosney, Herbert. *The Islamic Bomb: The Nuclear Threat to Isreal and the Middle East*. New York: Times Books, 1981.

Willrich, Mason. *Global Politics of Nuclear Energy*. New York: Praeger Publishers, Inc., 1971.

———. *International Safeguards and Nuclear Industry*. Baltimore: The Johns Hopkins University Press, 1973.

Willrich, Mason, and Taylor, Theodore, B. *Nuclear Theft: Risks and Safeguards*. Cambridge, Mass.: Ballinger Publishing Co., 1974.

Wyatt, Allan. *The Nuclear Challenge: Understanding the Debate*. Toronto: The Book Press, Ltd., 1978.

Yulish, Charles B., ed. *Soft vs Hard Energy Paths: 10 Critical Essays on Amory Lovins' "Energy Strategy: The Road Not Taken?"* New York: Charles Yulish Associates, Inc., 1977.

ARTICLES

Adams, Ian. "The Real McGuffin: Selling the Bomb, Confessions of a Nuclear Salesman." *This Magazine*, Vol. 16, No. 2, May 1982, pp. 18-19.

Aiken, A.M. "Marketing Nuclear Power Plants." *10th Annual Canadian Nuclear Association Conference*, May 1970, Paper No. 70-CNA-647.

Alesich, Ingrid. "Atomic Cafe: The Saskatchewan Version." *Briarpatch*, Vol. 13, No. 1, January-February 1984, pp. 8-10.

Anon. "Living with Radiation." Ottawa: AECL, January 3, 1981.

Baxter, C. "Our Reactor Made India's Bomb? Canadian A-Policy Facing Test." *Financial Post*, Vol. 59, October 9, 1965, pp. 1, 4.

Bennett, W.J. "Statement on Canada's Atomic Energy Program." Ottawa: AECL, 1955, AECL-168.

Bertell, Dr. Rosalie. "The Link Between Peaceful and Military Uses of Nuclear Power and the Health Effects of Uranium Mining." *Energy Probe*. December 1982, pp. 1-5. Copy provided by Energy Probe.

Bertin, L. "Our Scramble to Keep India's Atom Peaceful." *Maclean's*, Vol. 78, August 1965, p. 1.

Blake, L. "Design Problems in Rehabilitating the Glace Bay Heavy Water Plant." *Canadian Nuclear Association 16th Annual Conference*, Vol. 4, 1976.

Boggild, Kriss. "The Amax Controversy." *Alternatives*. Vol. 10, Nos. 2-3. Fall-Winter, 1982, pp. 40-54.

Bothwell, Robert. "Radium and Uranium: Evolution of a Company and a Policy." *Canadian Historical Review*. Vol. LXIV, No. 2, June 1983, pp. 127-146.

Bruman, Carol. "CANDU Sales and Setbacks." *Maclean's*, Vol. 96, August 22, 1983, p. 48.

"Canada's Position—India's Nuclear Test." *International Perspectives*. Vol. 3, July-August, 1974. p. 24.

Canadian Dimension. Vol. 14, July-August, 1979.

Carruthers, Jeff. "Canada May Promise Uranium as a Selling Point for Reactors." *The Globe and Mail*, July 4, 1974, p. B1.

_____. "What the Indian Nuclear Explosion Will Mean for Canada's Nuclear Policy." *Science Forum*, Vol. 7, August 1974, pp. 17-19.

_____. "How India's Nuclear Explosion Has Shaken Canada's Cabinet." *Science Forum*, Vol. 8, February 1975, pp. 16-18.

_____. "Continued Rise in Uranium Prices Viewed as Harmful to the Industry." *The Globe and Mail*, November 9, 1977. p. B2.

_____. "AECL to Buy Heavy Water Plant." *The Globe and Mail*. February 10, 1978, p. 3.

_____. "Romanian CANDU Deal Clears Second Stage." *The Globe and Mail*, July 29, 1978, p. B2.

_____. "Credit Line Is Arranged for Romania." *The Globe and Mail*. November 22, 1978, p. B1.

_____. "Four CANDU Response Credited to Financing." *The Globe and Mail*. December 21, 1978, p. B13.

Claridge, Thomas. "Ontario Hydro May Abandon Heavy Water Plant." *The Globe and Mail*. June 27, 1983, pp. 1, 5.

Clarkson, Stephen. "Just What Is Canada Accomplishing in India?" *Saturday Night*. Vol. 87, October 1972, pp. 15-17.

Clifford, Edward. "Big Potential Seen for Selling Electricity to the U.S." *The Globe and Mail*, February 14, 1983, p. B9.

Dixon, R.S. and Rosinger, E.L.J. *Third Annual Report of the Canadian Nuclear Fuel Waste Management Program*. Pinawa: Atomic Energy of Canada Limited, AECL-6821, December 1981.

Doern, G. Bruce. "'Big Science,' Government and the Scientific Community in Canada: The ING Affair." *Minerva*, Vol. VIII, No. 3, July 1970.

_____. "To Assume Safety in a Nuclear Age We Must Reform the AECB." *Science Forum*, Vol. 10, April 1977, pp. 3-5.

Dohle, Gordon. "Government Secrecy in Canada." *Indian Journal of Public Administration*. Vol. 25, No. 4, October-December, 1979, pp. 1025-1035.

Duff, Peggy. "What You Don't Know about the Arms Race." *Our Generation*. Vol. 13, No. 1, Winter 1979, pp. 7-22.

Edwards, Gordon. "Nuclear Power: A New Dimension in Politics." *Alternatives*. Vol. 5, No. 2, April 1976, pp. 26-30.

_____. "People Versus Nuclear Power." *Perception*, Vol. 2, March-April, 1979, pp. 31-33.

_____. "Canada's Nuclear Dilemma," *Journal of Business Administration*, Vol. 13, Nos. 1 & 2, 1982.

_____. "Fission Chips: Canada and the H-Bomb." *Transitions*. Journal of the Canadian Coalition for Nuclear Responsibility in *The Nuclear Free Press*, Spring 1983, p. 19.

Eggleston, Wilfrid. "The Nuclear Age in Canada." *Canadian Geographic Journal*, Vol. 71, December 1965, pp. 182-191.

Epstein, Edward. "Politicization and Income Distribution in Argentina: The Case of the Peronist Worker." *Economic Development and Cultural Change*. July 1975, Vol. 23, No. 4, pp. 615-631.

Foster, J.S. "The Canadian Nuclear Power Program." Ottawa, AECL, May 1976, AECL-5534.

———. "Marketing the CANDU—An Overview." *Canadian Nuclear Association International Marketing Seminar*. Ottawa, March 29, 1977.

Fox, M. "Ottawa Hesitant over Second (CANDU) Reactor for Argentina." *Financial Post*, Vol. 72, January 21, 1978, p. 11.

Franks, C.E.S. "The Development of Peaceful Nuclear Energy: Three Configurations of Knowledge and Power." *International Journal*, Vol. 34, Spring 1979, pp. 187-208.

Gordon, Sheldon. "AECL and the Huge Price of Success." *The Financial Post*, December 4, 1976, p. 5.

Gray, J.L. "A Statement of the Nuclear Power Development Program." Ottawa: AECL, February 1958, AECL-561.

———. "Why CANDU?: Its Achievements and Prospects." Ottawa: AECL, January 1974, AECL-4709.

———. "CANDU Milestones." *Proceedings of the 15th Annual Canadian Nuclear Association*. Vol. 2. *Development in Canada and Abroad*. Toronto: CNA, June 15-18, 1975, p. 94.

Gudmundson, F. "Saskatchewan Syndrome." *Canadian Dimension*, Vol. 14, July/August, 1979, p. 28.

Gupta, S.N. "Despite Ability, India Unlikely to Build Bomb." *Canadian Nuclear Technology*, Vol. 5, September-October, 1966, p. 40.

Hagg, Edmund V. "Whiteshell Centre on Nuclear Frontier." *Winnipeg Free Press*, December 17, 1983, p. 41.

Handelsman, S. "Is Canada Expanding Argentina's Killing Ground?" *Maclean's*, Vol. 89, October 4, 1976, p. 61.

Hanlon, Joe. "Repression Hits Physicists in the Argentine." *New Scientist*, Vol. 75, No. 1059. July 7, 1977, p. 5.

Harper, George. "A Do-It-Yourself A-Bomb." *New Scientist*, March 27, 1980, pp. 998-1001.

Havemann, Joan. "Food Irradiation—Brought to You by Atomic Energy of Canada Limited." *Briarpatch*, Vol. 12, No. 3, April 1983, pp. 18-19.

Haywood, L.R. "Heavy Water Supply and Demand." *Canadian Nuclear Association, 11th Annual Conference*, June 1971, Paper 72-CNA-306.

Hertsgaard, Mark. "Le president Reagan bouleverse les bases de la politique nucleaire." *Le Monde Diplomatique*, juin 1982, pp. 4-5.

———. "An Indestructible Industry: Why the Atomic Brotherhood Can Afford to Wait Us Out." *Mother Jones*, Vol. 8, No. 4, May 1983, pp. 26-31, 46, 48.

Horgan, Denys. "Protest over Argentinean Trade Ignored." *The Globe and Mail*, October 8, 1980, p. 3.

Hunt, Constance D. "Canadian Policy and the Export of Nuclear Energy." *University of Toronto Law Journal*, Vol. 27, No. 1, Winter 1977, pp. 69-105.

Hunter, W.D.G. "Canada's Uranium Industry: A Crisis of Survival." *Business Quarterly*, Vol. 26, No. 4, Winter 1961.

Jackson, Basil. "$100-Million Nuclear Order Shows AECL's Can Too." *The Financial Post*, March 24, 1973, p. 4.

———. "India's Bomb Test Won't Slow CANDU Sales Effort." *Financial Post*, Vol. 68, June 1, 1974, p. 15.

Jacobs, Paul. "What You Don't Know May Hurt You: The Dangerous Business of Nuclear Exports." *Mother Jones.* A copy provided by AECL (Pinawa) but a date was not included.

Jager, Manfred. "Scientist Favours Using North as World Nuclear Waste Dump." *Winnipeg Free Press*, February 22, 1984, p. 27.

Jennekens, Jon H. "Bill C-14: The Nuclear Control and Administration Act—Issues and Implications." *18th Annual Canadian Nuclear Association Conference.* Ottawa: June 1978.

Joskow, Paul L. "The International Nuclear Industry Today." *Foreign Affairs*, Summer 1977.

Kahrel, A.R. "Experience with Export of Nuclear Power Plants." International Atomic Energy Agency. Vienna: IAEA-SM-223/30, 1978.

Kapur, Ashok. "Peace and Power in India's Nuclear Policy," *Asian Survey*, Vol. 10, September 1970, pp. 779-788.

_____. "Nuclear Proliferation in the Third World: Some Aspects the West Neglects." *Science Forum*, Vol. 8, February 1975, pp. 16-18.

Keeley, James F. "Canadian Nuclear Export Policy and Problems of Proliferation." *Canadian Public Policy*, Vol. 6, No. 4, Autumn 1980, pp. 614-627.

Keys, David A. "Atomic Energy: Some Practical Applications." *Canadian Banker*, Vol. 58, Spring 1951, pp. 23-37.

Knelman, F.H. "Canadian Nuclear Energy—Who Needs It?" *Our Generation*, Vol. 13, No. 1, Winter 1979, pp. 23-34.

Krueger, Alice. "Irradiation Labelling Being Scrutinized: We May Not Be Told If Food's Been Treated." *Winnipeg Free Press*, September 17, 1983, p. 55.

Laclau, Ernesto. "Argentina: Imperialist Strategy and the May Crisis." *New Left Review*, July-August, 1970, No. 62.

LaPointe, Kirk. "Nuclear Waste from Canada Blocked at US Bridge." *The Globe and Mail*, July 24, 1980, p. 5.

Laurence, George C. "Early Years of Nuclear Energy Research in Canada." Chalk River Nuclear Laboratories: Atomic Energy of Canada Limited, May 1980.

Leist, G.T. "AECL Nuclear Power Marketing." *14th Annual Conference of the Canadian Nuclear Association.* Toronto, June 1974.

Lewis, W.B. "An Atomic Power Proposal." Ottawa: AECL, August 1951, AECL-186.

Lindsey, G. "Some Types of Nuclear Proliferation Are More Dangerous Than Others." *Science Forum*, Vol. 8, February 1975, pp. 10-12.

Long, Doug. "PM Issues 'Go to Court' Challenge: PC's Pledge to Force Price-Fixing Question." *The Ottawa Citizen*, August 6, 1977, p. 8.

Lovins, Amory B.; Lovins, L. Hunter; and Ross, Leonard. "Nuclear Power and Nuclear Bombs." *Foreign Affairs*, Vol. 58, Summer 1980, pp. 1137-1177.

McDowell, Michael. "CANDU has 'Slim' Hope in Japan." *The Globe and Mail*, January 22, 1983, p. 4.

McDowell, Stan. "Ottawa's Role in Nuclear Nightmare." *The Globe and Mail*, May 7, 1979, p. 8.

McElheny, Victor. "Few Nations Need Nuclear Plants: Exporting of Technology to Poorer Lands Finds Little Demand, Report Shows." *New York Times*, March 8, 1976, p. 38.

MacNabb, Gordon M. "Nuclear and Uranium Policies." *Canadian Nuclear Association Conference*, 1975.

Mahood, E. "Socialists and the Nuclear Power Issue." *Canadian Dimension*, Vol. 13, March 1979, pp. 5-7.

Malarek, Victor. "Eldorado Plant Regularly Warned of Inspections, Atomic Agency Says." *The Globe and Mail*, April 27, 1979, p. 5.

Mamorek, J. and Spinner, B. "Energy Overkill." *Canada and the World*, Vol. 42, April 1977, pp. 16-17.

Marossi, Ruth. "Canada's Uranium Crisis." *The Bulletin of the Atomic Scientists*, Vol. 17, No. 7, September 1961, pp. 281-286.

Marsh, David. "Argentina Could Be Top Dog in Latin American Natural Uranium Club." *The Globe and Mail*, April 30, 1979, p. B4.

Mathias, Philip. "'A Foot in the Door of the Future': Nova Scotia's Heavy Water Plant." *Forced Growth*. Toronto: James Lorimer and Co., Pub., 1971, pp. 103-123.

———. "Those CANDU Sales: Where Did the Money Go? Argentina: Who Gave What to Whom?" *Financial Post*, Vol. 71, November 19, 1977, p. 44.

———. "Those CANDU Sales: Where Did the Money Go? South Korea: Eisenberg's $18,5 Million." *Financial Post*, Vol. 71, November 19, 1977. p. 44.

Maynes, Clifford. "Boom and Bust: Canada's Uranium Industry Is Expanding Rapidly. But Who's Going to Buy the Uranium?" *The Nuclear Free Press*, Spring 1983, pp. 9-10.

Miller, Judith. "3 Nations Widening Nuclear Contacts: Some US Aides Feel South Africa, Israel, and Taiwan Are Helping Each Other Gain Atom Arms." *New York Times*, June 28, 1981, p. 15.

Morrison, Robert W. "Is Canada Peddling Nuclear Bombs World Wide in the Guise of Nuclear Reactors?" *Science Forum*, Vol. 10, December 1977, pp. 3-7.

Mrenica, Janet. "Power Exports Cultivate Adamant Opposition." *Transitions*. Journal for the Canadian Coalition for Nuclear Responsibility in *The Nuclear Free Press*, Spring 1983, pp. 17-18.

Orlando, F.W. "The Taiwan Research Reactor." Presented at *The 10th Annual Canadian Nuclear Association Conference*. Toronto, May 24-27, 1970. Toronto: CNA-70-CNA-662, 1970.

Patterson, Walter C. "Helping the Public Judge Contentious Issues Involving Science." *Science Forum*, Vol. 39, June 1974, pp. 3-5.

Polanyi, John. "Canada and the Spread of Nuclear Weapons: Editorial." *Science Forum*, Vol. 8, April 1975, p. 2.

Rogers, D.W.O. "Why Canada Should Stop Selling Its Reactors to the Third World Nations." *Science Forum*, Vol. 10, October 1977, pp. 9-12.

Ross, Oakland. "Mexicans May Need a Miracle to Weather Crisis." *The Globe and Mail*, February 1, 1983, pp. 1-2.

Rowan, Mary Kate. "AECL Not Certain 2-Reactor Accident Could Be Contained." *The Globe and Mail*, July 18, 1979, p. 4.

———. "Inspector Wouldn't Correct A-Plant Error." *The Globe and Mail*, August 9, 1979, p. 5.

Rubin, Norman. "Public Seeks Control over Atomic Board." *Winnipeg Free Press*, December 22, 1983, p. 7.

Sabato, Jorge. "Atomic Energy in Argentina: A Case History." *Development*, Vol. 1, 1973.

Salaff, Stephen. "A Fire to Suffocate." *Canadian Forum*, Vol. 60, September 1980, pp. 14-16.

Schreiner, John. "Uranium Supply 'Carrot' May Be Used to Boost CANDU Sales." *The Financial Post*, May 27, 1978 p. 3.

Schroeder, Denis. "Comment: The Nuclear Debate Moves to Rural Areas." *Science Forum*, Vol. 60, December 1977, p. 20.

Simmons, G.R.; Brown, A.; Davison, C.C.; and Rigby, G.L. "The Canadian Underground Research Laboratory." *International Atomic Energy Agency Conference on Radioactive Waste Management.* Seattle, Washington, May 16-20, 1983. Vienna: IAEA-CN-43/167.

Smillie, Elizabeth. "The Uranium Mining Industry Delivers..." *riarpatch*, October 1983, Vol. 12, No. 8, pp. 18-21.

Spicer, Keith. "Clubmanship Upstaged: Canada's Twenty Years in the Colombo Plan." *International Journal*, Vol. 25, 1969-70, pp. 23-33.

Von Stackelberg, Peter. "Weapons of War." *Goodwin's*, May 1983, Vol. 1, No. 1, pp. 15-20.

Stewart, Walter. "Lorne Gray's Gamble to Make Canada a Nuclear Great Power." *Maclean's*, September 1970, pp. 52-54.

_____. "How We Learned to Stop Worrying and Sell the Bomb." *Maclean's*, Vol. 87, November 1974, pp. 29-33.

Torgerson, Doug. "From Dream to Nightmare: The Historical Origins of Canada's Nuclear Electric Future." *Alternatives*, Vol. 7, No. 1, Fall 1979, pp. 8-17; 30; 63-64.

Torrie, Ralph. "People—and Other Hazards of Nuclear Technology," *Alternatives*, Vol. 7, Fall 1977, pp. 18-22.

_____. "Uranium Mine Tailings: What the Record Shows," *Alternatives*, Vol. 10, Nos. 2-3, Fall-Winter 1982, pp. 15-26; 31.

"Uranium City: More Than a Mine Is Closing." *One Sky Report*, May 1982.

Wohlstetter, Albert; Brown, Thomas A.; Jones, Gregory; McGarvey, David; Rowen, Henry; Taylor, Vincent; and Wohlstetter, Roberta. "The Military Potential of Civilian Nuclear Energy: Moving towards Life in a Nuclear Armed Crowd?" *Minerva*, Vol. 15, Nos. 3-4, Autumn-Winter, 1977, pp. 387-538.

"World List of Nuclear Power Plants." *Nuclear News*, August 1981, pp. 85-104.

REPORTS, PUBLIC DOCUMENTS, AND CONFERENCE PROCEEDINGS

Atomic Energy Control Board. *Annual Reports.* 1946-47 to 1981-82

Atomic Energy of Canada Limited. *Annual Reports*, 1952-53 to 1981-82.

Canada. Department of Energy, Mines, and Resources. *An Energy Policy for Canada.* Ottawa: Information Canada, 1973.

Canada. Department of Energy, Mines, and Resources. *The Management of Canada's Nuclear Wastes.* Chairperson: F.K. Hare. Ottawa: Supply and Services, Canada, 1977, Report EP77-6.

Canada. Department of Energy, Mines, and Resources. *Eldorado Uranium Refinery, R.M. of Corman Park, Saskatchewan: Report of the Environmental Assessment Panel.* Ottawa: Supply and Services, Canada, 1980.

Canada. Department of Energy, Mines, and Resources. *Uranium in Canada: 1979 Assessment of Supply and Requirements*, Ottawa: Supply and Services, Canada. Report EP-80-3, September 1980.

Canada. Department of Energy, Mines, and Resources. *Nuclear Policy Review Background Papers.* Ottawa: Supply and Services. Report ER81-2E, 1980.

Canada. Department of Energy, Mines, and Resources. *Policy Review of the Nuclear Power Industry.* Reiner Hollbach, Director. Draft report leaked to the Ottawa Press, June 1981. Montreal: Canadian Coalition for Nuclear Responsibility, 1981.

Canada. Department of Energy, Mines, and Resources. *Nuclear Industry Review: Problems and Prospects, 1981-2000*. Ottawa: Supply and Services, 1982.

Canada. Department of External Affairs. *Treaty Series*, 1945-1983. Ottawa: Supply and Services.

Canada. Department of External Affairs. *A Foreign Policy for Canadians*. Ottawa: Supply and Services, 1970.

Canada. Department of External Affairs. *Canada's Nuclear Safeguards Policy*. Ottawa: Supply and Services, 1978.

Canada. Department of Industry, Trade, and Commerce. *A Report by the Task Force on Canadian Export Marketing*. J.M. Douglas, Chairperson. Ottawa: Industry, Trade, and Commerce, 1978.

Canada. Department of Industry, Trade, and Commerce. *A Report by the Task Force on Canadian Export Marketing*. J.M. Douglas, Chairperson. Ottawa: Industry, Trade, and Commerce, 1978.

Canada. Federal Cabinet Briefing Document. An Energy Probe copy of the document leaked to *The Ottaws Citzen* ("Government Fears Argentine CANDU May Spawn Bombs," April 23, 1982).

Canada. Government of Ontario. Royal Commission on Electric Power Planning. *A Race against Time: Interim Report on Nuclear Power in Ontario*. Ontario: The Royal Commission on Electric Power Planning, 1978.

Canada. Government of Ontario. Royal Commission on Electric Power Planning. *The Report of the Royal Commission on Electric Power Planning, Vol. 1: Concepts, Conclusions, and Recommendations*. Chairperson: Arthur Porter, Ontario: Royal Commission on Electric Power Planning, 1980.

Canada. Government of Saskatchewan. *The Cliff Lake Board of Inquiry: Final Report*. Chairperson: E.D. Bayda. Regina: Saskatchewan Environment, 1978.

Canada. House of Commons. *Debates*, 1944-1982.

Canada. House of Commons. *1949 Special Committee on the Operations of the Atomic Energy Control Board*. Chairperson: G.J. McIlraith. Minutes of Proceedings and Evidence. Nos. 1-5.

Canada. House of Commons. *1952-53 Special Committee on the Operations of the Government in the Field of Atomic Energy*. Chairperson: G.J. McIlraith. Minutes and Proceedings of Evidence, Nos. 1-5. Ottawa: Queen's Printer, 1953.

Canada. House of Commons. Standing Committee on Public Accounts. *Proceedings*.

Canada. Senate. Special Committee on Science Policy. *A Science Policy for Canada*. 3 Volumes. Ottawa, 1970- 73.

Canadian Coalition for Nuclear Responsibility. *Time to Stop and Think: A Brief Presented to Prime Minister Trudeau, May 1977*. Montreal. Canadian Coalition for Nuclear Responsibility, 1977.

Canadian Nuclear Association. *Reports of the Annual Conferences*. 1961-1980.

Committee on Nuclear Issues in the Community. *Nuclear Issues in the Canadian Energy Context*. National Conference Proceedings, Vancouver, March 7-9, 1979. Ottawa: Royal Society of Canada for C.O.N.I.C.

Doern, G. Bruce. *The Atomic Energy Control Board: An Evaluation of Regulatory and Administrative Processes and Procedures*. Ottawa: A report produced for the Law Reform Commission of Canada, 1976.

Doern, G. Bruce, and Morrison, Robert W., eds. *Canadian Nuclear Policies*. Proceedings of a conference sponsored by the School of Public Administration and the Norman Patterson School of International Affairs, Carleton University and the Science Council of Canada. 8-10 November 1978. Montreal: The Institute for Research on Public Policy, 1980.

Eldorado Nuclear Limited. *Annual Reports*. 1968-1979.

Independent Commission on International Development. *North-South: A Programme for Survival*. The Commission's Report was chaired by Willy Brandt. London, Pan Books,1980.

International Atomic Energy Agency. *Market Survey for Nuclear Power in Developing Countries, 1974 Edition*. IAEA-165. Vienna: International Atomic Energy Agency,1974.

Ontario Coalition for Nuclear Responsibility, The. *Submission to the Royal Commission on Electric Power Planning with Respect to the Public Information Hearings*. Toronto: OCNR, September 23, 1976.

Torrie, Ralph D. *Half-Life: Nuclear Power and Future Society*. A research report prepared under the direction of the Ontario Coalition for Nuclear Responsibility with respect to the final hearings of the Royal Commission on Electric Power Planning, August 1977 (Revised January,1980).

Warman and District Concerned Citizens Group. *Why People Say No: A Report on the Environment Assessment for the Uranium Refinery at Warman, Saskatchewan*. Regina: Regina Group for a Non-Nuclear Society, 1980.

THESES

Casterton, James A. "The International Dimensions of the Canadian Nuclear Industry." Ottawa: MA Thesis, The Norman Patterson School of International Affairs, Carleton University, March 1980.

Sims, Gordon H.E. "The Evolution of AECL." Ottawa: MA Thesis, Carleton University, August 1979.

PERIODICALS

Alternatives, Fall 1977, Vol. 7, No. 1.

Ascent. The Magazine of Atomic Energy of Canada Limited. Vol. 1. (1980) to Vol. 3 (1982).

Asian Survey. Vol. 1. (1961) to Vol. 21 (1981).

irch Bark Alliance, The. No. 2 (Spring 1979) to Issue 13(Winter 1981-82). Succeeding title: *The Nuclear Free Press*.

ulletin of Peace Proposals. The International Peace Research Institute, Oslo. Vol. 1 (1970) to Vol. 11(1980).

ulletin of the Atomic Scientists. Vol. 4 (1948) to Vol. 39(1983).

usiness Quarterly. Vol. 16 (1951) to Vol. 47 (1982).

Canada Commerce. No. 105 (Jan. 1956) to No. 144 (Sept.1980).

Canadian Business. Vol. 22 (1949) to Vol. 54 (1981).

Canadian Forum. Vol. 27 (1947) to Vol. 60 (1981).

Canadian Nuclear Technology. Vol. 1 (1961) to Vol. 5(1966).

Energy Policy. Vol. 2 (1974) to Vol. 9 (1981).

External Affairs. Vol. 1-15, 1948-1963; Vol. 18-23, 1966-1971. Succeeding title: *International Perspectives*.

Far Eastern Economic Review. Vol. 37 (1962) to Vol. 116 (1982).

Foreign Affair. Vol. 26 (1948) to Vol. 59 (1981).

Indian and Foreign Review. Vol. 1 (1963) to Vol. 17 (1980).

International Canada. Vol. 1 (1970) to Vol. 10 (1979).

International Journal. Vol. 1 (1946) to Vol. 34 (1979).

International Perspectives. Vol. 1 (1972) to Vol. 9 (1980).
Maclean's. Vol. 64 (1951) to Vol. 95 (1982).
Minerva. Vol. 1 (1962-63) to Vol. 17 (1979).
New Scientist. Vol. 7 (1960) to Vol. 95 (1982).
Nuclear Free Press, The (superseded *The Birch Bark Alliance*) Issue 14 (Summer 1982) to Issue 20 (Winter 1983-84).
Saturday Night. Vol. 54 (1939) to Vol. 95 (1980).
Science Forum. Vol. 1 (1968) to Vol. 12 (1979).
Uranium Traffic in Saskatchewan. September 1981.

NEWSPAPERS

The Finanacial Post. 1949-1981.
The Globe and Mail. 1944-1983.
The New York Times. 1945-1981.

INTERVIEWS

Anonymous. Atomic Energy of Canada Limited (AECL), Pinawa, Manitoba. Telephone Interview, June 1983.

Brown, Dave. AECL, Pinawa, Manitoba. Telephone Interview, June 1983.

Casterton, James. Atomic Energy Control Board (AECB), Ottawa, Ontario. Telephone Interview, March 1984.

Lonergan, Terrence. Deputy Director of Nuclear Safeguards, External Affairs, Ottawa, Ontario. Telephone Interview, March 1984.

Sims, Gordon. AECB, Ottawa, Ontario. Telephone Interview, March 1984.

Smith, Robert. AECL, Pinawa, Manitoba. Telephone Interview, June 1983.

Spence, Hugh. AECB, Ottawa, Ontario. Telephone Interview, February 1984.

GLOSSARY OF TERMS AND ABBREVIATIONS

Advanced gas cooled reactor(AGR): a graphite-moderated, CO_2-cooled thermal reactor with slightly enriched uranium as a fuel.

AECL: Atomic Energy Of Canada Limited.

Atomic bomb: a bomb whose energy comes from the fission of heavy elements such as uranium and plutonium.

Atoms: the basic building blocks of all substances and indivisible by chemical means. Each element has its own distinctive arrangement of electrons and protons in its atom.

Baseload: the part of demand on an electrical grid that is constant in time. It is supplied by the power stations of lowest running costs, running as nearly continuously as possible so as not to tie up capital idly.

Biomass energy: energy derived from living organic material such as plants or from inorganic wastes, plant or animal; an indirect form of solar energy. Methane, or Biogas, production from organic wastes is a type of biomass energy.

Boiling water reactor(BWR): a light water reactor in which ordinary water, used both as a moderator and a coolant, is converted to high-pressure steam which drives the turbine.

Breeder reactor: a reactor that produces more fissile (fissionable) fuel than it consumes. The new fissile material is created by capture in fertile materials of neutrons from fission, a process known as breeding.

Calandria: a cylindrical reactor vessel that contains the heavy-water moderator. Hundreds of tubes extend from one end of the calandria to the other. The tubes contain the uranium fuel and the pressurized high-temperature coolant. The reactor core consists of all the components within the calandria.

CANDU: a Canada Deuterium Uranium reactor. The moderator is deuterium, or heavy water, and the fuel is natural uranium. Pressure tubes containing the fuel and coolant run the length of the reactor vessel, or calandria.

CEA: France's Commissariat d'Energie Atomique. The state body that oversees the power and military nuclear programs.

Chain reaction: a reaction that initiates its own repetition. In nuclear fission, a neutron induces a nucleus to fission and releases neutrons, which cause more fission.

Contamination: radioactivity where it should not be.

Containment: the structure within a reactor building—or the building itself—which acts as a barrier to contain any radioactivity which may escape from the reactor.

Coolant: a liquid or gas circulated through the core of a reactor to remove the heat of the fission process.

Cooling pond: a deep tank of water into which spent fuel is discharged upon removal from the reactor, there to remain until shipping for reprocessing.

Core: the part of the reactor where heat is produced by fission processes and transferred to the coolant; it contains the body of fuel and moderator.

Critical: nuclear material just capable of supporting a chain reaction is said to be "critical"; i.e., neutrons are captured and released at the same rate.

Criticality: the instantaneous condition when a sufficient mass of fissionable materials assembled in the right shape and concentration begins a self-sustaining chain reaction.

Decay: the disintegration of radioactive elements over time, releasing radiation.

Decontamination: the transfer of unwanted radioactivity to a less undesirable location.

Deuterium: an isotope of hydrogen whose nucleus contains one neutron and one proton and is therefore about twice as heavy as the nucleus of normal hydrogen. It is used as the moderator in the CANDU.

Diversion: a euphemism for theft, as applied to strategic or "special" nuclear material.

Dominant mutations: genetic effects that act on dominant genes and usually produce lethal and non-lethal mutations in the first few generations.

EMR: the Canadian Ministry of Energy, Mines, and Resources, Ottawa.

Enriched uranium: uranium in which the proportion of the uranium-235 isotope is higher than in the natural element (0.7%).

ERDA: US Energy Research and Development Administration, created in January 1975 after the split-up of the US Atomic Energy Commission (USAEC). The other agency was the US Nuclear Regulatory Commission.

Fallout: airborne particles and other material which fall to the ground following a nuclear explosion.

Fast breeder reactor (FBR): a reactor with little or no moderator, so that the neutrons from the reaction are not slowed down. It produces more fissile material than it consumes by "breeding" fissile material in a blanket of fertile material.

Fissile material: nuclear fuels in which the nuclei, when hit by neutrons, split and release energy plus further neutrons, which can result in a chain reaction. U-233, U-235, and PU-239 are examples of significant fissile materials, but only U-235 occurs naturally.

Fission: the splitting of a heavy nucleus into two or more parts, releasing energy.

Fissionable material: commonly used as a synonym for fissile material. The meaning of this term has been extended to include material that can be fissioned by fast neutrons only, such as uranium-238.

Fuel: material (such as natural or enriched uranium or uranium and/or plutonium dioxide) containing fissile nuclei, fabricated into a suitable form for use in a reactor.

Fuel bundle: an assembly of metal tubes containing nuclear fuel pellets ready for insertion in a reactor.

Fuel cycle: the series of steps involved in preparation and disposal of fuel for nuclear-power reactors. It includes mining, refining the ore, fabrication of fuel elements, their use in a reactor, chemical processing to recover the fissile material remaining in the spent fuel, re-enrichment of the fuel material, and refabrication into new fuel elements.

Fuel inventory: the amount of fissile material in the core of a reactor.

Fuel pellets: uranium dioxide, or other nuclear fuel in a powdered form, which has been pressed, sintered, and ground to a cylindrical shape for insertion into the sheathing tubes of the fuel bundle.

Fuel reprocessing: the processing of reactor fuel to recover the unused fissile material.

Fusion: the fusing together of certain light nuclei to form heavier nuclei. During the process, much energy is released and the reaction is the basis of the hydrogen bomb.

Gas centrifuge: a uranium enrichment device by which heavier uranium-238 atoms are slightly separated from lighter uranium-235 atoms by centrifuging uranium hexafluoride gas. Full-scale plants use many thousands of centrifuges in a cascade.

Gas-cooled reactor: a nuclear reactor in which a gas, such as carbon dioxide, is the coolant. In such a reactor, graphite is often used as the moderator.

Gaseous diffusion: a method of isotopic separation based on the fact that gas atoms or molecules with different masses will diffuse through a porous barrier at different rates. The method is used to separate uranium-235 from uranium-238.

Genetic effects: effects that produce changes to egg or sperm cells and thereby affect the offspring.

Half life: the time taken for half the atoms of a radioactive substance to disintegrate; hence, the time taken to lose half its radioactive strength. Each radionuclide has a unique half life, ranging from millionths of a second to billions of years.

Heat exchangers: a piece of apparatus that transfers heat from one medium to another. A typical example is the steam generator in the CANDU system where the hot pressurized heavy water coolant is used to convert ordinary water into steam to run the turbine.

Heavy water: water containing significantly more than the natural proportion (one in 6500) of heavy hydrogen (deuterium) atoms to ordinary hydrogen atoms. (See deuterium.)

Heavy water moderated reactor: a reactor that uses heavy water as its moderator. Heavy water is a good moderator and permits the use of natural (unenriched) uranium as a fuel.

High temperature gas-cooled reactor: a graphite-moderated, helium-cooled reactor using highly enriched uranium as a fuel.

Highly enriched uranium: uranium in which the proportion of uranium-235 has been increased to 90% or above.

Hydrogen bomb: a nuclear weapon that derives its energy largely from fusion (thermonuclear bomb).

IAEA: International Atomic Energy Agency, Vienna.

Irradiated: of reactor fuel, having been involved in a chain reaction, and having thereby accumulated fission products; in any application, exposed to radiation.

Isotope: species of an atom with the same number of protons in their nuclei, hence belonging to the same element, but differing in the number of neutrons. The chemical qualities are practically the same but the nuclear characteristics may be vastly different—eg., hydrogen (H_2) and deuterium (H_2), and U-235 and U-238.

Jet nozzle enrichment method: process of uranium enrichment based on pressure diffusion on a gaseous mixture of uranium hexafluoride and an additional light gas flowing at high speed through a nozzle along curved walls.

Kiloton energy: the energy of a nuclear explosion which is equivalent to that of an explosion of 1,000 tons of TNT.

Kilowatt: one thousand watts.

Laser enrichment: the separation of uranium-235 from U-238 by selective excitation of one isotope with a laser; potentially a short-cut to highly enriched uranium, which would present a serious problem as regards possible misuse of fissile material.

Light water: ordinary water(H_2O), as distinguished from heavy water (D_2O).

London Club/London Suppliers' Club: the group of countries which export nuclear facilities and which meet from time to time to devise guidelines for the supply of such facilities and materials.

Magnox: an alloy used as fuel cladding in first-generation British gas-cooled reactors, which are therefore called Magnox reactors.

Manhatten Project: the "Manhatten District" of the US Army Corps of Engineers—code name for the atomic bomb project.

Mass number: the total number of protons and neutrons in the nucleus of an atom (eg., U-235).

Material unaccounted for (MUF): the difference in the amount of a fissile material entering a facility and that coming out. It may indicate that diversion has occurred.

McMahon Act: the US Atomic Energy Act (1946), which banned any further transfer of nuclear information from the USA to the erstwhile allies, Britain and Canada, and set up the US Atomic Energy Commission (AEC) and the Joint Congressional Committee on Atomic Energy (JCAE).

Megawatt electric (MWe): the amount of power, in megawatts, generated by a reactor in the form of electricity.

Megawatt thermal (MWt): the amount of power, in megawatts, generated by a reactor in the form of heat. The MWt is approximately triple the MWe.

Megaton energy: the energy of a nuclear explosion which is equivalent to that of an explosion of one million tons (or 1,000 kilotons) of TNT.

Meltdown: the meltdown of a reactor core. The consequence of overheating which allows part or all of the solid fuel in a reactor to reach the temperature at which cladding and possibly fuel and support structure liquefy and collapse.

Moderator: a material, such as ordinary water, heavy water, or graphite, used in a reactor to slow down fast neutrons to increase the probability of further fission.

Natural uranium: uranium as found in nature, containing 0.7 percent of U-235, 99.3 percent of U-238, and a trace of U-234.

NPT: the Treaty for the Non-Proliferation of Nuclear Weapons or the Non-Proliferation Treaty.

NSSS: nuclear steam supply system—in a nuclear power station, everything up to but not including the turbine generators: the reactor and its facilities (refueling machine, control installation, fuel handling bay, cooling pond, steam generators if applicable).

Nuclear energy: the energy liberated by a nuclear reaction (fission or fusion) or by radioactive decay.

Nuclear explosive: an explosive based on fission or fusion of atomic nuclei.

Nuclear fusion: the formation of a heavier nucleus from two lighter ones with the simultaneous release of large amounts of energy.

Nuclear power plant: any device or assembly that converts nuclear energy into power. In such a plant, heat produced by a reactor is used to produce steam to drive a turbine that in turn drives an electric generator.

Nuclear weapons: bombs, missiles, and other devices in which the explosive power is derived from nuclear energy, ie., from fission and/or fusion. In a fission bomb (atom bomb), the energy is derived mainly from fission. In a thermonuclear bomb (hydrogen bomb), the energy may be derived either mainly from fusion or partly from fission and partly from fusion. The explosive power of a nuclear bomb is expressed in terms of the equivalent amount of TNT. In a kiloton bomb, the explosive power is equivalent to one thousand tons of TNT. In a megaton bomb, the explosive power is equivalent to one million tons of TNT.

Nuclear waste: the radioactive products of fission and other nuclear processes in a reactor.

On-line refueling: the replacement of reactor fuel while the reactor is still sustaining a chain reaction. A feature of the CANDU that makes it more difficult to safeguard.

OPEC: Organization of Petroleum Exporting Countries.

Organic coolant: an oil-like liquid having a high boiling point at low pressure used as coolant in the WR-1 test reactor at the Whiteshell Nuclear Research Establishment of AECL near Pinawa, Manitoba.

Plutonium: a radioactive human-made metallic element with atomic-number 94. Its most important isotope is fissile plutonium-239, produced by neutron irradiation of uranium -238. It is used for reactor fuel and in weapons.

Pile: the name of the original nuclear reactors, where "piles" of uranium were cooled by gas or water, and moderated by graphite or water. Named after the first reactor, Chicago Pile No. 1.

Power reactor: a reactor designed to produce nuclear-generated electricity, as distinguished from reactors used primarily for research or war.

Pressure tube reactor (PTR): a power reactor in which the fuel is located inside hundreds of tubes designed to with-stand the circulation of the high pressure coolant. The tubes are assembled in a tank containing the moderator at low pressure.

Pressurized water reactor: a power reactor in which heat is transferred from the core to a heat exchanger by water kept under high pressure to achieve high temperature without boiling in the primary system. Steam is generated in a secondary circuit. A type of light water reactor.

Radiation: particles or energy formed by spontaneous decay of radioactivity substances or during fission.

Radioactive decay: the gradual decrease in radioactivity of a radioactive substance due to nuclear disintegration, and its transformation into a different element. Also called radioactive disintegration.

Radioactive waste: equipment and materials (from nuclear operations) which are radioactive.

Radium: an intensely radioactive alpha-emitting heavy element.

Reactor (nuclear reactor): a device in which a self- sustaining fission chain reaction is maintained and, hopefully, contained.

Reprocessing: the extraction of fissionable material from spent fuel for later use by recycling.

Recycling: the reuse of fissionable material in irradiated fuel. It is recovered by reprocessing.

Safeguards: a term applied to keeping track of special nuclear material to prevent diversion.

Spent fuel: nuclear fuel that has been irradiated in a reactor to the extent that it can no longer effectively sustain a chain reaction; the fissionable isotopes have been consumed and fission-product poisons have been accumulated.

Tailings: the uranium ore left after the extraction of the uranium in the milling plant. It contains radium and emits radon.

Thermal efficiency: the percentage of the total thermal energy that is converted into electrical energy in a nuclear power plant. Only about 33% of the thermal energy is converted to electricity in a CANDU. The remainder is waste.

Thermonuclear: fusion.

Thermonuclear bomb: a hydrogen bomb.

Thermonuclear reaction: a reaction in which very high temperatures bring about the fusion of two light nuclei to form the nucleus of a heavier atom, releasing a large amount of energy.

Turnkey: sold at an all-inclusive price, ready to operate when the buyer turns a hypothetical key. The term reflects the influence of the automobile on North American culture.

UKAEA: United Kingdom Atomic Energy Authority.

Uranium: a radioactive element with the atomic number 92 and, as found in natural ores, an average weight of approximately 238. The two principal natural isotopes are uranium-235 (0.7% of natural uranium), which is fissile, and uranium-238 (99.3% of natural uranium), which is fertile. Natural uranium also includes traces of uranium-234. Uranium is refined at mines to U_3O_8 (an oxide called "yellowcake") and later to such forms as UF_6 and UO_2.

Uranium dioxide (UO_2): a compound used, with the natural concentration of uranium-235 unchanged, as the fuel in CANDU power reactors because of its chemical and radiation stability, good gaseous fission-product retention, and high melting point.

Uranium hexafluoride: a volatile compound of uranium and fluorine. UF_6 gas is the process fluid in the gaseous diffusion process.

USAEC: United States Atomic Energy Commission.

Vitrification: the fusing of high-level waste into glass-like solids.

Weapons grade material: a material with a sufficiently high concentration of the nuclides uranium-233 or uranium-235 or plutonium-239 to make it suitable for a nuclear weapon.

Yellowcake: a uranium compound consisting mainly of U_3O_8. The yellow powder is produced from uranium ore by an extraction process in a uranium mill.

Yield: the total energy released in a nuclear explosion. It is usually expressed in equivalent tons of TNT (the quantity of trinitrotoluene required to produce a corresponding amount of energy).

Zirconium: A naturally occurring metallic element. The material is used extensively in the construction of incore reactor components because it has a very high corrosion resistance to high-temperature water. It was assumed that it had a low neutron absorption rate, but the August 1983 accident at Pickering II (outside Toronto) may have disproved this theory.

Sources

Barnaby, C.F., ed. *Preventing the Spread of Nuclear Weapons.* Pugwash monograph I. London: Souvenir Press, 1969.

_____. *The Nuclear Age.* Stockholm International Peace Research Institute. Cambridge, Mass.: The MIT Press, 1975.

Durie, Sheila, and Edwards, Rob. *Fuelling The Nuclear Arms Race:* The Links Between Nuclear Power and Nuclear Weapons. London: Pluto Press, 1982.

Knelman, Fred H. *Nuclear Energy:* The Unforgiving Technology. Edmonton: Hurtig Publishers, 1976.

Lovins, Amory B. *Soft Energy Paths:* Toward a Durable Peace. New York: Harper Colophone Books, 1979.

Mueller, Peter. *On Things Nuclear:* The Canadian Debate. Toronto: Canadian Institute for International Affairs, 1977.

Patterson, Walter C. *Nuclear Power.* Harmondsworth: Penguin Books, Ltd., 1978.

Stockholm International Peace Research Institute. *Nuclear Energy and Nuclear Weapon Proliferation.* London: Taylor and Francis, Ltd., 1979.

Wyatt, Allan. *The Nuclear Challenge: Understanding the Debate.* The Book Press, Ltd., 1978.

The Coming of World War III

by Dimitrios Roussopoulos

It will never happen. It can happen. It will happen.

Politicians and military and scientific personnel working for various nation-states remain firmly convinced that their nuclear weapons policies are both logical and righteous while also believing that there will never be a nuclear war.

A large group of scientists, journalists and academics believe that the possibilities of a nuclear 'accident', a computer error, for example, in which missiles are launched by mistake, or the deliberate use of these weapons, can lead to a nuclear holocaust.

After working with the disamament movement for more than 20 years, and having just completed a thorough investigation of the intensified arms race and the emergence of the new disamament movements in Europe and North America, Dimitrios Roussopoulos believes a third world war will happen, because not enough is being done to prevent it. This conclusion has a number of radical implications for activists in the peace movement, sympathisers to its aims and those interested in social change.

Dimitrios Roussopoulos founded the Combined Universities Campaign for Nuclear Disamament in 1959 and the journal SANITY, monthly newspaper of the Canadian CND, as well as OUR GENERATION AGAINST NUCLEAR WAR, a peace research journal. He was also a founding member of the International Confederation for Disarmament. THE COMING OF WORLD WAR III is the fruit of eight months of research and travel covering 10 countries.

Paperback ISBN: 0-920057-02-0   **$12.95**
Hardcover ISBN: 0-920057-03-9   **$22.95**

Toward an Ecological Society

by Murray Bookchin

2nd printing

In this exciting new collection of essays, which will stand beside Bookchin's well-known classic **Post-Scarcity Anarchism** (with its seven printings, translated into five languages), the author deals with all dimensions of social ecology.

"Murray Bookchin may be the orneriest political theorist alive... he's worth arguing with... Bookchin is capable of penetrating finely indignant historical analyses... [This book] is another stimulating, wideranging collection... [with] several excellent essays on urban planning, the future of the city, new developments in ecologically sound technology, and the history of utopian thought..." — IN THESE TIMES.

"A revolution needs a prophet, the green revolution no less than others, and there is no shortage of aspirants. Now there are a few names on the lists: Petra Kelly, Rudolf Bahro — and Murray Bookchin... [This] collection of essays... are brilliant and exciting exercices...' — RESURGENCE.

"[This book] is always a provocative work that gives abundant evidence of its author's position at the center of debate... It therefore deserves the careful attention of anyone seriously interested in constructive social thought... It is a work of crucial importance." — TELOS.

"Bookchin's great virtue — which he shares with some other modem anarchist thinkers like Paul Goodman and Colin Ward — is that he constantly relates his theories to society as it is — not a an abstraction, but a human reality, and to what people can do at the basic social levels." — GEORGE WOODCOCK.

"The strength of a book like this is that the repetition and reformulation of clusters of ideas, attitudes and values from essay to essay make the overall vision compelling." — JOHN FEKETE, CANADIAN ASSOCIATION OF UNIVERSITY TEACHERS REVIEW.

320 pages
Paperback ISBN: 0-919618-98-7   **$12.95**
Hardcover ISBN: 0-919618-99-5   **$29.95**
Ecology/Philosophy

TURNING THE TIDE

The U.S. and Latin America
by Noam Chomsky

Regarding U.S. policy in Latin America, *Turning the Tide* succinctly provides the most cogent available descriptions of what is going on, and why. It will be a central tool for everyone who wants to promote peace and justice in the Americas.

Noam Chomsky reveals the aim and impact of U.S. policy in Latin America by examining the historical record and current events. With this as backdrop, he also shows the connection between Latin American policy and broader nuclear and international politics and explains the logic and role of the Cold War for both super-powers. Finally, Chomsky looks at why we accept Reaganesque rhetoric in light of the role of the media and the intelligentsia in the numbing of our awareness. He concludes by describing what we can do to resist.

Turning the Tide is a succinct volume ideal for understanding the broad factors governing U.S. policy in Latin America, the role of the Cold War, and the role of the media and intellectuals with respect to each.

Noam Chomsky is professor of Linguistics and Philosophy and Institute Professor at M.I.T.; recipient of honorary degrees from the University of London, University of Chicago, Delhi University, and four other colleges and universities; fellow of the American Academy of Arts and Sciences, member of the National Academy of Arts and Sciences, and member of the National Academy of Sciences; author of numerous books and articles on linguistics, philosophy, intellectual history and contemporary issues.

298 pages
Paperback ISBN: 0-920057-78-0   **$14.95**
Hardcover ISBN: 0-920057-76-4   **$29.95**

THE NUCLEAR POWER GAME
by Ronald Babin
translated by Ted Richmond

The establishment of the nuclear power industry in our society is not a simple evolutionary step in the history of our techno-scientific civilization. Its introduction, including the production of nuclear weapons, is the determined, conscious work of a small techno-bureaucracy with tremendous power and a deeply held desire for secrecy and centralized power.

Ronald Babin offers us a remarkable investigation not only of this dangerous caste of technocrats, but also the widespread popular opposition to it. Examining the growth of the nuclear industry in Canada which is encouraged by both private industry and the State, the author shows the relationship between public policy and the citizen movements that claim a public space on this issue and the right to determine matters that affect their daily lives. The relationship between public policy and protest lies at the centre of this book.

Ronald Babin works in the Departement de Sociologie, Université de Montréal.

236 pages
Paperback ISBN: 0-920057-31-4   **$14.95**
Hardcover ISBN: 0-920057-30-6   **$24.95**

Printed by
the workers of
Editions Marquis, Montmagny, Québec
for
Black Rose Books Ltd.